THE ART OF WAR

D0836050

THE ART OF WAR

NICCOLÒ MACHIAVELLI

A Revised Edition of the Ellis Farneworth Translation
With an Introduction by
NEAL WOOD

DA CAPO PRESS

Library of Congress Cataloging in Publication Data

Machiavelli, Niccolò, 1469-1527.
  [Arte della guerra. English]
  The art of war: a revised edition of the Ellis Farneworth translation / Niccolò
Machiavelli: with an introduction by Neal Wood.
      p.   cm.
  Translation of: Arte della guerra.
  Reprint. Originally published: Indianapolis: Bobbs-Merrill, 1965.
  Includes index.
  ISBN 0-306-80412-3
  1. Military art and science—Early works to 1800. 2. War—Early works to 1800.
3. Torpedoes—Early works to 1800. I. Title.
U101.M1613   1990   90-3794
355.02—dc20   CIP

Niccolò Machiavelli: 1469–1527
The Art of War was originally published in 1521

4 5 6 7 8 9 10   02 01 00 99

This Da Capo Press paperback edition of *The Art of War*
is an unabridged republication of the edition published
in New York in 1965. It is here reprinted by
arrangement with Neal Wood.

Published by Da Capo Press, Inc.
A member of the Perseus Books Group

All Rights Reserved

Manufactured in the United States of America

CONTENTS

THE ART OF WAR

BOOK FOUR   110

BOOK FIVE   130

BOOK SIX   150

BOOK SEVEN   183

INTRODUCTION

Unquestionably Niccolò Machiavelli is one of the great political theorists and literary artists of our civilization. But his importance as a military thinker has been generally overlooked in the English-speaking world, perhaps because many historians have tended to ignore the theory and practice of war. To some extent, the neglect of this aspect of Machiavelli's virtuosity may be remedied by reprinting the eighteenth-century translation by Ellis Farneworth of the *Arte della guerra*, the least known of the major "non-literary" works of the Florentine. However, another reason for the reprinting exists. Only by the careful consideration of *The Art of War* in relation to *The Prince* and *The Discourses* can one fully grasp the relevance of Machiavelli's military thought for his political ideas, a relevance seldom appreciated by scholars.

The introductory essay, therefore, will serve a dual purpose: to discuss the work as a military classic, and to suggest the nature of the connection between the author's military and political theory. Readers who are concerned primarily with military history will have a special interest in the first three sections. Students of political ideas may find more to their taste in the last four sections.

1. MACHIAVELLI: HIS MILIEU AND HIS MILITARY EXPERIENCE

Machiavelli's lifelong preoccupation with military affairs should surprise no one who is familiar with the politics of his day, with his activity in the Florentine civil service, and with his intellectual pursuits. Born in 1469, Machiavelli reached manhood at the close of Italy's long period of relative isolation from European affairs.[1] By the middle of the fifteenth century, an unstable balance of power began to characterize the relations among the various Italian republics and principalities, a harbinger of the nation-state system which was to crystallize later in Western Europe. The Italian experience produced the new diplomacy with resident ambassadors and the beginnings of regularized procedures in the intercourse of states. But the reduction of tensions and overt military conflict that resulted from a balance of power in miniature was abruptly terminated in 1494 by the invasion of the French under Charles VIII, who was bent upon the conquest of Naples. Until 1529 the peninsula was a battleground in the struggle for power among the rulers of France, Spain, and Germany. Four French expeditions followed that of Charles, one organized by Louis XII in 1499, and three by Francis I, in 1515, 1525, and 1527. French intervention ended in 1529 with a renunciation of all claims to Italian territory and a permanent withdrawal. The internal condition of Florence—like the domestic politics of her neighbors—had to a great extent become a function of the international conflict on Italian soil. For example, the citizens of Florence had twice managed to throw off the rule of the Medici, in 1494 and 1527; in both cases, however, the intervention of Spanish troops returned the family to power: first in 1512, serving the Holy League of Julius II, and then in 1529, serving the Emperor Charles V. Affairs of the city were rendered more difficult by the fact that two of the Popes were Medici, Leo X (1513–1521) and Clement VII (1523–1534). So actively engaged was the Church in the complex diplomatic maneuvering and political intrigue of the age, that it alternated support between France and Spain some ten times, changes in policy that resulted from the personal ambitions of the Popes.

In an age of constant warfare, of alliance and counter-alli-

[1] The political struggle in Renaissance Italy and the birth of modern diplomacy are described acutely by Garrett Mattingly in *Renaissance Diplomacy* (Boston: Houghton Mifflin and Co., 1955).

ance, of assassination and coup d'état, the only feasible solution to the civic ills of a small state like Florence might very well appear to a contemporary observer to be of a military nature, as suggested perhaps by the exploits of Cesare Borgia, son of Pope Alexander VI. Initially aided by Louis XII, the young Borgia, who combined violence and cunning with a rough justice toward his subjects, had created between 1498 and 1503, in a very vigorous and ruthless manner, the basis for a unified, powerful papal state. Had it not been for his own illness at the time of his father's death and the election of Julius II to be Pope, Cesare might well have become the supreme force in Italian politics. To the patriotic, republican Machiavelli, a Borgia-like figure could very well be the answer to Italy's predicament. A savior with a sword—in the style of the classical hero-founder—might, by replacing the customary mercenary troops with a citizens' militia, be able to carve an orderly commonwealth out of tumultuous north-central Italy, drive forth the foreign barbarians, and end the temporal ambitions of Rome. So Machiavelli pleaded in the final chapter of *The Prince,* to which he added a brief explanation of the technical military innovation by which he believed his dream would become an actuality.[2]

Machiavelli's faith in a military remedy for the ills of Italy is certainly in part a reflection of his own practical experience in government. Although never a soldier, as a bureaucrat he was extremely active in military matters.[3] The fourteen years (1498–1512) during which he served Florence in a permanent official capacity were largely devoted to the problems of war

---

[2] *Prince,* 26. The new method, Machiavelli believes, combines the advantages both of the Swiss pikemen, effective against cavalry but not against infantry, and of the Spanish short-swordsmen, effective against infantry but not against cavalry.

[3] The following is based largely upon Charles C. Bayley, *War and Society in Renaissance Florence: the "De Militia" of Leonardo Bruni* (Toronto: The University of Toronto Press, 1961), pp. 240–315; and Roberto Ridolfi, *The Life of Niccolò Machiavelli,* tr. Cecil Grayson (London: Routledge and Kegan Paul; Chicago: The University of Chicago Press, 1963).

and defense. In 1498 he was appointed second Chancellor
and Secretary of the Ten on Liberty and Peace, an executive
body concerned with military and foreign affairs. Most of his
diplomatic missions, in the course of which he was to visit
France, Switzerland, and Germany, were either directly or
indirectly related to military concerns and provided him with
the occasion to broaden his knowledge of the art of war by
observation and discussion. Between diplomatic missions he
was often occupied with military duties, which were neces-
sitated primarily by his government's continual efforts to
reconquer Pisa after her successful revolt in 1495. In fact,
Machiavelli's first official mission was in regard to the Pisan
war in 1498. His career as a theorist began and ended with
state papers on military subjects: in 1498 he wrote *The Discourse on the War with Pisa,* and in 1526 he reported to the
Pope on the defenses of Florence. Apparently his initial experience with an actual military operation came in the summer of 1500 when he was secretary to the two Florentine Com-
missioners of War who had been assigned to oversee the army
of Gascon and Swiss mercenaries at the siege of the rival city
on the River Arno. The recalcitrance of the troops over a
question of payment turned the campaign into a fiasco. Because of this unfortunate experience and previous ones of a
similar nature, Florence, in order to be less dependent upon
mercenaries, began to rely increasingly upon levies of conscripts from the rural areas for auxiliary garrison and pioneer
duties. In preparation for what proved to be the unsuccessful
summer campaign of 1503 against Pisa, Machiavelli was
charged with raising 2,000 rural conscripts as an auxiliary
force for some 3,500 mercenaries. The failure of the campaign
apparently emboldened Machiavelli's advocacy of the replace-
ment of mercenaries by a regular combat militia. He found
an enthusiastic supporter of the scheme in Cardinal Francesco Soderini, brother of Piero Soderini who had been elected
Gonfalonier of Justice, or Chief Magistrate, of Florence for
life in 1502. But Piero and other Florentine leaders evidently
believed that for the present the institution of a citizens' mili-

tia was politically unfeasible. In the summer of 1504 Machia-velli was associated with the highly imaginative but imprac-tical effort to divert the Arno so as to cut Pisa's line of communication to the sea. This ingenious venture, with which Leonardo da Vinci seems to have been connected, may have been the brain-child of the Secretary. Finally in December 1505, after another disastrous summer campaign, Soderini and the Ten, at the end of their resources, authorized Machia-velli to raise a militia. However, full legislative approval was not sought until the Secretary could show something for his efforts.

Like other medieval city-states, Florence had in times past depended upon a citizens' army. Since the beginning of the fourteenth century, increasing prosperity and the refusal of the wealthy to bear arms had resulted in a general reliance upon mercenaries by the Italian commercial states. The con-dottieri often proved more dangerous to their civic employers than to the enemy. In order to extract funds from their em-ployers, soldiers of fortune might unnecessarily prolong a cam-paign, or engage in a kind of sit-down strike, or threaten to retire altogether in an hour of crisis. Many did not hesitate at blackmail or treachery if profit were involved, and some even seized power for themselves in the states that they were supposedly defending. Besides endangering the finances and civic order of a commonwealth, the condottieri were often militarily ineffectual.[4] Perhaps the chess game style of their mode of warfare has been exaggerated; nevertheless, mercenary captains tended to be more intent upon preserving their own forces and drawing their ample stipends than upon destroying the enemy. The military weakness of the condottieri became all too apparent in their appalling defeat at the battle of Fornovo on July 6, 1495, inflicted by the numerically inferior —but seasoned and determined—troops of Charles VIII.

Clearly some answer to the problem of the condottieri had

[4] On the other hand, it is arguable that the condottieri were the first modern military specialists, and that without their expertise the art of war could scarcely have advanced as it did.

to be discovered if civil order in Florence were to be secure internally and externally. Yet no alternative to an army of native or foreign mercenaries was without serious objections. A professional standing army of citizens would be an exhaustive drain upon the already depleted finances of the state and could very well become an instrument of a would-be tyrant. A militia, recruited from volunteers, would probably be numerically inadequate, while a conscripted militia might, like a standing army, constitute a menace to the republic. In addition, a part-time militia, volunteer or conscript, might be incapable of mastering the complexities of modern warfare against fully trained and experienced soldiers. Machiavelli, enchanted as he was with the idea of the ancient republican citizens' armies of Greece and Rome, believed that the conscription of a combat militia was the only viable course for his city. The nature of the Florentine state, however, presented an obstacle to the project. Any large body of disciplined infantry could not be recruited from the city itself, for citizens would expect to serve in the cavalry and certainly were more eager to command than to be commanded. Hence, Machiavelli concluded that instead of citizens of full status, the subjects of the city would have to be conscripted; of these subjects, the residents of the *cantado,* the rural areas, were to be preferred to the inhabitants of subjugated urban centers, such as Arezzo and Pistoia, within Florentine territory. The difficulty with the plan was that a militia of non-citizens from the *cantado* would never display the loyalty and enthusiasm of citizens in defending the interests of the republic. Nevertheless, since there was no very obvious alternative, the chance would have to be taken. Just after Christmas Day 1505, Machiavelli left the city with his commission to begin to enroll a militia from the *cantado.* His efforts were interrupted by the routine affairs of office in the spring of 1506, and again in October by the task of supplying the troops of Julius II, which were passing through the territory. At this time Machiavelli estimated that more than 5,000 men had been recruited. Since the Florentine citizenry seemed less skeptical about a militia after seeing the fruits of the Secretary's year of labor, the famous militia ordinance, largely drafted by Machiavelli, was passed on December 6, 1506. The ordinance provided for the enlistment of at least 10,000 infantry by the summer of 1507 to consist, after the model of the Swiss formations, of seventy per cent pikemen; the remaining thirty per cent was to be made up of all other arms. Responsibility for implementing the statute naturally fell to Machiavelli who was named Secretary of the newly constituted Nine of Militia. After two busy years we find him, in the spring of 1509, at the siege of Pisa where he is superintending the three camps of the Florentine army, directing their supply, keeping the behavior of the men under constant surveillance, and informing his government of all developments. The laurel for Machiavelli's long and arduous toil was the fall of the city on June 8, with the resulting glory for his victorious militia. Authority was soon granted to raise a force of light cavalry, a commission at which he worked intermittently for the next two years. A cavalry ordinance was passed on March 23, 1512, under the threat of an invasion by Imperial forces. Machiavelli skillfully mobilized the 12,000 militiamen for the city's defense. But the amateur citizen-soldiers were completely routed by the professional Spanish troops of the Emperor. The Medici and their followers, banished since 1494, once more came to power. Unjustly accused of participating in a treasonable conspiracy, Machiavelli was imprisoned and tortured early in 1513. After a month of confinement he was released and allowed to live in retirement at Sant' Andrea, seven miles from Florence, on the small estate that he had inherited from his father.

Although he was never to regain his former office, he was once more to participate in Florentine military affairs during the last year of his life. Visiting Rome in 1525 to present Clement VII with the completed *History of Florence,* which the Pontiff, as Cardinal Giulio de'Medici, had commissioned in 1520, Machiavelli failed to convince his old friend Francesco Guicciardini, the President of the Romagna, that a militia should be raised for the defense of that realm against the

Emperor Charles V, the recent victor at Pavia. Machiavelli's failure, however, must have been somewhat lightened by learning that he was again eligible to hold public office in Florence. In the spring of 1526 he was called upon by Guicciardini, who was acting for the Pope, to assist Count Pietro Navarra, a distinguished military engineer, in strengthening the fortifications of Florence. Machiavelli's report to Rome included a proposal for a design that has been lauded by modern experts. Subsequently, he was appointed Secretary of the newly created Five of the Walls, which was to supervise the renovation of the city's defenses. During the next months, almost up to his death, Machiavelli was in the field with the papal armies serving his city and the newly appointed Lieutenant General of the allied forces, Guicciardini.

Fortune, however, was as fickle as ever, for the Medici-controlled government of Florence, whose full confidence Machiavelli appears to have won after so many years, was overthrown by the republican party. As in 1512, Machiavelli lost his position; a month later on June 21, 1527, he died. Ironically his end came just when it seemed that a new force of militia would be created. Since the early part of the year, a heated debate had been taking place about the advisability of reviving the militia to prepare for the attack of Charles V. Following the successful May revolution, Clement VII settled his differences with Charles, who in turn promised to return the Medici to power after the capture of Florence. The matter of raising a militia for the defense of Florence, therefore, was of the utmost urgency. Conscription of citizens, as well as of noncitizens from the *cantado,* was authorized by an ordinance of November 6, 1527, which was drafted and executed by the secretary of the newly resurrected Ten, Donato Gianotti, an old friend and admirer of the author of *The Art of War.* Florence fell in 1530 but not before the urban militia had given a courageous account of itself. Among the fallen conscripts of that year, was Lodovico Machiavelli, son of Niccolò.

Machiavelli's actual participation in the military affairs of Florence was combined with a keen intellectual interest in the

art of war. He was sensitive to the traditional humanistic ven-
eration for the military greatness of the Romans, and to the
pleas of Petrarch and Salutati for an Italian resurgence, beginning with the expulsion of the foreign barbarians. Another
important influence was the continuing debate during the
Quattrocento concerning the relative merits of militia and
mercenary forces, and the position taken by men like Leonardo
Bruni and Flavio Biondi—wholehearted protagonists of a
militia to be patterned along the lines of a Roman legion.
But the principal fount of the military ideas of Machiavelli
was the thought of the ancients. The standard classical military treatises by Frontinus, Aelian Tacticus (Aelianus), Vegetius, and Modestus were readily available. They were published in a single volume in Rome in 1487 by Eucharius Silber,
reprinted in 1494 and 1497, and also appeared in a Bolognese
edition, 1497. Both Latin and Italian translations of the works
of Xenophon—Machiavelli did not know Greek—also existed.
Xenophon wrote only one technical military manual, the
Hipparchicus (On the Cavalry Commander), and Machiavelli
may have read it. However, the views upon military and civic
leadership and organization expressed in the *Hiero* and in the
Cyropaedia, a work described by Major General Fuller as
"largely a textbook on generalship," [5] would seem to have
influenced the Florentine.[6] After Livy, Xenophon is the most
widely cited author in *The Discourses.*[7] Whereas Livy along
with Frontinus, Plutarch, Polybius, Tacitus, and Vegetius were
to a great extent used by Machiavelli as compendia of facts
about ancient politics and war, Xenophon may well have been
an important source of idea and insight. Machiavelli's intellectual interest in the art of war is by no means confined to anti-

[5] J. F. C. Fuller, *The Generalship of Alexander the Great* (New Brunswick, N. J.: Rutgers University Press, 1960; London: Eyre and Spottis-
wood, 1958), p. 53.

[6] A similar opinion is also expressed in Leo Strauss, *Thoughts on Machiavelli* (Glencoe: Free Press, 1958), pp. 162, 291, 293. See my forthcoming
essay, "Xenophon's Theory of Leadership."

[7] *Discourses,* II, 2, 13; III, 20, 22, 39; also, *Prince,* 14.

quity; numerous examples from modern history are cited in his writings. Early evidence for his research into modern military history is the description in his handwriting of the battle of Anghiari found in Leonardo da Vinci's manuscript known as the Codex Atlanticus; it is there to guide that artist in a painting for the city of Florence, one of the many commissions he never executed. Machiavelli's intellectual passion for the military art, however, is not so much demonstrated by referring to the numerous military examples and precepts cited in his works as it is by realizing that for him, as for Xenophon, a military model is apparently crucial for a theory of politics.[8]

2. STRUCTURE AND SOURCES OF THE TEXT

Machiavelli's reputation as a military theorist rests primarily upon *The Art of War* (1521), the only one of his major works to be published during his lifetime, and the one which he may have believed to be his most important.[9] Even if he had never written the book, his name would still figure in military annals as an early champion of a popular militia, and because of his recommendations on warfare in *The Prince* and *The Discourses*. These scattered recommendations are elaborated in *The Art of War*, in dialogue form, a common Renaissance genre for certain kinds of technical treatises. The preface of the work, dedicated to a young friend, Lorenzo Strozzi, to whom Machiavelli was indebted for a recent kindness, explains the intimate relationship existing between military and civic affairs. Book I discloses a convivial scene during 1516 in the gardens of the Florentine gentleman, Cosimo Rucellai, who died in

[8] A view concerning Xenophon that is developed in my forthcoming essay, "Xenophon's Theory of Leadership."

[9] L. Arthur Burd, "Florence (II): Machiavelli," *Cambridge Modern History* (Cambridge: Cambridge University Press, 1931), I, 211–212. One of the best general discussions of *The Art of War* is Pasquale Villari, *Niccolò Machiavelli e i suoi tempi*, ed. Michele Scherillo (4th posthumous ed.; Milan: Hoepli, 1927), II, 304–343.

1519. Those present besides the host are his guest of honor, the Papal Captain, Fabrizio Colonna,[10] who has paused for rest and refreshment upon his way to Rome from the wars in Lombardy, and a group of Cosimo's intimates: Zanobi Buondelmonti, Battista della Palla, and Luigi Alamanni. Dinner and entertainment concluded, the friends escape the afternoon sun in a shaded corner. In fact, the gathering is the Orti Oricellari, a circle for literary, philosophical, and political discussion founded by Bernardo Rucellai and revived by his grandson, Cosimo.[11] Machiavelli, who probably joined this society of intellectuals in 1515 or somewhat later, wrote for its edification *The Discourses,* which is dedicated to Cosimo and Zanobi. Another work, *The Life of Castruccio Castracani* (1520), is inscribed to Zanobi and Luigi Alamanni. The seven books in *The Art of War* are virtually the monologue of Fabrizio about the military precepts of the ancients and their application to the reformation of contemporary military science. Cosimo, the principal interlocutor of the first two books, retires in favor of Luigi in the third book; the last four books are divided between Zanobi and Battista. Always referring to the practice of the ancients, Fabrizio begins by analyzing the deplorable condition into which the Italian art of war has fallen. He strongly urges the resuscitation of the art by means of a citizens' militia and discourses at length upon the recruitment of the men and officers for such an army. Next, in Book II, he discusses the proper arming, organization, and training of the militia. Two books follow on the order of battle. Book III offers a detailed examination of classical battle formation and method, and includes a description of a model battle

10 Colonna (d. 1520), who had served both the French and the Spanish in Italy, was evidently a first-rate soldier, a cut above the usual mercenary commander. See Colonel Marie Henri François Élizabeth Carrion-Nisas, *Essai sur l'histoire générale de l'art militaire* (Paris, 1824), I, 468 and n. 1.

11 Felix Gilbert, "Bernardo Rucellai and the Orti Oricellari: a Study in the Origin of Modern Political Thought," *Journal of the Warburg and Courtauld Institute,* XII (1949), 101–131.

which incorporates the lessons previously learned. The subjects of Book IV are tactics, planning, stratagems to be used before, during, and after a battle, generalship, and morale. In the last three books the topics are the order of march (V); encampment, including decampment, and the provisioning and welfare of troops (VI); and the defense and attack of towns and fortresses (VII). Fabrizio concludes with a comment upon the superior discipline and military skill of a militia organized according to ancient practice, condemns mercenary armies, and laments that fortune has never provided him with the opportunity of creating and leading the kind of ideal army he has been describing.

The Art of War is the first full-scale modern attempt to revive and popularize classical military thought. While Machiavelli was working on the book, he referred to it by the Latin title *De re militari.*[12] The principal ancient sources upon which he relies are Vegetius, Frontinus, Polybius, and Livy.[13] In addition he makes use of Caesar, Josephus, Plutarch, and others. Aelian Tacticus, the early Greek mathematician who wrote on the formation and drill of the phalanx, may also have been employed. At least Aelian was available to Machiavelli in Latin translation in the various one-volume editions of the time that included Vegetius and Frontinus. Clearly, Vegetius, the author of the famous *De re militari* (4th century of the Christian Era), a compendium on Roman military practice, is the primary source. Machiavelli follows very closely the organization of *De re militari,* which is divided into five books: selection and training of soldiers (I); organization (II); tactics (III); sieges and fortifications (IV); naval warfare (V). The final book, of course, is not employed by Machiavelli, since he is not concerned with naval warfare. In his first book, Machiavelli's remarks about the nature of the men to be se-

[12] Ridolfi, *Life,* p. 178.

[13] With regard to the ancient sources, I am particularly indebted to L. Arthur Burd's invaluable "Le fonti letterarie di Machiavelli nell' *Arte della Guerra,*" *Atti della Reale Academia dei Lincei,* Series V, Vol. IV (1896), Pt. I, 187–261.

lected for military service rely heavily upon the first part of
Book I of Vegetius. Polybius is also followed for the procedures
of Roman recruitment. The discussion of the training of
troops, their drill, and exercise, in the second book of *The
Art of War* draws upon the second part of Book I of the *De
re militari*. The description of Roman weapons and armor
is largely taken from Polybius. Book III of *The Art of War,*
which deals generally with the order of battle, reaches a climax
in the description and discussion of a model battle. Fewer
classical sources are used in this section than in any other.
Although Machiavelli's model battle is usually thought to be
unprecedented in military literature,[14] he may have been inspired by the lengthy description in Xenophon's *Cyropaedia*
of the battle between Cyrus the Great and the forces of King
Croesus of Lydia before the city of Sardis. Certainly the details
of the battle as told by Xenophon are fictional, designed to
demonstrate the military principles that his life of Cyrus is
an excuse for expounding.[15] Concerned as he is in Book IV
with tactics and generalship, Machiavelli turns to the third
book of Vegetius. Here, for the description of the various stratagems used in ancient times, he relies extensively upon Frontinus, as he does throughout the remainder of the book.[16]
Machiavelli's concern with the order of march in Book V

---

[14] The uniqueness of Machiavelli's battle and its importance is emphasized by Felix Gilbert in his "Machiavelli: the Renaissance of the Art
of War," *Makers of Modern Strategy*, ed. E. M. Earle (Princeton: Princeton University Press, 1944), pp. 16–18. Professor Gilbert's essay is indispensable to any student of the subject.

[15] Xenophon, *Cyropaedia* VII. The whole of Book VI is devoted to the
preparation of the campaign against Croesus. Undoubtedly Xenophon
possessed historical sources that are no longer extant, but it seems un-
likely that his meticulous description is an historical account. It seems,
rather, to be fiction designed to teach various lessons in the art of war.
Herodotus, for example, in the *Persian Wars* I. 80, provides us with only
a fraction of the information about the battle found in Xenophon.

[16] Frontinus is the source for the stratagems enumerated in the following passages of *The Art of War:* IV, 116–120, 123–124, 128–129; V, 148–
149; VI, 171–179; VII, 192–198.

draws to a limited extent upon the corresponding section in the third book of Vegetius. Although Machiavelli's prescriptions for the ideal encampment in Book VI are his own, the model is the lengthy treatment of Polybius; [17] Vegetius is also of some importance.[18] In his final book, Machiavelli makes good use of the material on sieges in the fourth book of the *De re militari*. But he does not simply use the classical sources for factual information. For example, key passages from Vegetius on the principles of war are reproduced almost word for word by Machiavelli.[19]

With all his reliance upon, and plagiarism of, the ancient sources, Machiavelli has done something more in *The Art of War* than to produce an anthology of classical military theory. In a way, he has compiled a critical synthesis of ancient military wisdom, modified to some extent to suit the changing times. He selects and discusses the methods of the ancients, weighing one against the other, and choosing and combining those that seem to be the most advantageous for the modern era. Although Roman practice predominates, examples are cited from the Greeks, Carthaginians, Gauls, Scythians, and Assyrians. Nor are the techniques of the moderns—the Swiss, the Spanish, and the French—overlooked. To a limited degree he does realize that the technology of his age renders some of the procedures of the ancients obsolete; for instance, the use of artillery requires fundamental modifications in battle formations.[20] Despite his dependence upon Vegetius, Machiavelli

[17] Polybius, *Histories* VI. 27–42.

[18] Machiavelli had also undoubtedly read Xenophon's description of an ideal encampment in *Cyropaedia* VIII. 5. 2–14.

[19] Compare the following passages in *The Art of War* with those of the *De re militari*, given in parentheses: IV, 124–125, estimation of factors (III. 9); V, 143–144, precautions to be taken on the march (III. 6); VI, 166–167, the health of the army (III. 2); VII, 202–204, basic precepts of the military art (III. 26). A translation of the *De re militari* is in Thomas R. Phillips (ed.), *Roots of Strategy* (Harrisburg, Pa.: The Military Service Publishing Company, 1940), pp. 73–175.

[20] *Art of War*, IV, 113.

differs with him on a number of essentials. Whereas the fourth-
century commentator, who was writing in the period of
Roman military decline, believes in the desirability of a professional standing army, Machiavelli returns to the more ancient Roman republican institution of a popular militia. The
use of cavalry is given slightly greater emphasis by Machiavelli, although for both writers the infantry is the core of the
army. Machiavelli's combination of pikemen and short-swordsmen within the same basic tactical unit is a departure from
the views of the Roman. Vegetius says little about actual battle, a subject which is at the heart of *The Art of War*. Differences also exist between the two thinkers upon the questions
of recruitment, promotion, weapons, combat methods, the
ordering of troops, and encampment. A final word of caution
is necessary in regard to Machiavelli's use of the classical
sources. Although he was influenced appreciably by the Romans, it should be stressed that he misunderstands certain aspects of the Roman art of war. Apparently he never realizes
that Vegetius fails to distinguish between early and late Roman practice, treating examples of both as if they coexisted.
Moreover, the important role of Roman missile weapons and
the use of pikes tends to be overlooked by the Florentine in
his historical researches.

Although Machiavelli's military theory is fundamentally
Roman, it breaks radically with many elements of medieval
practice still in vogue in the Quattrocento.[21] Emphasis in this
respect must be upon the difference from medieval practice,
rather than theory, because the actual conduct of war violated
the precepts of Vegetius, who paradoxically was the most

[21] Still one of the best and most convenient summaries in English of
the medieval art of war is Hoffman Nickerson, "Warfare in the Roman
Empire, the Dark and Middle Ages, to 1494 A.D.," Part II of *Warfare: A
Study of Military Methods from the Earliest Times,* by Oliver Lyman
Spaulding, Hoffman Nickerson, and John Womack Wright, with a Preface
by General Tasker H. Bliss (New York: Harcourt, Brace and Co., 1925),
pp. 191–411. Much of what follows owes a great deal to this and to Part
III, "Warfare, in Modern Times: to the Death of Frederick the Great,"
by Spaulding and Wright, esp. pp. 415–496.

studied and honored military writer during the Middle Ages. The absence of any centralized state, the general lack of any idea of nationhood or national citizenship, and the whole unique structure of feudal society left their imprint upon the medieval art of war. Armies were little more than *ad hoc* collections of local contingents; companies were commanded by the various royal tenants who rallied to the king's assistance as part of their obligation under the feudal system of land tenure. Organization, staff services, and hierarchy of command in the modern sense were nonexistent. Codes of military law were lacking. Each company captain believed that he was the equal of the others. Regular training and discipline were practically unknown. The typical medieval army was always formed just prior to the campaign and disbanded immediately afterward. Moreover, the rank and file of each company possessed no sense of loyalty to the whole; their allegiance was only to their manor, their village, their county. Consequently, a sustained military effort on a large scale was virtually impossible. The complicated tactics of a long strategic retreat could not be entertained, much less executed. If for some reason the king was not ready to give battle to his opponent, his only practical alternative was to retire to a well-fortified stronghold which would protect him from the enemy while he was able to complete his preparation, and which at the same time would serve to prevent his army from disintegrating. Cavalry, consisting of the knights and their men-at-arms, was the major force; the basic strategic principle was to give immediate battle with a mass charge. After the initial clash, in which maneuverability was at a minimum, the medieval battle became a melee of individual struggles. With all the defects of the medieval military art, the medieval soldier displayed great courage and enthusiasm, toughness and fighting spirit.

Christianity had a part in fashioning medieval warfare in both theory and practice. The central idea of a just Christian war for the sake of punishing evildoers was perhaps of little real significance for practice. But the same cannot be said of

the military guild of knighthood with its strong individual-
istic moral code of chivalry shaped by a common Christian
outlook. Widespread belief in the chivalrous virtues and in
the Christian faith, the idea of common membership in the
Republica Christiana, may have helped to prevent warfare
from becoming the very bloody and total kind of activity that
it had been among the ancients. Between medieval foes there
was the bond of Christian conduct and gentlemanly behavior
that tended to mitigate the nature of the punitive action
resorted to by the victor. This may account for the fact that
medieval commanders did not make full use of the stratagems
that had been a common part of the classical military leader's
repertoire. Conversely, the medieval commander seemed particularly susceptible to the employment of deception and
trickery by a ruthless and unchivalrous opponent. Finally, it
should be noted that the medieval soldier could think only
of his Christian faith as the supreme end to which all other
activities were subordinate, an attitude completely alien to
the idea that religion could be an effective means of increasing the morale, determination, and loyalty of the soldier, a
means to the ultimate military goal of victory. If the good
military commander instinctively realized this, he was never
able to conceptualize it, as did classical writers and commanders like Polybius. Machiavelli has little sympathy for these
medieval values. War for him is war, a no-holds-barred contest. Victory is the aim to which all other considerations on
the battlefield must be subordinated. Behavior toward the
enemy is not subject to common moral considerations. Every
type of trickery and violence is legitimate when used against
the enemy. The ideal military commander is one capable of
constantly devising new tactics and stratagems to deceive and
overpower the enemy.

3. SIGNIFICANCE AND INFLUENCE OF THE TEXT

Historians of modern military thought are as quick to point
out the strength of Machiavelli's general principles as they are

to criticize them for their weakness. Almost unanimous praise
is bestowed upon his idea that politics and war constitute
a kind of functional unity, with war serving as an instrument
of politics. The author of one of the first histories of military
theory, Colonel Carrion-Nisas, is quite eloquent in his enthusiasm.[22] As one might expect from the nation of Scharnhorst
and Clausewitz, the great German students of the history of
war like Max Jähns and Hans Delbruck find the idea particularly congenial.[23] F. L. Taylor summarizes the consensus
by writing that Machiavelli "is the first secular writer to attempt to allot to the practice of arms its place among the collective activities of mankind, to define its aims, to regard it
as a means to an end." [24] And this has been the general emphasis given to Machiavelli's political doctrine and its influence
by the German philosophic historians who have examined the
rise of the *Machtstaat* and *Realpolitik,* and the development
of the idea of *Staatsräson* in the modern world.[25]

Wide approval, even by the usually hostile Sir Charles
Oman,[26] is also accorded Machiavelli's condemnation of the
condottieri and their method of waging war, and to his desire
to replace them with national troops who would have a vital
stake in the defense of their country. All are critical, however,

[22] Carrion-Nisas, *Essai,* I, 466–467.

[23] Max Jähns, *Geschichte der Kriegswissenschaften vornehmlich in
Deutschland* (Munich and Leipzig: R. Oldenbourg, 1889), I, 457, 469;
Hans Delbruck, *Geschichte der Kriegskunst im Rahmen der politischen
Geschichte* (Berlin: G. Sticke, 1920), IV, 133.

[24] F. L. Taylor, *The Art of War in Italy, 1494–1529* (Cambridge: Cambridge University Press, 1921), p. 157.

[25] For instance, Friedrich Meinecke, *Machiavellism: the Doctrine of
Raison D'Etat and Its Place in Modern History,* tr. Douglas Scott, Introduction by W. Stark (New Haven: Yale University Press, 1957). This is
a translation of *Die Idee der Staatsräson in der neuren Geschichte* (Munich and Berlin: R. Oldenbourg, 1925). See also Gerhard Ritter, *The
Corrupting Influence of Power,* tr. F. W. Pick, Foreword by G. P. Gooch
(Hadleigh, Essex: Towerbridge Publications, 1952).

[26] Sir Charles Oman, *A History of War in the Sixteenth Century*
(London: Methuen and Co., 1937), p. 94.

of his conviction that part-time citizen-soldiers, instead of a standing army of professionals, would be a viable substitute for foreign mercenaries in a period when war was becoming an increasingly complex activity. This criticism is tempered occasionally by some charitable remark, such as Jähns' that Machiavelli is the "true prophetic spirit" of the modern conscript army.[27] However, it is usually unrecognized that political advantage counts for more than military advantage in Machiavelli's calculations. First, the armed citizenry would be a very definite obstacle in the path of anyone who contemplated seizing power. Second, a militia would always, in Machiavelli's speculations, serve as the fundamental instrument of civic education, a means of instilling a people with respect for authority and a sense of common purpose. Third, a militia would be less costly to the state than a standing army. In sum, a militia is always an instrument and a bulwark of republicanism. Moreover, whatever the military demerits of the citizens militia, the inglorious defeat of the Florentines at Prato in 1512 was hardly a fair trial of Machiavelli's views.[28] We have previously observed that the militia then assembled was a compromise required by the peculiar circumstances of Florentine society and politics, not the embodiment of Machiavelli's ideal. The militia was composed of non-citizens, the Florentine subjects of the rural *cantado,* not of the citizens with a patriotic devotion to their country as prescribed by Machiavelli in *The Art of War.* On this score the behavior of the non-citizen conscripts of 1512 should always be com-

[27] Jähns, *Geschichte,* I, 468.

[28] This seems to be the only conclusion that can be drawn from the superb examination by Professor Bayley, *War and Society,* pp. 268–284. Martin Hobohm, especially in the first volume of his two-volume work, *Machiavellis Renaissance der Kriegskunst* (Berlin: Curtius, 1913), is the first to analyze meticulously the serious military inadequacies of the Florentine militia, and of Machiavelli's whole concept of a militia. In respect to the Florentine militia, Hobohm's criticism has been met in Villari, *Machiavelli,* II, Appendix I, 579–582. The chief point made in the appendix is that much of the military ineffectiveness of the militia resulted from political necessity.

pared to the fortitude of the armed citizenry in 1530, although they too were defeated. Moreover, the discipline and unity of the 1512 force were seriously affected by the continuation in the ranks of the old local jealousies and feuds between rural communities, by the poor and sporadic remuneration of the troops, and by the completely inadequate peacetime training resulting from the government's financial straits. Finally, before they confronted the Spanish veterans in 1512, the militia from the *cantado* had never faced competent, well-trained opponents in the field, an experience altogether different from participating in the lengthy siege of Pisa.

Machiavelli's emphasis upon the infantry as the "nerve of the army," with cavalry relegated to a supporting function, in opposition to the practice of the Middle Ages and of the condottieri, is warmly applauded by the commentators. On this point as in so many of his other recommendations, the author of *The Art of War* is clearly adhering to Roman practice, yet he is by no means oblivious to the increasing prominence of the infantry in his day. Swiss and German pikemen and Spanish short-swordsmen were proving to be the most formidable fighters in Europe, and Machiavelli took the contemporary lesson to heart. But his concept of the infantry suffers from several glaring deficiencies which are singled out by the critics. Infantry, he explains in *The Art of War* and elsewhere, should combine the advantage of the phalanx and of the legion, and consequently of the Swiss pikemen and the Spanish swordsmen. Small-arms have a meager role to play in all his speculations. In actual practice pikemen continued to be used, albeit in decreasing numbers, until the invention of the socket bayonet and its general adoption by the beginning of the eighteenth century; the swordsman was replaced, in the main, by the musketeer before the end of the Cinquecento. The companies of Maurice of Nassau consisted approximately of an equal number of pikemen and musketeers, with no swordsmen; somewhat later, in the army of Gustavus Adolphus, the balance tipped in favor of the musketeer. Besides Machiavelli's grievous underestimation of the significance of small-arms in modern warfare, he fails to assign to artillery more than a very minor part in combat. Perhaps, in part, this neglect can be explained by his fixation on what he thought was the quintessential element of all warfare, the human factor, the quality of the soldier. And, of course, the new missile weapons were crude, inefficient, and unreliable. Also, the reader must remember that Machiavelli is always the zealous advocate who constantly resorts to overstatement and exaggeration in an effort to make the most favorable case for his proposals. He also slights the potential of a well-ordered force of heavy cavalry; to him cavalry means light cavalry, useful in scouting and skirmishing, but never as a major force with a major tactical role. Machiavelli does, however, include more cavalry in his legions than either of his two authorities, Polybius and Vegetius, who are describing Roman practice. Finally, on the basis of his 1526 report on the defenses of Florence with its recommendations for some innovations, Machiavelli may be the first modern writer on the subject of fortifications; but since the report was not published, his impact upon subsequent developments seems negligible.[29]

The full story of Machiavelli's influence upon subsequent military theory and practice has never been told. I do not intend to do so here, although a few remarks, mainly suggestions and speculations as to the nature and direction of the influence, are necessary. Evidently, *The Art of War* was widely read and highly esteemed throughout the sixteenth century. Besides the two Florentine editions of 1521 and 1529, there were six other Italian editions before the end of the century.[30] In Valencia the work was plagiarized in the seven books of Diego de Salazar's *Tratado de re militari* (1536). Perhaps the very fact that in the dialogue Salazar substitutes the great Spanish captain, Gonzalo de Córdoba, for Fabrizio Colonna, indicates the value he placed upon the doctrine of Machiavelli.

[29] Villari, *Machiavelli*, II, 335–339; Maurice J. D. Cockle, *A Bibliography of Military Books up to 1642*, Introduction by Sir Charles Oman (2nd ed.; London: The Holland Press, 1957), p. xxi.

[30] Venice, 1540, 1541, 1546, 1550, 1554; Palermo, 1587.

A French translation by Jehan Charriers, in a volume that included his translation of Onasander's *Strategicus,* was published in Paris in 1546.[31] Peter Whitehorne's English translation appeared in London in 1560, and was reprinted in 1573 and 1588. In the early part of the next century, Latin and German translations were published. Just as important as these numerous editions in the dissemination of the Florentine's military ideas was the 1548 publication in Paris of the anonymous *Instructions sur le faict de la guerre,* often attributed to Guillaume du Bellay, but actually the labor of Raymond de Beccarie de Pavie, sieur de Fourquevaux (1508–1574), distinguished French soldier and diplomat. Fourquevaux's book is one of the most notable and frequently cited works of the time.[32] Not only the organization, but also the substance of the work owes more to *The Art of War* than to any single source.[33] Indeed, the Frenchmen's debt to Machiavelli is acknowledged by the new title given to the edition of 1549, *Instructions sur le Faict de la Guerre, extraicts des livres de Polybe, Frontin, Vegece, Cornazon, Machiavelle, et plusiers autres bons autheurs.* Machiavelli's growing prestige as a military thinker is perhaps indicated by the juxtaposition of his name with those of the ancients, a prestige which is seemingly confirmed in a similar way several decades later by Montaigne's observation:

It is related of many military leaders that they had certain books in particular esteem, as the great Alexander did Homer; Scipio Africanus, Xenophon; Marcus Brutus, Polybius; Charles the Fifth, Philip

---

[31] A description of the edition is found in Victor Waille, *Machiavel en France* (Paris: A. Ghio, 1884), pp. 164–165. Unfortunately, Albert Cherel's survey, *La pensée de Machiavel en France* (Paris: L'Artisan du Livre, 1935) does not deal with the influence of Machiavelli's military ideas.

[32] Cockle, *Bibliography,* no. 41; G. Dickinson (ed.), *The Instructions sur le Faict de la Guerre of Raymond de Beccarie de Pavie, Sieur de Fourquevaux* (London: University of London, The Athlone Press, 1954), pp. v, cix. The various sixteenth-century editions are as follows: French, 1548, 1549, 1553, 1592; Italian, 1550, 1571; Spanish, 1567; English, 1589; German, 1594.

[33] Dickinson, *ibid.,* pp. cxx–cxxii, cxxvi–cxxix.

de Commines; and in our times it is said that Machiavelli is still held in repute in other countries.[34]

Perhaps Machiavelli's most immediate, and, indeed, most significant contribution to the development of modern military science resulted from his revival of the idea of Roman legion organization, and all that is entailed by such organization. His proposal for tactical organization is based upon the Roman army of 24,000 men, divided into four legions. The legions would consist of ten battalions, each of 450 men. In theory this arrangement, as presented in *The Art of War*, would seem to be a definite tactical advance over the medieval army, which was a motley assembly of companies of varying size incapable of a planned and coordinated action of complexity. In practice, a legion divided into four battalions is still a cumbersome unit for modern warfare. Actual proof of this came with the institution in 1534 of legion organization for the French provincial militia by Francis I, guided, perhaps, by the recommendations of the Florentine Secretary. Although the French legions proved to be tactically ineffective and generally failed to distinguish themselves in battle, they did constitute the nucleus of the Crown's infantry during the Wars of Religion; in the seventeenth century, the two legions that had not been disbanded were the basis of the regiments of Champagne and Picardy. Fourquevaux's *Instructions,* inspired by Machiavelli, was addressed to the reform of the French legionary system. But if Machiavelli in theory and the French in practice had failed to exploit fully the tactical possibilities of legion organization, others who followed did not. Roman legion organization was the source for the ideas of Maurice of Nassau and his famous disciple, Gustavus Adolphus, who between them launched the modern art of war. In order to achieve maximum flexibility, maneuver, and control, Maurice ultimately decided to divide his army into units of 1,000 men, comprising groups of 80 to 100 soldiers.

But the essence of the Roman legion was discipline. And this

[34] Michel de Montaigne, "Observations on Julius Caesar's Method of Making War," in *The Essays of Michel de Montaigne,* tr. and ed. Jacob Zeitlin (New York: Alfred A. Knopf, 1935), II, 387.

discipline depended upon the careful selection of recruits, extensive drill and training, a hierarchical chain of command, functional arrangements defined by rules, and a code of military law. To Machiavelli, discipline is of paramount importance, particularly because of his advocacy of pikemen. As he knew from the Swiss experience with the phalanx, nothing but the most severe discipline and drill would make this method of combat successful. In addition, Machiavelli's combination of pikemen and swordsmen within the same basic unit required even greater discipline than might otherwise be needed. If, in the actual development of modern warfare by Maurice of Nassau and Gustavus Adolphus, legion organization was greatly modified, the iron discipline of the legion became even more significant because of the very nature of the modifications. Once infantry, equipped with firearms and pikes, becomes the major combat force, and once small tactical units, singly and in varying combinations, are expected to execute with exactitude their different combat missions without endangering the unity of the battle plan, disciplined coordination must supercede individual virtuosity. The army must operate with machine-like precision.

Regardless of Machiavelli's lack of prescience in regard to professionalism, small-arms and artillery, and cavalry, his emphasis upon infantry as the nerve of the army and upon legion organization indicated a direction to be taken by military reform, while his insistence upon the revival of ancient discipline truly heralded the future. All of this is suggested by Voltaire, who was far from enchanted with the Florentine:

Let us observe that the arrangements, the marching, and the evolution of battalions, nearly as they are now practiced, were revived in Europe by one who was not a military man—by Machiavel, a secretary at Florence. Battalions three, four, and five deep; battalions advancing upon the enemy; battalions in square to avoid being cut off in a rout; battalions four deep sustained by others in column; battalions flanked by cavalry—all are his. He taught Europe the art of war; it had long been practiced, without being known.[35]

---

[35] Voltaire, François-Marie Arouet, "Battalion," *A Philosophical Dictionary*, tr. from the French (London: W. Dugdale, 1843), I, 198. The remainder of the article is an attack upon Machiavelli.

The Art of War, then, is the first classic of modern military science.[36] Machiavelli's achievement is the rejection of medieval practice and the attempt to revive the ancient art of war. From a technical point of view, he is not a particularly keen observer or accurate analyst of either ancient or contemporary military affairs. His is not a scientific or logically rigorous mind. Deeply in love with everything Roman, he is the impassioned littérateur whose very passion not only tends to blind him to the significance of the military developments in his world, but also to some features of antiquity. But it is precisely this ardent love affair with mistress Rome that is responsible for his deep imprint upon the emergence of modern military science. This is the reason why Sir Charles Oman's verdict is at once true and irrelevant:

> But unfortunately for his reputation as a prophet in the military sphere, all his recommendations of a practical sort bear no relation whatever to the actual development of tactics and organization during the later years of the century. He "backed the wrong horse" in almost every instance; he thought that artillery was going to continue negligible, that the day of cavalry in battle was quite over, that infantry was going to continue in very huge units, like the legion, and that the pike was destined to be put out of action by short weapons for close combat, like the sword of the ancient Roman or of the Spanish footman of Gonsalvo de Cordova. In every case his forecast was hopelessly erroneous.[37]

Sir Charles fails to understand that the revolution in warfare in early modern Europe owed less to technology—the invention and application of small-arms and artillery—than to changes in human relations established by Maurice of Nassau and Gustavus Adolphus in their model armies. The revolution in discipline and drill wrought by these military virtuosi made the efficient use of modern missile weapons possible, a

[36] The consensus of the most serious historians of the subject since the French Revolution. For example, see Carrion-Nisas, *Essai,* I, xliii–xliv; 231, n. 1; General Étienne Alexandre Bardin, *Dictionnaire de l'armée de terre,* ed. General Oudinot de Reggio (Paris, 1841–1851), I, 440, 462; Jähns, *Geschichte,* I, 456–457, 468–469; Delbruck, *Geschichte,* IV, 117, 132–133; Gilbert, "Machiavelli," pp. 20–25.

[37] Oman, *History,* pp. 93–94.

fact succinctly expressed by Max Weber almost half a century ago:

The kind of weapon has been the result and not the cause of discipline. . . . It was discipline and not gunpowder which initiated the transformation. The Dutch army under Maurice of the House of Orange was one of the first modern disciplined armies. . . . Gun powder and all the war techniques associated with it became significant only with the existence of discipline—and to the full extent only with the use of war machinery, which presupposes discipline.[38]

German military historians have long recognized that the new emphasis upon discipline and drill is directly related to the revival of interest in the ancient military art.[39] Before Machiavelli's time, the systematic conception of troop formations is virtually unknown; after his time, ancient drill manuals and military ordinances are translated. The ancient orders of battle, of the march, and of the camp are resurrected; even ancient weapons become models to be imitated.

The great value given to military discipline during the second half of the sixteenth century is indicated in two fundamental ways. One is the development of military law. Fourquevaux's book stresses the subject of military justice, and contains the first complete code of military discipline in the French language.[40] It is followed by Gaspard de Coligny's *Le Règlement au siege de Boulogne* (1551), which is gener-

[38] Max Weber, *From Max Weber: Essays in Sociology*, tr. and ed. H. H. Gerth and C. Wright Mills (New York: Oxford University Press, 1946), pp. 256–257. The selection is from Weber's *Wirtschaft und Gesellschaft* (Tübingen: Mohr, 1922). A penetrating criticism of the "technocratic theory of history" is to be found in the essay of David Rapoport, "Military and Civil Societies: the Contemporary Significance of a Traditional Subject in Political Theory," *Political Studies*, XII (June 1964), 178–201.

[39] See Hobohm, *Kriegskunst*, II, 191 ff., 399, 402–403; Delbruck, *Geschichte*, IV, 117 ff.; Werner Hahlweg, *Heeresreform der Oranier und die Antike* (Berlin: Junker und Dünnhaupt, 1941), esp. pp. 26–29. Also of importance in this connection are the two articles by Gerhard Oestreich, "Der römische Stoizismus und die oranische Heeresreform," *Historische Zeitschrift*, CLXXVI (1953), 17–43; and "Justus Lipsius als Theoretiker des neuzeitlichen Machtstaates," *ibid.*, CLXXXI (1956), 31–78.

[40] Dickinson, *Instructions*, pp. lxxvi, lxxxix.

ally believed to be the foundation of modern military law. A second expression of the new premium placed upon discipline is the appearance of a variety of tactical tables for the convenience of the commander in planning operations; in these, men are reduced to numbers to be manipulated arithmetically. Among the first of the compilations of tactical tables was that of the military engineer, Girolamo Cataneo, who also wrote on fortifications and bombardment.[41] Mathematics, of course, was being applied increasingly to the problems of military engineering and artillery. But the tactical tables represent the application of mathematics to the organization and control of human beings. The use of the quantitative method for the planning and direction of troop formations and maneuvers presupposes an emphasis in theory and practice upon discipline and drill. About the same time that the men who were revolutionizing warfare were applying mathematics to questions of military organization, the pioneers of modern science were beginning to describe the relations of natural phenomena in quantitative terms. The marriage of the two interests is found in the person of the illustrious astronomer and mathematician, Thomas Digges. Highly esteemed by Tycho Brahe, this fascinating figure of Elizabethan England, was a Copernican who, however, rejected the idea of fixed stars. He is most widely known for his theory of the infinity of the celestial system which he advanced before Giordano Bruno's views were known. From 1586 to 1593 he served as mustermaster-general of English forces in the Netherlands, a position acquired through the influence of his patron, the Earl of Leicester. Evidently one result of his military experience

---

41 *Tavole brevissime per sapere con prestezza quante file uanno à formare una giustissima battaglia* (Brescia, 1563). The full title of the English translation of 1574 is *Most briefe tables to know redily howe manye ranckes of footemen armed with Corslettes, as vnarmed, go to the making of a iust battayle, from an hundred vnto twentye thousande. Next a very easye, and approved way to arme a battaile with Harkabuzers, and winges of horsemen according to the vse at these daies Newlye increased, and largelye amplified both in the tables, as in the declarations of the same, by the Aucthour himselfe.*

was the publication in 1590 of *An arithmetical warlike treatise named Stratioticos*, the revised edition of a book which first appeared in 1579.[42] Described by Cockle as "one of the best military books of the time," [43] it includes a treatise on arithmetic and algebra, calculations for the officer, the duties of the officer, a discussion of military law, and mathematics for artillery. On the basis, then, of books like those by Cataneo and Digges, it seems that military arithmetic preceded Sir William Petty's discovery of political arithmetic by a century. Notions of a mechanistic system of nature and a mechanistic military system seem to have arisen about the same time. The application of mathematics to military organization suggests that the army began to be thought of as a deliberately created system of interacting parts,[44] the movements of which are susceptible to quantification, years before Thomas Hobbes, the first modern political thinker, employed the Galilean method to describe the state as a mechanical contrivance. These facts and conjectures underscore Max Weber's argument that the new military discipline, rather than the new technology, is the fundamental factor in the transformation of military science during the early modern period, and they suggest the crucial role of Machiavelli's plea for rational military organization.

As we have seen, although in a form somewhat different from his intentions, the ideal of Machiavelli was to a great extent realized in the efficient military mechanism created by Maurice of Nassau, who was evidently acquainted with the precepts of the Florentine both directly through *The Art of War* and indirectly through the writings of Fourquevaux and Fran-

---

[42] Thomas Digges had also collaborated with his father, Leonard, upon a treatise concerned with military applications of mathematics, *A Geometrical Practise, named Pantometria* (London, 1571). A second edition was published in 1591. The subjects are topography, artillery, and military and naval architecture.

[43] Cockle, *Bibliography*, no. 25.

[44] Gilbert, "Machiavelli," pp. 17–18, asserts that Machiavelli "conceived of a battle as functioning like a well-oiled mechanism, because this concept corresponded to the course of a real battle."

cesco Patrizi (1529–1597).[45] However, the thinker more than any other responsible for shaping the outlook of the prince is the all but forgotten Justus Lipsius (1547–1606).[46] While the Belgian savant, famed for his critical edition of Tacitus (1575), was teaching at the University of Leyden between 1579 and 1591, the young Maurice was his student for a brief time. In 1589 Lipsius published his *Politicorum Libri Sex* and presented a copy to the prince. Fifteen editions of the book appeared in the next decade as well as translations into Dutch, French, English, Polish, and German, and somewhat later, into Spanish and Italian. The treatise is judged by Oestreich to be the theoretical foundation for the military reforms of Maurice [47] and a prime intellectual force upon the distinguished Austrian generalissimo, Montecuccoli, the first to attempt rigorously to systematize the art of war.[48] If this estimation of the impact of Lipsius is correct, then Machiavelli must be allotted a share in the honors. For Lipsius, a devotee of the Florentine, is one of the few modern writers to couple his idol with the venerated names of Plato and Aristotle.[49] Machiavelli is the only modern thinker whom he recommends to his readers. Lipsius, like his master, roundly condemns the use of mercenary troops, and dwells upon the indispensability of the careful selection, training, and discipline of soldiers.[50] However, Lipsius calls for a national cadre-conscript army instead

---

[45] Patrizi, *Parralleli Militari . . . Ne' quali si fa paragone delle Milizie antiche, in tutte le parti loro, con le moderne* (Rome, 1594).

For the relation between Machiavelli and Maurice see the two essays of Oestreich cited above p. xxxiv, n. 39, and Jähns, *Geschichte*, I, 471; Delbruck, *Geschichte*, IV, 181–183; Hahlweg, *Heeresreform*, p. 185, n. 197.

[46] Revival of interest in Lipsius in regard to these matters is largely due to the two essays of Oestreich. See also the informative analysis of Lipsius in Rapoport, "Military and Civil Societies."

[47] Oestreich, "Justus Lipsius," esp. p. 46.

[48] *Ibid.*, pp. 66–67.

[49] *Ibid.*, p. 41. On Lipsius and Machiavelli, see also Giuseppe Toffanin, *Machiavelli e il "Tacitismo"* (Padua: Draghi, 1921), pp. 174–178.

[50] Oestreich, "Justus Lipsius," pp. 61–63, for his comparison. In addition, see his "Römische Stoizismus," pp. 25–27.

of a militia. The most interesting intellectual link between the two thinkers is in Lipsius' concept of a neo-stoic military morality or ideology. Central to the concept is the idea of constancy which involves duty, self-control, temperance, life-giving energy, and strength of soul. Here is a distinct echo of the Machiavellian *virtù,* one that was destined to become the military counterpart of the Calvinistic outlook in the economic world.[51]

From the time that the importance of discipline and training began to be taken for granted by soldiers, that is, from the time of the pioneer achievements of Maurice and Gustavus, and of the emergence of the national professional army, Machiavelli's reputation as a military thinker suffered.[52] Obviously, many of his technical recommendations could not be followed in the newly developing warfare of maneuver, movement, and firepower. The decline of his reputation was also related to the abuse directed against his political views, the moral indignation with Machiavellism expressed in a series of anti-Machiavellian tracts, the most famous of which was by Frederick the Great. Accordingly, from the middle of the seventeenth century until the early part of the nineteenth, his military ideas are openly criticized; his name is seldom mentioned in the military classics then being written. But the chief critics are often men of little military reputation, while the obligation of some of the major military classics to his ideas is very obvious. Among the critics were Brantôme, Algarotti, and Maizeroy. The notorious *Mémoires* of Brantôme (1540–1614) were not published until 1665–1666. Although the work is a valuable exposé of the life and manners of the sixteenth-

[51] Gustavus Adolphus' demands upon his commanders are: virtue, knowledge, prudence, authority, and success. Virtue consists of uprightness of life, zeal in enterprise, diligence in service, valor in danger, hardiness in action, swiftness in execution. Nils Ahnlund, *Gustav Adolf the Great,* tr. Michael Roberts (Princeton: Princeton University Press, 1940), p. 142.

[52] Jähns, *Geschichte,* I, 471–472, is a useful guide, as are the various articles in Bardin, *Dictionnaire.*

century French court, the author's historical naïveté is quite evident. A soldier of considerable experience, Brantôme nevertheless was more of a courtier than a military figure; he gained a greater reputation for his boudoir adventures than for his skill on the field of battle. A second critic, Count Algarotti (1712–1764), the friend of Voltaire and Frederick the Great, although of some importance in the sphere of art and literary criticism, is scarcely a judge of military questions. Of these critics, Maizeroy (1719–1780), who served with distinction under the great Marshal de Saxe in Bohemia and Flanders, and who devoted many years to a study of the ancient military art, is the only one fully qualified to evaluate Machiavelli's military thinking. Much of his criticism, particularly of Machiavelli's understanding of ancient military practice, is sound and erudite. But taken as a whole, Maizeroy's analysis tends to be more pedantic than illuminating.

Of the five classic military thinkers writing in the eighteenth century—Montecuccoli, Folard, Saxe, Frederick the Great, and Guibert—only Folard mentions and praises Machiavelli. Raimond de Montecuccoli (1608–1681), the skillful antagonist of Turenne, was too cautious and prudent, too much of a Fabius Maximus, to rank among the greatest of the military practitioners. Great he was, nevertheless, and even greater was his posthumous fame of being the modern Vegetius, which was gained by his *Mémoires,* first published in Vienna in 1718. His theoretical exploits have been likened to those of Bodin in political science and Bacon in philosophy.[53] He was the first to conceive of the art of war as a science by attempting to systematize its principles. The father of the Prussian military reforms at the opening of the nineteenth century, Scharnhorst, found a stimulus and a model in the conception of Montecuccoli.[54] He is quite definitely the intellectual heir of Machiavelli and Lipsius. Yet, unlike them, Montecuccoli brings to

[53] Rudolf Stadelmann, *Scharnhorst: Schicksal und geistige Welt* (Wiesbaden: Limes Verlag, 1952), p. 95.

[54] *Ibid.,* pp. 91–99, for the influence of Montecuccoli upon Scharnhorst.

his material the sure touch of the experienced man of war, with a discerning eye for the logic of the activity he has mastered. The very organization of the work and the terse prose style testify to a new approach. The first book explains the principles of military science in an extremely concise, systematic, and forceful way; maxims that are relevant to various principles are contained in the second book; a more detailed application of some of the principles is illustrated in the third book by the author's reflections upon the war with the Turks in Hungary from 1661 to 1664. Characterized by an absence of rhetoric, the work opens with the statement that the purpose of war is victory; and victory depends upon the preparation, the disposition, and the action of the troops.[55] Three lengthy chapters on each of these factors follow. Preparation is concerned with the quality, arms, training, and discipline of soldiers and officers, with artillery, munitions, supply, and money. Disposition of troops is contingent upon the nature of the forces to be used, the country in which the action is to take place, and the nature of the operation: whether it is for attack, defense, or relief. Action in marching, camping, and battle should be executed with resolution, secrecy, and rapidity. Not the least interesting of Montecuccoli's remarks are on generalship.[56] The general must have certain natural or inborn characteristics: a warlike spirit, vigorous health, majestic appearance. Much more essential are the acquired attributes, of which the most important is a vast knowledge of war to be learned, not from books, but from long military experience. Next among the acquired qualities is *la vertue morale:* prudence, justice, temperance, and *force.* The last, which embraces courage, fortitude, energy, and determination, is the uniquely military virtue, the attribute of the good soldier, and especially the good officer. By setting an example of *force* the good general will be able to stir his army to a vigorous and skillful attack. In times of adversity his *force* will in-

[55] Raimond de Montecuccoli, *Mémoires* (Amsterdam and Leipzig, 1756), IV, 1–2.

[56] *Ibid.,* IV, 7, 216–222.

spire his soldiers with the powers of resistance, endurance, and steadfastness. *Force* is the inner spiritual strength of the man of war. Here is the *virtù* of Machiavelli, the neo-stoic *constantia* of Machiavelli's disciple, Justus Lipsius. Whatever Folard, Saxe, Frederick the Great, and Guibert may think of the Florentine, they laud this modern Vegetius.

After Montecuccoli, the Chevalier Folard (1669–1752) is the first theorist of significance. Folard was an experienced soldier of valorous service with the Swedish forces of Charles XII as well as with the French. Because of his difficult and fiery temperament—in this respect he was a kind of military Rousseau—he never rose beyond the rank of Master-of-Camp. His commentary upon the *Histories* of Polybius was published from 1727 to 1730 and went through several editions, enlarged and revised by the author during his lifetime. The detailed analysis of ancient practice in the work is an excuse for the exposition of his own tactical views. Despite the antagonism that his vigorous and polemical arguments aroused, his work continued to be read for many years. His single comment upon Machiavelli is both a eulogy, and an attempt to discredit *The Art of War*. Folard, in treating *coup d'oeil*, the able commander's intuitive grasp of the military situation, cites and praises Machiavelli's stress upon hunting as a means to this end.[57] *The Art of War*, however, is a thinly disguised plagiarism, hardly worthy of the author of the immortal works, *The Prince* and *The Discourses*, which warrant the careful scrutiny of all men of war. Thus the irascible Chevalier is the sole military thinker of stature to dismiss unreservedly *The Art of War*.

Whether Folard's one-time pupil, the renowned Marshal Maurice de Saxe (1695–1750) would agree with his mentor's abrupt dismissal of *The Art of War* is doubtful, since he pays homage to the Florentine in spirit, if not by name, in *Mes Rêveries* (1757).[58] This facinating essay is claimed by its au-

[57] Jean-Charles Folard, *Histoire de Polybe avec un commentaire* (Amsterdam, 1774), I, 222–223. The citations from Machiavelli are, *Prince*, 14; *Discourses*, III, 39.

[58] An excellent English translation is in Phillips, *Roots*, pp. 189–300.

thor to have been completed in December of 1732 after thirteen nights' work in an effort to dispel his boredom.[59] The advocacy of conscription; the concern with the human factor in war and with the quality, welfare, and morale of the troops; the admiration for the Roman legion and the proposal for the modification of legion organization which is in effect the anticipation of the divisional army; the attention to the problem of discipline; the perceptive remarks upon leadership—all bring Machiavelli to mind.[60]

For Frederick the Great (1712–1786), a firm admirer of Saxe, *The Art of War* was a "favourite book." [61] A number of themes of the Prussian King's *Military Instructions*,[62] originally written in 1747 to be circulated secretly among his top commanders, would tend to indicate the influence of Machiavelli: discipline, estimate of factors, supply, encampment, secrecy, and deception. The good general must conceal his thoughts, for he should always be an actor on stage, thereby able to shape the mood of his army.[63] But there are important differences in the outlooks of the two men. Although Frederick is convinced that knowledge of terrain is essential to good generalship, he does not recommend the chase as a means of acquiring this knowledge.[64] Moreover, his belief in firepower and in the tactical role of cavalry is at variance with the teachings of the Florentine. But in spite of such differences, the true Machiavellian spirit is manifested in Frederick's constant emphasis, in theory and practice, upon the attack. Even when on the defensive, one should always attempt to seize the initiative in an audacious manner. The best defense is a vigorous and purposeful offense. Frederick's boldness and daring as a military commander won the praise of Napoleon.

A more striking parallel to some of the ideas of the Ren-

---

59 *Ibid.*, pp. 210, 276, 300.

60 *Ibid.*, pp. 193–201, 210–224, 243, 245–249, 270, 294–300.

61 According to Cockle, *Bibliography*, no. 12.

62 Reprinted in Phillips, *Roots*, pp. 311–400.

63 *Ibid.*, p. 346.

64 *Ibid.*, pp. 338–342.

aissance thinker is found in the influential *Essai général de tactique* (1773) by the Comte de Guibert (1743–1790)—so much so that Carrion-Nisas notes the absence of any acknowledgement.[65] It is particularly in the preliminary discourse that the hand of Machiavelli is seen,[66] although his influence can also be detected in parts of the technical treatment of tactics, for example, in regard to the march.[67] From Guibert's dedication to his fatherland, to his concluding plea for a national leader of genius to regenerate France, the discourse is animated by a fervent patriotism. One wonders whether *The Prince* was a model. The heart of the introductory statement is reminiscent of Machiavelli's opening and concluding statements in *The Art of War*. Guibert begins by describing the corruption of France, and of Europe in general, contrasting this self-seeking world of avarice and luxury, in which all sense of the common interest has been lost, with the hardiness, vigor, and solidarity of Rome. He insists upon the intimate connection between military and civic life.[68] The military skill of the Romans and the amazing prowess of their legions, on the one hand, and their manners and values, their social and political arrangements, on the other, were mutually sustaining. Hannibal, despite his consummate military ability, was doomed in his contest with Rome because his army and men were the products of a corrupt city.[69] Once Rome found a general to equal the Carthaginian, her triumph was assured. The chaotic condition of the art of war of his day, Guibert contends, arises from the corrupt civic order. A new foundation, which will be at once political and military, is the only solution; a founder-hero is the only means by which the new order can be achieved.[70]

[65] Carrion-Nisas, *Essai*, I, 382.
[66] Jacques Antoine Hippolyte Guibert, *Essai général de tactique* (London, 1773), I, iii–xliii.
[67] Carrion-Nisas, *Essai*, I, 483.
[68] Guibert, *Essai*, esp. I, xxxiii.
[69] *Ibid.*, I, xxiii–xxiv.
[70] *Ibid.*, I, xx–xxii, xxxvi–xxxvii.

Napoleon Bonaparte in many ways is the embodiment of the ideals of Machiavelli and Guibert. *Le grand constructeur,* as Madelin calls the Corsican,[71] studied Guibert closely, and read and admired Machiavelli.[72] He respected *The Art of War;* [73] he commented upon *The Prince;* [74] he carried *The Discourses* with him on his campaigns; [75] he outlined *The History of Florence.*[76] In 1808 the Emperor ordered a special portable library of one thousand volumes, including *The Discourses,* which was to be used in the field.[77] His library in the Trianon contained a nine volume edition of Machiavelli's works, translated by Guiraudet.[78] Napoleon turned to Machiavelli the military thinker for broad principles rather than for technical advice.[79] War as a political instrument, the purpose of which is to defeat the enemy, is axiomatic for both thinker and soldier. Similarly, they believed—the one in theory, the

[71] Louis Madelin, *Napoléon* (Paris: Dunod, 1935), p. 447.

[72] *Ibid.,* p. 40; Waille, *Machiavel,* pp. 142–143, 153; Cherel, *La Pensée de Machiavel,* pp. 249–253.

[73] Waille, *Machiavel,* pp. 142–143; Spencer Wilkinson in *The Rise of General Bonaparte* (Oxford: The Clarendon Press, 1930), p. 149, is less positive than Waille that Napoleon had read *The Art of War.* He feels that in all likelihood he did so.

[74] *Machiavel commenté par N^on Buonaparte; Manuscrit trouvé dans le carrosse de Buonaparte après la Bataille de Mont-Saint-Jean, Le 18 Juin 1815* (Paris, 1816). The book consists of a new French translation of *The Prince* with Napoleon's comments. Annotated excerpts from *The Discourses* are also included. The preparation of the volume and the introduction were the work of the Abbé Aimé Guillon. Neither Waille, *Machiavel,* p. 251, nor Cherel, *La Pensée de Machiavel,* pp. 251–253, 335, nor item 443 under Napoleon I in *Bibliothèque Nationale: Catalogue Générale des Livres Imprimés,* Vol. XXII, indicates that this work is spurious.

[75] J. Colin, *L'Éducation militaire de Napoléon* (Paris: R. Chapelot, 1900), pp. 115–116.

[76] William Milligan Sloane, *The Life of Napoleon Bonaparte* (New York: The Century Company, 1912), I, 150.

[77] *Correspondance de Napoléon I* (Paris, 1854–1869), XVII, no. 14207, as quoted in J. M. Thompson, *Letters of Napoleon* (Oxford, Basil Blackwell, 1934), pp. 223–225.

[78] Antoine Guillois, *Napoléon, l'homme, le politique, l'orateur d'après sa correspondance et ses œuvres* (Paris: Perrin, 1889), II, 578.

[79] Colin, *L'Éducation,* pp. 114–118, 371.

other in practice—in the importance of careful planning, of seizing the initiative, of the use of deception, and of swift execution. Again the human factor in war is vital for each. Finally, the role of the leader is essential to success: his courage, energy, foresight, and *coup d'oeil.*

When we turn from *le grand constructeur,* himself, to nineteenth-century military practitioners, theorists, and historians who were influenced by his accomplishments in war, we find high praise for the Florentine man of letters. Marshal Gouvion-Saint-Cyr (1764–1830), referred to by Napoleon as a "military genius" and who was responsible for the important military reform of the French army after the Restoration, esteemed the writings of Machiavelli, Montecuccoli, and Frederick the Great.[80] He regarded Machiavelli as a great man of war, although ignorant of the actual practice of arms. Colonel Carrion-Nisas, classmate and officer of Napoleon, one of the first competent military historians, urges his readers to study carefully *The Art of War.*[81] He compares Machiavelli to Polybius; just as Polybius stands between the Greeks and the Romans, so the Florentine bridges the ancient and modern military worlds.[82] General Bardin believes that no educated man of war can dispense with reading *The Art of War.*[83]

Not least among the admirers and interpreters of Napoleon's military prowess is Karl von Clausewitz (1780–1831), whose *Vom Krieg,*[84] published posthumously by his wife in 1832, became the foundation for the far-reaching changes in the art of war in the nineteenth and twentieth centuries. Clausewitz, the protégé and intellectual heir of Scharnhorst, is without doubt the greatest military theorist of the West. His doctrines

---

[80] Waille, *Machiavel,* p. 141.

[81] Carrion-Nisas, *Essai,* I, 231, n. 1; Jähns, *Geschichte,* I, 472, concurs in general with the high estimate of Machiavelli by Carrion-Nisas.

[82] Carrion-Nisas, *Essai,* I, 462. Delbruck, *Geschichte,* IV, 133, also compares Machiavelli to Polybius.

[83] Bardin, *Dictionnaire,* I, 462.

[84] Karl von Clausewitz, *On War,* tr. J. J. Graham, Introduction and notes by F. N. Maude (London: K. Paul, Trench Trübner and Co. Ltd., 1911), 3 vols.

of unlimited war and of war as an extension of politics are found in Machiavelli. Much of the insight of the Florentine is summarized in Clausewitz's view of the central problem of war: to gain "a preponderance of physical forces and material advantages at the decisive point." [85] A similarity to the ideas of Machiavelli is seen in the Prussian's concern with the estimate of factors, knowledge of terrain, and his comparison of the conduct of war to the "workings of an intricate machine." [86] Evidence of the legacy of Machiavelli is also apparent in Clausewitz's stress upon the principle of attack in his discussion of strategy. Use one's "entire forces with the utmost energy" is his famous maxim.[87] In fact, Clausewitz hails Machiavelli as possessing "a very sound judgement in military matters." [88] But to one who has read Clausewitz for the first time, his treatment of the moral factors in war provides the most striking parallel to the precepts of Machiavelli. The analysis of the qualities of generalship and of military virtue can be interpreted as an illuminating commentary upon Machiavelli's concept of *virtù*.[89] Since war is conceived of by Clausewitz as "perpetual conflict with the unexpected," [90] two qualities in the general are needed above all: a "lucid intellect" and a "great moral courage," reminiscent of Machiavelli's *prudenza* and *virtù*. Clausewitz's "lucid intellect" is *coup d'oeil* in a broad sense—the ability to penetrate swiftly to the reality of a situation that is not apparent to the average mind. An emotional force, the source of energy, bravery, and spiritual strength are included in the meaning of moral

85 Clausewitz, *Principles of War*, tr. and ed. Hans W. Gatzke (Harrisburg, Pa.: The Military Service Publishing Company, 1942), p. 12. This is a new translation of Clausewitz's memorandum to the Prussian crown prince. The memorandum is also included in vol. III of the Graham translation of *Vom Krieg*.

86 Clausewitz, *Principles*, p. 61.

87 *Ibid.*, p. 46.

88 Clausewitz, *Strategie* (Hamburg: Eberhard Kessel, 1937), p. 41, as quoted in Gilbert, "Machiavelli," p. 25.

89 Clausewitz, *On War*, esp. I, 46–75, 177–192.

90 *Ibid.*, I, 50.

courage. Its foremost characteristic is boldness, the dynamic creative power that in armies must be subject to obedience, and that in generals must be directed by great intellect.[91] The military genius is born with boldness; a mark of his genius is the ability to instill his army with boldness. Clausewitz's final advice in the memorandum to the Prussian crown prince, the future King Friedrich Wilhelm IV, might have been penned by Machiavelli to Lorenzo de' Medici, duke of Urbino, to whom he dedicated *The Prince*:

Be audacious and cunning in your plans, firm and persevering in their execution, determined to find a glorious end, and fate will crown your youthful brow with a shining glory, which is the ornament of princes, and engrave your image in the hearts of your last descendents.[92]

4. THE RELATION OF THE POLITICAL AND THE MILITARY ARTS

Machiavelli evidently believes that the basic relationships between the arts of war and of politics are as follows:

1. Military power is the foundation of civil society.
2. A well-ordered military establishment is an essential unifying element in civil society.
3. A policy of military aggrandizement contributes to the stability and longevity of civil society.
4. The military art and the political art possess a common style.
5. A military establishment tends to reflect the qualities of the civil society of which it is a part.

The first three need to be discussed only briefly because of their more or less explicit treatment by Machiavelli. But the last two warrant a more detailed examination because they

[91] *Ibid.*, 186–187.
[92] Clausewitz, *Principles of War*, p. 69.

are only implicit in his writing. In addition, analysis of these two relationships proves to be the most rewarding in the attempt to ascertain the role of the military in his political thought.

The preface to *The Art of War* contains a clear formulation of the close tie between military power and the civil order. A current opinion maintained that military and civilian life are antithetical. The transformation in the behavior of the civilian who dons uniform and engages in soldiering endangers the peace and order of his city. Machiavelli challenges the universality of this generalization, although he admits its veracity as a description of the corrupt situation in Italy. He contends that ancient history demonstrates that the military and the civilian need not be in opposition. All that men cherish—art, science, religion, and civic order—depends upon the security provided by military might. Laws, no matter how well-designed, are of little value in safeguarding internal order unless the military establishment is sufficient to protect a community from foreign aggression. Without benefit of such protection, a state is like a splendid palace filled with rich furnishings and costly jewels, yet exposed to the elements because of the lack of a roof. That in our hostile world of perpetual struggle, "No state . . . can support itself without an army," [93] is Machiavelli's conclusion, one which he had already expressed by the aphorism that good laws rest upon good arms.[94] Machiavelli's quite natural preoccupation with military security is further manifested in his description of the civil ruler. Mastery of the art of war is absolutely essential to successful civic leadership.[95] Indeed, Machiavelli, sometimes, uses the term *principe* to designate army commander as well as civil ruler. Scrupulous attention should be given to military affairs in times of peace as well as in war. Constant training and discipline will keep an army in top form, ready for instant

[93] *Art of War*, I, 30.
[94] *Prince*, 12.
[95] *Prince*, 14.

action. Moreover, the ruler and his subordinates must themselves always be in the excellent physical condition necessary for service in the field. For this purpose the best peacetime school for the prince and his associates is the chase.[96] On this score Machiavelli alludes to Chiron, the centaur, fabled tutor of the princes of antiquity, who included in his curriculum the art of hunting, a gift bestowed upon him by the Gods.[97] Hunting is an imitation of war which involves strenuous physical exertion on all kinds of terrain in all weather, and the employment of various stratagems in order to outwit and track down the prey. Intimate acquaintance with the lay of the land of his dominion, and an intuitive feel for topography in general can also be acquired by the prince who energetically practices the art. Constant study of history and of the actions of the military figures of the past, whose examples are worthy of emulation, should be the foremost way of training the intellect of the prince.

A well-ordered army, besides guarding civil society against outside interference, should have a primary integrating and stabilizing function in internal affairs. Along with family upbringing and religion, the military training received by the citizen who actively participates in a militia is fundamental to civic education. Machiavelli attributes Roman supremacy

[96] *Ibid.*, and *Discourses*, III, 39. Machiavelli, like Xenophon, to whom he refers in both passages, emphasizes the value of hunting in military education. Machiavelli may have read Xenophon's treatise on the chase, *Cynegeticus*, the twelfth chapter of which is particularly relevant. More probably he was following Xenophon's views on the subject in the *Cyropaedia* I. 2. 9–11; 3. 14; 55. 5–15; II. 4. 25; VIII. 1. 34–38. The recommendation of hunting for a military education is traditional. See Plato, *Laws* I. 633; VI. 763; VII. 823–824. Oliver Lyman Spaulding in *Pen and Sword in Greece and Rome* (Princeton: Princeton University Press; London: H. Milford, Oxford University Press, 1937), p. 146, refers to the appendix of the *Strategicon*, by the sixth-century Byzantine Emperor Maurice, which describes the organization of a mass hunt to be used for training an army. At least as late as the eighteenth century, the chase was prescribed as an important means of acquiring *coup d'oeil*. See Folard, *Histoire*, I, 221; Guibert, *Essai*, II, 97.

[97] *Prince*, 18; also, Xenophon, *Cynegeticus* I.

to her excellent military organization which schooled the populace in discipline.[98] Hence, the civic agitations for which the Republic was noted stayed within bounds and had an invigorating rather than a debilitating effect. At least as Machiavelli views Roman history, from the time of the Tarquins to the Gracchi—a period of over four hundred years—the continual internal conflict was never so serious as to necessitate the widespread infliction of penalties, either exile or execution, or fines against individual citizens. Social conflict, he claims, never degenerated into the factional menace to the public welfare that it did in many lesser states. Romans who served in the legions learned to be loyal, to love peace and order, and to fear the Gods. Respect for law and authority, a spirit of self-sacrifice, and exceptional personal courage were other qualities acquired from the common military experience. Good military organization making for good civic discipline was, therefore, a decisive factor in the stability and grandeur of the republic. An important reason, Machiavelli believes, for the serious decline of parental, religious, and civic authority in his own Italy is the lack of good military organization. Schooling the populace in civic discipline by establishing citizens' armies would be one of the surest ways of arresting internal disintegration at the same time that maximum security against external dangers is being provided.[99]

Machiavelli also suggests what might be called a general theory of human "salvation" through the military.[100] The word "salvation," however, must be used rather gingerly in reference to Machiavelli's ideas, because his radically pessimistic view of man and human relations precludes his envisioning the possibility of attaining permanent temporal peace and well-being in a rationally organized and regulated society. No civil society, however well-constructed, will endure

[98] *Discourses,* I, 4; III, 36.

[99] *Art of War,* I, 40–41.

[100] The following ideas are discussed in far greater detail in my forthcoming book on Machiavelli.

forever, as the story of the world's two most durable and stable civic orders, Rome and Sparta, indicates. At best, all that men can hope for, before the inevitable decay and death of the body politic occur, is a long prosperous civic life free from the worst of the more common afflictions. Premature decline can be avoided, and unity and vigor can be maintained if our approach to political problems is rational. But the flux of history and institutions cannot be permanently stayed; change will always win out in the long run. Delay of the inevitable fall, then, is the only hope of earthly salvation that Machiavelli extends to us. The military can be crucial in this postponement of doom; nothing will prevent the ultimate fall.

Man's inherent egoism means that conflict is the basic pattern of social behavior. Individuals, families, and states exist in a condition of ceaseless tension and war. Civil society produces two qualitatively different kinds of conflict, corrupt and ordered. Corrupt conflict is the struggle among men for aggrandizement and domination without respect for the authority of law, religion, and age, and without concern for the common good. In the corrupt civil society, one dominated by corrupt conflict, economic avarice is the common mode of behavior, and sensual gratification by means of the money wrested in the social contest is the common goal. Politically speaking, corruption means factionalism, violence, conspiracy; in republics, an alternation between anarchy and tyrannical rule. Ordered conflict takes place within a framework of law, and is always subordinate to the common good, never erupting into violence and civil war. Religious belief prevails in the good society; parents and elders are esteemed and respected. Citizens generally fulfill their civic duties and obligations. Honesty is the rule in private and public affairs. Men are not judged upon the basis of their wealth—economic ends are the least esteemed—but by their dedication to the community. Honor and glory in the service of the fatherland are the most highly regarded values. Self-discipline and frugality, rather than the uncontrolled pursuit of power, wealth, and sex, are the cherished principles of personal conduct. Whereas Florence typifies the corrupt civic order, the Roman Republic is the model of the good society. To each Machiavelli devotes a work of analysis, *The History of Florence* and *The Discourses.*

Corruption is the central domestic problem of the statesman. In order to prevent a good civic order from being corrupted or to make a corrupt society good, the ruler must understand the causes of corruption. Corruption appears in an overly successful society whose collective efforts no longer have to be concentrated for the sake of survival upon a particular aim, for example, the resisting and taming of nature, constant vigilance against a potential external threat, continual active struggle with an enemy, or a program of military aggrandizement. The conquest of nature, the removal of the potential external threat, the destruction of a traditional enemy, or the consummation of military policy by conquering all there is to conquer, causes a people to relax their effort, to seek to live the luxurious life, to become soft and self-seeking. Expansionism seems to be the most viable means of preserving social solidarity and morale, and of strengthening the virtues of courage and endurance, and thereby, of holding corruption in check. Military expansionism is preferable to any of the alternatives because it enables a people to exert greater control over their own destinies than if they were to struggle against nature, or continually to counter the threats and attacks of neighboring powers. A society must act boldly and purposefully if it is not to become the plaything of fortune. And the initiative once seized should always be held firmly. Keeping the example of the doughty Roman republicans ever before him, Machiavelli contends that the strongest possible instrument of expansionism is the well-ordered force of citizen-soldiers who will be fighting for their own honor and glory. Corruption, therefore, can be checked in a republic that sends its sons out to perform valorous deeds. But success in these martial adventures is ultimately its own undoing; with no more worlds to conquer, corruption can no longer be contained. Salvation by the military will postpone, not prevent, the inevitable decay. Of course education—in the broadest sense to include the instruments of social control such as religion and law, if rationally utilized—can deter civic corruption. But without some perennial challenge to existence, education alone is insufficient.

5. THE COMMON STYLE OF THE TWO ARTS

By stipulating that the successful statesman must be a capable general, Machiavelli closely associates the political and the military arts. For a single individual to be proficient in both arts would be an exceedingly difficult and rare accomplishment unless a single style or mode of activity were common to both. Machiavelli seems in every way to suggest exactly this. Founders and reformers of states and military commanders are grouped together with founders of religions and men of letters as those who achieve the highest fame.[101] Again, statesman and soldier are linked in the only two examples given by Machiavelli of double glory and double shame. He who founds and maintains a state or an army will win double glory; he who is given a state or an army and loses it will be disgraced by double shame.[102] Four specific references to artistic activity occur in *The Prince, The Discourses,* and *The Art of War.*[103] Two of these are observations that a sculptor can carve a much finer statue if he starts with a piece of unblemished stone. In one case Machiavelli compares sculpture to statecraft, in the other, sculpture to generalship. The founder of a state will be able to create a more perfect work by beginning with a simple, rustic, uncorrupted people like the Swiss.[104] The general will be able to create a better army out of untrained and untried citizens than if he attempts to

---

[101] *Discourses,* I, 10.

[102] For state, *Prince,* 24; for army, *Discourses,* III, 13.

[103] *Prince,* Epistle Dedicatory; *Discourses,* I, Introduction, 11; *Art of War,* VII, 209–210.

[104] *Discourses,* I, 11.

use the military adventurers and riffraff that fill mercenary armies.[105] Once more, then, Machiavelli has placed statecraft and generalship in juxtaposition. The reason is obvious: both are creative arts concerned with molding raw human material into the form desired; and the models to be imitated, Machiavelli never tires of repeating, should be taken from classical antiquity.[106]

Another example of the close connection between the military and the political in Machiavelli's mind is his concept of *virtù*.[107] Although his use of *virtù* is often confusing, much of the apparent ambiguity in his general theory is dispelled as soon as the special meaning that he often gives to the term is clarified. *Virtù* is a necessary quality of effective military and political leadership, and it is essential to the survival and well-being of a people in this alien and hostile world. Whether an individual or a people, a general or a statesman are being discussed by Machiavelli, *virtù* in the special sense is basically a military quality. There is no synonym for this use of *virtù*. Machiavelli employs it to characterize masculine

---

[105] *Art of War*, VII, 209–210.

[106] Machiavelli's concept of statecraft as creative activity is in the classical tradition. On cosmic and creative activity see the discussion of Plato as "political demiurge" in Glenn R. Morrow, *Plato's Cretan City: An Historical Interpretation of the Laws* (Princeton: Princeton University Press, 1960), pp. 10–13, 568–569, 571–572, 591–592. Also see the brief, excellent comparison of the three orders of creativity—cosmic, political, poetic—in Richard Kuhns, *The House, the City, and the Judge: the Growth of Moral Awareness in the "Oresteia"* (Indianapolis and New York: The Bobbs-Merrill Company, Inc., 1962), pp. 100–101, 145. Michael Oakeshott in *The Voice of Poetry in the Conversation of Mankind: an Essay* (London: Bowes and Bowes, 1959), p. 15 and n. 1, distinguishes between the modern view of politics as "practical activity" and the classical view as "poetic activity," the object being the achievement of glory, a tradition to which he assigns Machiavelli.

[107] The problem of *virtù* in Machiavelli is much too complicated to be treated adequately here. See my forthcoming study, "Machiavelli's Concept of *Virtù* Reconsidered." Important references to *virtù* in Machiavelli's writings are as follows: *Prince*, 6–8, 17, 19, 24–25; *Discourses*, I, 9–11; II, 1–2; III, 1, 21, 36; *Art of War*, II, 76–81.

and aggressive conduct that is exhibited in a dangerous and uncertain situation of tension, stress, and conflict. The concept entails the idea of tremendous force of will and inner strength that will enable one to overcome the most recalcitrant opposition and to endure the most perilous adversity. Among the attributes included in *virtù* are boldness, bravery, resolution, and decisiveness. A tour de force, military or political, results from the vital creative energy so much a part of *virtù*.

True *virtù* in an individual or in a people always involves the greatest discipline and training. Without these, there will not be the vital capacity for endurance and firmness, the necessary resilience, the power of sustaining a course of action until the end is achieved. The leader possessing extraordinary *virtù* is born with certain qualities that are strengthened and shaped by conditioning; a people usually acquire *virtù* by being conditioned in the proper way. A people like the Gauls may be naturally warlike and spirited, but because they lack adequate discipline, their natural propensity will soon be weakened in any test of endurance. The Romans, not so warlike and spirited by nature as the Gauls, are nevertheless a people of exceptional *virtù* because their conduct has been molded by excellent civic education and organization. *Virtù*, therefore, is not simply unruly energy, unbridled ferocity, and a rapidly exhausted boldness. *Virtù* to be a virtue must be *virtù ordinata*.

Just as no single term can do justice to Machiavelli's special meaning of *virtù*, so no word alone can stand for the opposite quality. One possible antonym is *ozio:* indolence, inaction, a lack of energy. In a sense, all that characterizes a woman in Machiavelli's view is opposed to *virtù:* faintheartedness, irresolution, and hesitancy. The archetypal product of *virtù* is the foundation of a state or an army; the archetypal figure of *virtù* is the military hero-founder, Romulus or Cyrus the Great. *Virtù* may be associated with extreme wickedness and with the pursuit of power and self-aggrandizement by any means and at any price; for example, the career of the bloody and ferocious Roman emperor, Septimius Severus, displays

virtù. But when superior *virtù* is found combined in an individual with pre-eminent *prudenza,* as in Romulus and Cyrus,
dedication to the common good will characterize his behavior.
Machiavelli believes that the strongest motive for altruism is
a selfishness directed by intelligence. For the prudent man of
virtù will soon recognize that his labor in behalf of the common good will bring him the greatest personal power and
security from conspiracy, and will win for him the truest
glory. On the other hand, leaders like Piero Soderini and
Numa Pompilius, the successor of Romulus, who are interested
in the well-being of the citizenry, may not be men of great
virtù. And some leaders, petty tyrants especially, may lack
both *virtù* and a concern for the common good.

If generalship and statecraft are creative activities requiring extraordinary *virtù,* what of the techniques employed
in the two arts? Does Machiavelli think that they are similar
in any significant respects? He writes that "every art has its
general rules and principles upon which it is founded." [108]
The inference can be drawn from all that he says that a single
set of "general rules and principles" is common to both the
art of war and the art of politics. Furthermore, it is arguable
that these common rules and principles are of an essentially
military nature. Machiavelli's conception of politics and the
political art may well be derived in part from his theory of
war and the art of war. Much of one activity appears to be
similar to the other activity. The style of the statesman re-
sembles in many ways the style of the military commander.
According to Machiavelli, whose gloom in certain respects is
Augustinian, man is incurably perverse, avaricious, and power-
seeking; selfishness is the heart of all human relations.[109] Consequently, life in general, and political life in particular, tend

[108] *Art of War,* III, 102.

[109] See Herbert Deane's illuminating discussion of Augustine's concept
of human nature, and of some of the parallels in the views of modern
thinkers, including Machiavelli, but especially Hobbes, in *The Political
and Social Ideas of St. Augustine* (New York: Columbia University Press,
1963), pp. 39–77, 221–243,

to be vicious struggles for domination and aggrandizement, potentially or actually conditions of war. Each new political situation in civil society is comparable to a battle between the "army" of the political leader and the forces of his enemies. The outcome of the struggle depends upon the strategy, tactics, and leadership of the opponents. Whether one side emerges with a clear victory, or whether—and much more likely—the conclusion of the engagement is indecisive, new conflicts between new antagonists arise in a never-ending sequence.

What kind of argument will help to demonstrate that Machiavelli often conceives of the art of politics in military terms? To begin with, his approach to politics differs substantially in several respects from all previous political thinkers in the western tradition. His focus is always upon the detailed mechanics of acquiring, holding, and increasing political power. Before him, Xenophon alone had concentrated upon the techniques of effective military and civic leadership, but the Greek never went so far as Machiavelli in the advocacy of force and deception against fellow-citizens, for reasons which will soon be made clear. Aristotle, in the fifth book of the *Politics*, discusses the seizure of power; however, it is always as an illegitimate kind of political activity. Nor does he dwell extensively upon the minutiae of method and organization necessary for a successful coup. An important reason for these differences between Machiavelli and the ancients is the idea so prominent in the classical outlook: the fundamental distinction between friend and foe, and the different treatment which should be accorded to each. The result is a basic intellectual—if not practical—division of labor. Ancient political theory is almost entirely concerned with the proper relationships among friends or fellow-citizens. Military theorists take for their sphere of activity the relation between friend and foe. Ideally, the citizens of a classical polity are thought to be partners, joined by an intimate bond of friendship and common values, who seek the good life through mutual aid and cooperation. The ideal nature of the relationship desired among fellow citizens is to some extent expressed by the meaning of *societas,* a fraternity or group of comrades. Among friends—for example, the citizens of a *polis*—differences of opinion are resolved in an orderly fashion by rational discourse without resort to deception or violence. Anyone of the friends who refuses to conform to the commonly accepted rules is subject to punishment; if his transgression is serious enough, he may be expelled from the circle of friends into the external world of foes. Ancient works of political thought are always addressed to the partners in the common life of the city. The purpose is to enlighten them as to the nature of the ends for which they should strive and to describe the social arrangements needed for their attainment. The conduct between friend and foe is expected to be different from the conduct between friends. Deceit, trickery, and violence against a foe are justifiable. The classical military treatise is the analysis of just how this behavior may be most effectively applied to the defeat and the capture of the foe. Xenophon made the brilliant discovery that an army, like a city, is a community of friends. Although, like Machiavelli, he often sees statecraft in the image of generalship in this regard, he thinks always of the general's relation to his own army as one to a community of friends. Xenophon never recognizes that fellow-citizens or fellow-soldiers can be treated legitimately as foes. Machiavelli, of course, would be the first to admit that a statesman needs loyal friends and allies just as a general requires a devoted army. But he recognizes that at best a civil society and an army are complex mixtures of friends and foes, individuals and groups contending for different interests; they are certainly never a totality of friends completely united in pursuing a common good. Within the group immediately supporting the political leader, the friendship of some is usually more apparent than real. The allegiance of the "friend" may be only temporary, ready to be transferred to someone else when advantage is to be gained. Even the most intimate of friends may, without warning, prove unfaithful in an hour of need, because the strongest self-discipline implanted by convention under certain circumstances is not enough to prevent the outburst of the self-seeking ego. Friendship, Machiavelli seems to imply, is not so much the precious union of hearts so dear to the classical theorists, as it is a tenuous, external bond of self-interest. By the very fact of their egoistic natures men are forever isolated and alone, whether they are friends or foes. With Machiavelli the classical distinction between friend and foe is blurred. Since every friend is a potential foe, there is considerably less reluctance to employ deception and violence in dealing with a fellow-citizen. The ways of peace are in many ways now like the ways of war because peace is no longer thought of as the natural condition of man, a time for the positive pursuit of the common good. Civic peace to Machiavelli is an interlude between wars in which overt conflict and violence diminish but do not disappear, in which tensions accumulate below the surface to erupt anew.

If Machiavelli does not agree with classical theorists about important aspects of the nature of politics, he does tend to discuss politics as classical military writers discuss the art of war.[110] For example, there follow forty-three topics or categories of stratagems listed and analyzed by the Roman Frontinus (*ca.* A.D. 35 or 40–103),[111] general, consul, and governor of Britain:

1. On concealing one's plans
2. On finding out the enemy's plans

[110] Among the most important in chronological order from the 4th century B.C. to the 4th century of the Christian Era are: Aeneas Tacticus, Xenophon, Polybius, Asclepiodotus, Onasander, Aelian Tacticus, Frontinus, Arrian, Modestus, and Vegetius. Xenophon and Polybius were also political theorists. Unfortunately the technical military treatises of Polybius have not survived.

[111] Frontinus, *Strategemata*, tr. Charles E. Bennett [Loeb Classical Library] (Cambridge, Mass.: Harvard University Press; London: W. Heinemann, 1925). Topics 1–12 are discussed in Book I; topics 13–25, in Book II; and topics 26–43, in Book III. The topics in Book IV have been omitted because it is usually not attributed to Frontinus.

This catalogue listing the precepts of the military art recommended by Frontinus is strikingly similar to a collection that might be made of Machiavelli's political principles. The same could not be said of Plato or St. Thomas. The military rules, of course, must be adapted to the political context.

It is quite possible to isolate and describe something approaching a style that is, in certain respects, peculiar to the outlook, thought, and behavior of military theoreticians and practitioners since the century of Xenophon and Alexander the Great. Military leaders approach a military situation from a particular perspective. Their task, as they see it, is to solve the problem presented by all factors involved, according to certain necessary procedures, and then to translate the solution into action that will defeat the enemy. Toward non-military situations, they tend to think and to act in a similar fashion. Now the so-called *Principles of War,* the standards for planning and executing military operations, provide us with the main features of this military attitude. Although the principles are found in varied combination and phrasing in different treatises and manuals, military experts nevertheless agree as to the essentials.[112] A military operation must be secretly and meticulously planned upon the basis of the detailed assessment of all information and intelligence collected about the enemy. The forces, reserves, and allies that are available and that can be relied upon are to be ascertained, and an estimation is then made of all advantageous and disadvantageous factors. This informed calculation will determine the fundamental objective of the operation, the direction and nature of the central and auxiliary thrusts, and the general disposition of troops. A clearly defined and rationally devised strategy requires the choice of techniques for implementation that are adequate for the prevailing conditions and that are flexible enough to be changed with changing conditions. One's own base of operations and forces must be secured. The initial blow should be delivered with rapidity and energy at the decisive moment in as economic and concentrated a fashion possible at the enemy's weakest point. Throughout the operation, the advantage of surprise and deception must be fully exploited. After the initial blow, the impetus of the attack cannot be allowed to slacken. Finally, the most carefully devised strategy and tactics are of little purpose unless the commander can control and direct his own forces with great precision. His troops must be loyal, determined, spirited, and disciplined, ready to follow their leader through the direst perils. Leadership is the key to victory; the ability to exact willing and devoted obedience is the test of leadership.

In large measure these are Machiavelli's major concerns in his discussion of domestic politics as well as in his advice

112 The subsequent summary is not intended to be a complete statement. It does indicate the more important elements and is derived from American and British military manuals, the views of Clausewitz, and the lucid account of Major General Fuller, *Generalship of Alexander the Great*, pp. 284–305.

on the conduct of foreign affairs and warfare. The military style or cast of mind, just described, informs not only the purely military proposals of *The Art of War* and his other works, but also the political analysis and recommendations of *The Prince* and *The Discourses.* The necessity of foresight, planning, and preparation for the future constitutes a favorite political theme of Machiavelli,[113] one that emphasizes the need of expert advice and the gathering of intelligence, the importance of gaining friends and allies as insurance against contingencies in the future, the estimate of factors, and the rational calculation of the objective. Trickery, depending upon secrecy, deception, and surprise, are axiomatic to the political theory of Machiavelli.[114] Flexibility, the ease with which one can continually adapt one's plans and behavior to the changing times and circumstances, is among the chief requisites of success on a domestic political level.[115] Machiavelli constantly warns the leader against the half-way measure, the practice of taking a middle course, the attempt to have the best of two possible and diametrically opposed modes of behavior.[116] The blow must not be delivered against the political opponent until all preparations have been made. Until they are, a policy of temporizing must be followed. But once the political forces are ready, there can be no hesitation; the attack must be launched vigorously and decisively.[117] The skillful statesman always seeks to seize the initiative in domestic and foreign affairs and to cling to it tenaciously. He must do more than react to the maneuvers and pressures of

[113] *Prince,* 3, 6–7, 22–25; *Discourses,* I, 30, 33, 52; III, 2, 6.

In all that has preceded and in all that follows, I certainly do not mean to deny that Machiavelli's rational, calculating attitude toward politics owes much to the commercial spirit of his times. I am simply arguing that the "counting-house" ideology does not alone seem to explain adequately his style of political thought.

[114] *Prince,* 18–19; *Discourses,* I, 44; II, 13; III, 6. Both works, of course, are filled with examples.

[115] *Prince,* 25; *Discourses,* III, 6, 8, 9.

[116] *Prince,* 3, 21, 25; *Discourses,* I, 26; II, 23; III, 2, 6.

[117] *Prince,* 8; *Discourses,* I, 33, 45; II, 27; III, 6.

others. Whenever possible it is he who must set the pace, who must see that every action of the enemy is a reaction to the behavior of his own forces which are operating according to clearly defined plans and purposes. A knockout blow should always be sought in preference to a long war of attrition. Before the major political conflict comes to a head, the leader should safeguard his position and those of his supporters as best he can.[118] In addition, he should block the political ambitions of others by seeing that the governmental offices which they covet are securely filled by his own friends and allies.[119] One of Machiavelli's lasting preoccupations is the problem of political and military leadership in which the command-obedience relation is central.[120] Whether he is writing on civic matters or generalship, he stresses the methods whereby willing obedience can be exacted and hatred avoided. Hatred of an army for its commander, or of a citizenry for its ruler, is the prime evil that jeopardizes all leadership.

The general, therefore, seems to be a model for Machiavelli's statesman in the handling of supporters and in the tactics to be used against the domestic political enemy. Perhaps another indication of Machiavelli's military style is his assumption that the end of the political struggle is power, just as the military commander's goal is power over the enemy. The political art and the military art, therefore, are largely a matter of the means necessary to achieve a common aim of aggrandizement. Both statesman and general are principally concerned with devising and using instruments by which they can exert their will over the will of others: those of violence, deception, manipulation, and control. Important differences, however, exist between their respective activities—differences fully appreciated by Machiavelli. The statesman can never be so ruthless about the use of force as the general is against his enemy. Moreover, his use of the various techniques re-

118 *Prince,* 19; *Discourses,* I, 46; III, 6.
119 *Discourses,* I, 52; III, 6.
120 Cf. *Prince,* 16–21 and *Discourses,* III, 19–23.

quired in the struggle to gain and maintain power must be disguised from the view of fellow-citizens. His power will be imperiled if he gains the reputation for being brutal and deceitful. Brutality and deceit may well prove necessary, but the political leader should, as much as possible, never appear to have to resort to them in domestic politics.

6. CONSPIRACY AND COUNTER-CONSPIRACY

It is evidently the military animus of so much of his thought that leads Machiavelli to emphasize the conspiratorial and counter-conspiratorial nature of politics and to outline the first general theory of political conspiracy in western thought.[121] Classical political thinkers have little to say about conspiracy, except to condemn its practice. Although historians since Herodotus describe many conspiracies, some in great detail, only military theorists—before Machiavelli—had attempted to systematize the art of conspiracy by formulating general rules for its conduct. Conspiracy falls quite naturally within the classical military perspective, since it is a friend-foe relationship attaining a characteristic military form in civil war. The ancient military thinkers had contributed to a theory of conspiracy in several ways. They had suggested methods by which discontent and unrest, and even armed uprisings, could be incited within the enemy forces, particularly within an armed fortress or city that is besieged, and they had dis-

[121] This achievement has seldom been acknowledged by commentators. The articles, "Political Conspiracy" and "Coup d'État," in the *Encyclopedia of the Social Sciences* (New York: The Macmillan Company, 1930–1935) do not refer to Machiavelli. Neither does his name appear in connection with a theory of conspiracy in either of two recent books on the subject: Donald J. Goodspeed, *The Conspirators: A Study of the Coup d'État* (New York: Viking Press, 1962); Feliks Gross, *The Seizure of Political Power in a Century of Revolutions* (New York: Philosophical Library, 1958). Goodspeed is interested in developing a general theory of conspiracy on the basis of a number of recent coups which he has studied. His conclusions (pp. 208–238) do not differ substantially from those of Machiavelli in *Discourses*, III, 6.

cussed counter-measures.[122] In their more general consideration of tricks and ruses to be used to deceive, confuse, and overpower the enemy in the field, they had provided numerous tactical procedures that could be applied by conspirator and counter-conspirator to any intra-mural engagement of their forces. Machiavelli discovers two fundamental political situations. One is the foundation of a new state, or the radical reform of an already existing civil order—two activities that are practically identical. Each is a conspiratorial operation entailing the transformation of an existing arrangement of things. Many individuals and groups, having a vested interest in the prevention of change, will resort to force and treachery to block the endeavors of the founder or the radical reformer. The second political situation, the maintenance of an already founded or reformed civic order, requires that conditions unfavorable to conspiracy must be fostered by the ruler. Close vigilance over the populace must be exercised by the ruler so that he may detect and eliminate any plot or intrigue against his regime. Political power is acquired by conspiracy and is preserved by counter-conspiracy. To be proficient in either requires a thorough acquaintance with the other. The nature of conspiratorial politics is examined in each of Machiavelli's "political" works. *The Prince* can be divided roughly into two parts: the first (Chapters 1–11), deals with the conspiratorial phase; the second (12–26), stresses the counter-conspiratorial aspect. Chapter 7 of the first section treats in detail the conspiracy of Cesare Borgia, abetted by his father Pope Alexander VI, to found a strong united papal state; Chapter 19, at the very center of the second half, is devoted to the problem of maintaining power by the prevention of conspiracy. In *The Discourses,* Chapter 6 of Book III, "On Conspiracies," is the longest of the work. It is the first systematic treatise on the conspiratorial art in the West, and it is

122 For instance, see the only surviving work of the first western technical military writer, Aeneas Tacticus, *On the Defense of Fortified Positions,* tr. The Illinois Greek Club, "Loeb Classical Library" (Cambridge, Mass.: Harvard University Press; London: W. Heinemann, 1923).

the clearest expression in all the author's writings of his debt to military science. The essay, Machiavelli explains at the beginning, is written to aid rulers in understanding the nature of conspiracy so that they will be able to take every precautionary measure to prevent it. Actually, the information provided is as helpful to conspirators as it is to counter-conspirators. An indication of the importance of the chapter is its place in the context of the work as a whole. *The Discourses* are divided into three books: the first analyzes the domestic affairs of the Romans; the second, the foreign and military affairs; and the third, the contribution to Rome's greatness made by the virtuous actions of some of her outstanding citizens. The statement describing the purpose of the third book comes at the end of its opening chapter; there Machiavelli stresses the importance of periodically bringing a body politic back to its first principles in order to arrest the growth of corruption and the accompanying civic disorder. This perennial revitalization of a people can be accomplished either by the activity of an exceptionally virtuous individual or by vigorously executed laws, which, of course, also depend upon the intervention of virtuous individuals. There follow seven chapters dealing specifically with conspiracy and counter-conspiracy in domestic Roman politics, and including the theoretical discussion, "On Conspiracies." The story of the plot led by Junius Brutus, the liberator of Rome, against his uncle Tarquinius Superbus is the example dwelt upon most extensively. The irony in the example of Junius Brutus is that his very success in expelling the Tarquins subsequently involved him in the task of participating in the trial and execution of his sons who conspired against the new republican order then being established. Even Tarquinius Superbus, who was unable to oppose the coup of Junius and his fellow republicans, had himself acquired power by assassinating his predecessor, Servius Tullius, whose crown had in turn been gained by conspiracy. The lesson is obvious: conspiracy in the acquisition of power is of no avail unless firm measures to prevent conspiracy can be taken once power is achieved. Even in the best ordered republic, Machiavelli affirms that the danger is ever-present; he cites a number of other Roman conspiracies, and concludes Book III with a reference to three of the most famous, the methods that were employed to put them down, and a eulogy to Q. Fabius Maximus Rullianus for his part in ending one of them. Most of Book III, however, is concerned with recounting the measures taken by Roman military leaders against the enemies of the Republic and with the way in which they managed and disciplined their troops; it is an extremely significant discussion in view of our argument, for it further suggests that conspiracy and war are closely related activities. Civic and military leaders must contend with the problem of maintaining discipline and preventing conspiracy and mutiny among their followers. Machiavelli's last major work before his death, *The History of Florence*, more a theoretical treatise on civic corruption than a particularly trustworthy chronicle of his city, describes one conspiracy and counter-conspiracy after another. Its final book, devoted explicitly to the theme of conspiracy, commences with two chapters on the Pazzi plot against Lorenzo de' Medici, a discussion which proceeds along the general lines of the precepts set forth in "On Conspiracies." It is more than fitting that a work which is the natural history of a single city's civic corruption should close with such a topic, since Machiavelli insists that the best preventive measure against civic conspiracy, i.e., the best form of counter-conspiracy, is to see that a polity is well ordered.[123]

Machiavelli's approach to counter-conspiracy is most adequately summarized by his belief that, "Government is the management of citizens so that they are neither able nor inclined to oppose you." [124] The task is the same for the general who commands an army and for the statesman possessing supreme political power. At the heart of all leadership is the problem of obedience, the problem of the ways and means of

[123] Substantially the same opinion as that of Goodspeed, *The Conspirators*, p. 238.

[124] *Discourses*, II, 23.

exacting obedience from one's troops and subjects and of avoiding their contempt and hatred. Disorder and conspiracy will inevitably result from the leader's failure to win the respect of his followers. In *The Prince* and *The Discourses,* Machiavelli largely examines the problem of obedience in terms of whether the leader should seek to command on the basis of love or of fear. The conclusion in the earlier work, that deals primarily with the relation of the civic leader to his subjects, is that ideally a ruler should be both loved and feared by his people; but if there must be a choice between the two, fear is preferable to love, providing the fear is of a quality to induce respect, and not hatred and contempt.[125] Machiavelli reasons that the prince can more effectively control his citizens by fear than by love, because fear arouses a greater sense of obligation than love, and because fear is dependent upon the will of the prince, whereas the source of love is the will of the people. To avoid being hated, the prince must take pains to gain an excellent reputation. Negatively, this means that he should avoid unreasonable, tyrannical violation of the possessions, the persons, and the honor of his subjects. Positively, he must always appear to be good, even if for reasons of state he has to act in a cruel and ruthless fashion. One of the crucial ingredients in successful leadership is the talent to appear to be what one is not, as long as actual ability is not counterfeited. In addition, the prince must punish evil severely, reward the skill, competence, and goodness of his subjects, and everywhere encourage initiative, enterprise, and industry. Finally, the performance of great enterprises, both domestic and foreign, will bring the ruler great prestige and fame, and his state, glory and honor. This princely mode of behavior, when joined with energy, foresight, and determination, with a majestic manner marked by a lack of pride and arrogance, and when supported by a rationally organized state founded upon informed policy decisions, the rule of law, and good arms, is the best insurance against conspiracy. Machiavelli is never an advocate of tyr-

[125] *Prince,* 16–22.

anny, in the sense of the unrestrained and arbitrary use of cruelty and force to satisfy the irrational caprice and appetite of a sovereign. Civil order is not the order of the graveyard. Tyranny arises in a weak corrupt society, and is, despite its appearance of absolute sovereignty, a relatively feeble, unstable form of government, an ideal breeding ground for every kind of disorder and conspiracy. The position of *The Discourses* on the proper relation between the general and his troops [126] is similar to the recommendations of *The Prince* on the behavior of the civic ruler. Machiavelli thinks that if a military commander is competent, it makes little difference whether he is severe or humane in the handling of his men. But humane or severe, he can never afford to lose the respect of his troops by becoming an object of contempt or hatred. Humaneness must be firm without any sign of weakness or indecisiveness. Severity must be tempered by moderation and justice, and distinguished by an absence of arrogance.

In *The Art of War,* Machiavelli draws attention to the fact that of all social organizations, an army is the one requiring the greatest discipline. Like civic discipline, military discipline depends to a great extent upon the reputation and conduct of the general. Unless he acts properly, he will fail in his efforts to create an efficient military instrument. Military law should be rigorous and severe. Decimation and running the gauntlet were among the chief punishments by which the Roman armies became the most disciplined forces the world has known. Machiavelli recommends that punishment by the soldiers themselves, and in civic society by the citizens, is an important deterrent to violation of the law. Ringleaders of any conspiracy or mutiny must, of course, be dealt with in an exemplary fashion. Just as the general should be ruthless in his punishment, so he should be generous in rewarding and praising good conduct. Perhaps the most suitable policy is to maintain order in camp by fear and punishment, and in the field by hopes and rewards. Each soldier should be paid well and what is due him; all booty is to be distributed

[126] *Discourses,* III, 19–23.

equitably. Caring for the physical well-being of an army is an important way by which the general can secure a willing obedience and avoid the perils of disunity and low morale. When not engaged in battle, troops can be kept from mischief by seeing that they are continuously occupied in various labors. Gambling and women, always a source of trouble in camp, should be strictly prohibited. All soldiers are entitled to a secure rest from their work; and a rationally designed, well-defended encampment will allow them to do so, as well as enabling the commander to keep their actions under the closest surveillance. Good health in the camp, another basis of good discipline, will be the responsibility of an adequate medical staff. Daily exercise of all troops and a sufficient but not luxurious diet are also means to this end. Other techniques of ensuring discipline are suggested throughout the book. Rational organization, in which each man knows his place and function, what is expected of him and what he can expect from others, is basic. Religion is one of the strongest bulwarks of morale and martial spirit. An army which is rigorously and continuously trained in times of peace will be much less likely to disobey in attack and retreat. Commands can only be obeyed if they are understood; hence, clear and intelligible communication is decisive. The quality of the communication is also important. Orders should be designed to inspire obedience, courage, and spirit. A good military commander should also be an effective orator, able to arouse his troops to enthusiastic devotion to the enterprise which is being undertaken. Other devices, such as regimental colors and music, are aids in instilling self-confidence and a determination to overcome the enemy, in addition to their usefulness to the general in the direction and control of his army. By rotating his subalterns' commands and by ensuring that no officer commands troops from his own district, the general can take precautions against the possibility of the formation of potential nuclei of insubordination and mutiny. A kind of fundamental social division of power between an infantry recruited from the rural areas and an urban cav-

alry may also contribute to the same end. In the course of
his experience, the able commander learns that restlessness
and discontent among his own troops will give way to a
high degree of unity resulting from fear of the enemy. This
is particularly true when the army is in a do-or-die situation,
one of necessity, in which there appears to be no alternative
to victory except death. The demand of unconditional sur-
render by the enemy may prove a potent weapon that can be
turned against them. For general and statesman, the danger
of mutiny and conspiracy can be minimized by a rationally
conceived and prudently executed policy of control.

7. THE MILITARY MODEL OF THE RATIONAL COMMUNITY

The study of Machiavelli's social and political thought
might well begin with *The Art of War,* rather than in the
conventional fashion with *The Prince* and *The Discourses.* By
reading first *The Art of War,* the student might grasp more
readily the nature of a well-ordered state and of able civic
leadership as discussed in the other works. One of Machiavelli's assumptions, although it is never clearly articulated,
is that an army tends to reflect the quality of the civil society
of which it is a part. To observe an army in training, in camp,
on the march, and in combat, is to observe how a people act
in the most arduous circumstances. A factional, corrupt society
will put a feeble and undisciplined fighting force in the field.
The army of a well-ordered polity will perform with spirit
and efficiency. Military behavior, in fact, tends to magnify
civic characteristics; the strengths and weaknesses of the civil
parent are more easily perceived and identified in the military offspring. But why can we not apply this insight to the
analysis of Machiavelli's ideas? The theory of military organization and leadership in *The Art of War* does seem to represent in rather bold relief what Machiavelli values in regard to
political organization and leadership. Moreover, when used
in this way, *The Art of War* does help to clarify some of the

apparent ambiguities, vaguenesses, contradictions, and omissions in the political works. It is neither as diffuse as *The Discourses* and *The History of Florence,* nor as compressed as *The Prince.* In writing on highly controversial political, moral, and religious issues, a man of the Cinquecento might find plain speaking extremely dangerous. However, a technical military treatise would be another matter; everything was to be gained by being lucid and precise.

The army depicted by Machiavelli in *The Art of War* is a supremely rational mechanism. Its function can be succinctly defined as military victory over the enemy. Every part and activity of the military community exist simply and solely for the sake of this primary function assigned to the whole. Rational efficiency in terms of the best possible means to the end of victory is the criterion by which all arrangements and kinds of conduct are instituted or permitted to exist. Direction of this community is assured by a hierarchy based upon function. At the top there is a unity of direction in the hands of a single individual, and from him a regularized chain of command extends downward. Each person in the chain is directly responsible to the person above him for all that goes on below him. His rights and duties are fully and clearly prescribed by the rules which govern the community as a whole, setting forth routinized procedures to be followed by all, and stipulating the punishment for their violation. All of this contributes to the sense of security and well-being felt by the individual who is a part of the system. He is able to predict the consequences of his activities, to know what he can and cannot do with impunity. Remuneration is in proportion to the function performed. Advancement in the hierarchy depends upon one's ability to perform his allotted function. It is quite possible for the individual who first enters the society at the bottom of the hierarchy to advance to the top on the basis of personal merit. In fact, the leading members of the hierarchy are expected to have passed through and gained experience in all the levels below them. Selection for membership in the military community is in strict accordance with rational criteria such as age, physical condition, occupation, and moral character, all with an eye toward the contribution that the individual will be able to make. Training for the various functional roles is determined by detailed regulations prescribing the nature and frequency of the exercises, the type of arms, equipment to be used, etc. The military community is divided into different kinds of functional units, each kind identical in composition and equipment. Operations of the community whether in camp, on march, or in battle are conducted in a routinized, orderly fashion according to the methods learned while training. If the military community is the most rational of communities, its most rational aspect, perhaps, is the encampment which Machiavelli describes in considerable detail. It is a triumph of planning and functional efficiency. Designed for an army of 24,000, the camp is in the form of a square with a regular grid of streets, and plazas designed for particular functions. The camp will always be the same, facing the same direction, no matter where it is erected. Encampment and decampment proceed according to the most efficient method that can be devised. Within the camp, each man and his unit will always occupy the same position, and the different kinds of units will be distributed in accordance with the kind of contribution they can make to the defense of the camp. Internal and external security are the main considerations in the over-all design.

With certain changes and with a decrease in the degree of regularity and discipline, the ideal military community that is prescribed by Machiavelli in *The Art of War* becomes something like the well-ordered civic community which he advocates in *The Prince* and *The Discourses*. The civic community should also be a rational mechanism so designed and operated as to make the citizens secure and prosperous. Rational functioning in terms of the most efficient means to achieve these social ends characterizes the good civic order. The individual's contribution to the functioning of the civic mechanism determines his position in the social scale and his share in the distribution of honors and rewards. Advancement is on the basis of personal merit. A system of rules controls social behavior. Over-all direction and the power to enforce conformity to the stipulated norms of conduct are concentrated at the top of the social hierarchy. Regardless of the frequent organic analogies to be found in his writings,[127] Machiavelli's conception of the civic community is mechanistic. The state possesses neither a life, nor a soul, nor a personality, nor an interest of its own. No higher end, final cause, or spiritual meaning, gives purpose and orientation to the state's existence. Both military and civic communities are artifices constructed by men to prevent human beastliness from reducing life to primitive anarchy. Man's primordial and destructive first nature is kept in check by the imposition of a second nature through rational social organization. Discipline and courage, self-control, self-sacrifice, and cooperation—qualities so vital to what we call civilization—are the products of social artifice and invention. Far from being a natural harmony of the inner spiritual life common to all men, the order upon which civilization depends is the welding together of a variety of conflicting interests by the instruments of force, law, example, and religion. Civic mechanisms do not grow of their own accord. They must be designed, constructed, maintained, and adapted to changing conditions by the conscious and purposeful efforts of men.

If Machiavelli's rational military order serves as a model for his concept of civil society, his idea of the nature of civic law and civic leadership seems also in part to be derived from the same source. Law in one of Machiavelli's important senses is the command of *il principe*, either the general, the prince, or the legislative assembly.[128] Law arises historically from the human need for social unity and protection. By rewarding or punishing soldiers and citizens for obedience or disobedience, law can be one of the principal instruments of social control. Machiavelli judges all laws by their utility in advancing the

---

[127] For a few of these analogies, see *Discourses*, I, Introduction; II, 5, 30; III, 1, 49.

[128] Machiavelli's definition of public law is in *Discourses*, I, 18.

ends which are dear to him. The test, therefore, of a good law is its contribution to maintaining a disciplined, spirited, and rational social organization, to preventing or checking corruption, and to promoting the subjects' security and well-being. If law is to control social behavior effectively it cannot be the arbitrary whim of an arbitrary ruler. All laws must be made known to all soldiers and citizens, and should never be retroactive. Each law must apply equally to all under the law; each infringement must be punished no matter who the culprit is. Bills of attainder and *ex post facto* laws defeat the very purpose for which Machiavelli conceives the law to be instituted. He whose command is the law, should always, if only on expediential grounds, set an example before his subjects of scrupulous obedience to his own directives. Law, military and civil, cannot be changed too frequently without seriously disturbing the security and contentment of the subjects. Yet legal change is necessary to meet changing conditions. Flexibility of law is a requisite of a rational society as long as the orderly routine of a people is not constantly upset by too much and too radical change. Substantively, civil law—and we should ever keep in mind the military counterpart—must sustain and strengthen the other levers of social control: the religious and military establishments. The lives and possessions of all under the law are to be scrupulously safeguarded. A degree of social equality is to be assured, and a life given over to lust and avarice is to be discouraged by strictly enforced sumptuary laws which are imposed to suit the need of the times. Industry and enterprise in every sphere of socially beneficial activity should be rewarded; sloth and the absence of initiative, penalized. Law then is the framework of rules holding together the civil and the military mechanisms in order that they may function. Laws are good or bad as they add to, or subtract from, the rational functioning, as defined by Machiavelli, of these mechanisms.

As we have emphasized, traits of the competent general characterize *il principe,* the source of law. This means that the

ideal statesman is a cool, rational, calculating individual who
prudently plans his action and adjusts his style to fit the circumstance. He cannot fail to use force and deception when
necessary to ward off threats to his power. If, on occasion, he
must be violent and ruthless, he must never lust for blood or
relish cruelty. No good general loves to kill for the sake of
killing; no good statesman can be a sadist. *Il principe* plays
the part demanded by the situation in which he finds himself.
The test of his prowess is not only a facility in assuming many
roles, but also a chameleon-like aptitude to suit the right role
to the particular situation. Emotional self-discipline as well as
energy is at the root of what Machiavelli means by virtuous
leadership. Even if the leader has to take on a charismatic aura
for the purpose of consolidating and manipulating his followers, he always remains beneath the disguise a man who has
critically examined himself, who knows his own strengths and
weaknesses, and who acts rationally in the light of this self-
knowledge. To act like God may be essential for the statesman;
to think that he is God is the end of his skill and the beginning of his downfall. Despite the concessions which the
leader has to make to satisfy popular sentiment for a *dux*, he
must be of sterner stuff than the common rabble-rouser or
idol of the masses. Machiavelli's ideal seems to be the vigorous,
courageous, and noble Roman republican, a man of first-rate
mind, whose leadership depends more upon his military virtuosity and humaneness than upon fear. It is to the "liberal"
and "great-souled" Scipio Africanus that Machiavelli is inclined instead of to the outspoken, doughty moralist, Marcus
Cato Major.[129] Of statesmen today, Charles de Gaulle seems
to be in some ways the type Machiavelli has in mind. But the
Florentine's preferences cannot be easily stereotyped, for certainly he would have approved of much of Lenin's activity.
However inconclusive such speculations may be, we can be
positive that neither Mussolini, nor Hitler, nor Stalin were
Machiavellian types, even if *The Prince* was their bedtime

---

[129] Machiavelli's feeling for Scipio is expressed by a lengthy eulogy in
his poem, *Ingratitude*.

companion. The first became a debauchee, the second was a madman, and the last ended his days as an oriental despot.

The argument that Machiavelli's concept of the ideal army is in many respects relevant to his view of the rational civic order should not suggest that he identifies or confuses the civic community with the military community. The two communities are distinct, yet related, although the relation is not one of parity. Machiavelli is quite explicit that the rational military mechanism should never be confounded with the rational civic mechanism. The well-ordered state should be governed by its citizens; the army cannot be governed by its soldiers. An army is an instrument of the state, and should always be subordinate to it. War is only one of the means, albeit a very important one, at the disposal of civil society to achieve its goals. The aim of the general and his army is victory over the enemy for the sake of the civic purpose of security and prosperity. All soldiers should be citizens, but soldiering should be only a part-time occupation of the citizen. Besides the relation of subordination between the military and civil communities, there is also another important distinction. Civil society is always much less organized, less rationalized, and less disciplined than the military mechanism. The civic mechanism always will be, and always should be, less of a rational mechanism than the army. To borrow a distinction made by Aristotle in his criticism of Plato's republic, an army acts in *unison,* while a civil society should be a *harmony.* The unison of the military mechanism precludes internal conflict. Harmony in the civic community precludes neither conflict nor competition. Conflict in the form of an open clash of diverse interests will destroy the army. Within certain limits, such conflict is a source of strength and vigor for civil society. These limits are a respect for authority, a desire to abide by the rules, and a consideration for the interests of others that will lead to a belief in the primacy of a common good. A conflict of interest arises from the very nature of man. It may be temporarily eliminated as in an army, or directed, contained, and utilized as in civil society, but its total extinction is found only among the dead. Machiavelli is too much of a republican, too much of the very kind of man he is so fond of describing as "human nature," too much of an admirer of Rome, ever to believe that the civil order should be an army.

NEAL WOOD

SELECTED BIBLIOGRAPHY

The following works are essential for an understanding of various aspects of Machiavelli's military thought. Whenever available, English translations have been listed.

BARDIN, GENERAL ÉTIENNE ALEXANDRE. *Dictionnaire de l'armée de terre.* 17 vols. Edited by General Oudinot de Reggio. Paris, 1841–1851.

BAYLEY, CHARLES C. *War and Society in Renaissance Florence: the "De Militia" of Leonardo Bruni.* Toronto: The University of Toronto Press, 1961.

BURD, L. ARTHUR. "Le fonti letterarie di Machiavelli nell' *Arte della Guerra,*" *Atti della Reale Accademia dei Lincei,* Series V. Vol. IV (1896), Pt. I, 187–261.

CARRION-NISAS, COLONEL MARIE HENRI FRANÇOIS ÉLIZABETH. *Essai sur l'histoire générale de l'art militaire.* 2 vols. Paris, 1824.

CLAUSEWITZ, KARL VON. *On War.* 3 vols. Translated by J. J. Graham. New and revised edition with introduction and notes by F. N. Maude. London: K. Paul, Trench, Trübner and Co. Ltd., 1911.

COCKLE, MAURICE J. D. *A Bibliography of Military Books up to 1642.* Introduction by Sir Charles Oman. Second edition, London: The Holland Press, 1957.

COLIN, J. *L'Éducation militaire de Napoléon.* Paris: R. Chapelot, 1900.

DELBRUCK, HANS. *Geschichte der Kriegskunst im Rahmen der politischen Geschichte.* 7 vols. Berlin: G. Stike, 1900–1936.

DICKINSON, G., ed. *The Instructions sur le Faict de la Guerre of Raymond de Beccarie de Pavie, Sieur de Fourquevaux.* London: University of London, The Athlone Press, 1954.

FOLARD, JEAN-CHARLES. *Histoire de Polybe avec un commentaire.* 7 vols. Amsterdam, 1774.

FRONTINUS. *Strategemata.* Translated by Charles E. Bennet. Loeb Classical Library. Cambridge, Mass.: Harvard University Press; London: W. Heinemann, 1925.

GILBERT, FELIX. "Machiavelli: the Renaissance of the Art of War," in *Makers of Modern Strategy.* Edited by E. M. Earle. Princeton: Princeton University Press, 1944.

GUIBERT, JACQUES ANTOINE HIPPOLYTE. *Essai général de tactique.* 2 vols. London, 1773.

HAHLWEG, WERNER. *Die Heeresreform der Oranier und die Antike.* Berlin: Junker und Dünnhaupt, 1941.

HOBOHM, MARTIN. *Machiavellis Renaissance der Kriegskunst.* 2 vols. Berlin: Curtius, 1913.

JÄHNS, MAX. *Geschichte der Kriegswissenschaften vornehmlich in Deutschland.* 2 vols. Munich and Leipzig: R. Oldenbourg, 1889–1891.

LIPSIUS, JUSTUS. *Sixe Bookes of Politickes or Civil Doctrine.* Translated by William Jones. London, 1594.

———. *Tvvo Bookes of Constancie.* Translated by Sir John Stradling. Edited by Rudolf Kirk with notes by C. M. Hall. New Brunswick, N. J.: Rutgers University Press, 1939.

LIVY. *History of Rome.* 14 vols. Translated by B. O. Foster, R. M. Geer, E. T. Sage, A. C. Schlesinger. Loeb Classical Library. Cambridge, Mass.: Harvard University Press; London: W. Heinemann, 1919–1959.

MATTINGLY, GARRETT. *Renaissance Diplomacy.* Boston: Houghton Mifflin and Co., 1955.

MEINECKE, FRIEDRICH. *Machiavellism: the Doctrine of Raison D'Etat and Its Place in Modern History.* Translated by Douglas Scott. Introduction by W. Stark. New Haven: Yale University Press, 1957.

MONTECUCCOLI, RAIMOND DE. *Mémoires.* 4 vols. Amsterdam and Leipzig, 1756.

OESTREICH, GERHARD. "Justus Lipsius als Theoretiker des neuzeitlichen Machtstaates," *Historische Zeitschrift,* CLXXXI (1956), 31–78.

————. "Der römische Stoizismus und die oranische Heeresreform," *Historische Zeitschrift*, CLXXVI (1953), 17–43.

OMAN, SIR CHARLES. *A History of War in the Sixteenth Century.* London: Methuen and Co., 1937.

PHILLIPS, BRIGADIER GENERAL THOMAS R., ed. *Roots of Strategy.* Harrisburg, Pa.: The Military Service Publishing Company, 1940. Contains translations of Vegetius, *De re militari;* Maurice de Saxe, *Mes Rêveries;* Frederick the Great, *Military Instructions.*

PIERI, PIERO. *Introduzione all'Arte della guerra di N. Machiavelli.* Rome: Edizioni Roma, 1936.

POLYBIUS. *The Histories,* 6 vols. Translated by W. R. Paton. Loeb Classical Library. Cambridge, Mass.: Harvard University Press; London: W. Heinemann, 1960.

RIDOLFI, ROBERTO. *The Life of Niccolò Machiavelli.* Translated by Cecil Grayson. London: Routledge and Kegan Paul; Chicago: The University of Chicago Press, 1963.

RAPOPORT, DAVID C. "Military and Civil Societies: the Contemporary Significance of a Traditional Subject in Political Theory," *Political Studies,* XII (June 1964), 178–201.

SPAULDING, OLIVER LYMAN. *Pen and Sword in Ancient Greece and Rome.* Princeton: Princeton University Press; London: H. Milford, Oxford University Press, 1937.

SPAULDING, OLIVER LYMAN, NICKERSON, HOFFMAN, and WRIGHT, JOHN WOMACK. *Warfare: A Study of Military Methods from the Earliest Times.* Preface by General Tasker H. Bliss. New York: Harcourt, Brace and Co., 1925.

TAYLOR, F. L. *The Art of War in Italy, 1494–1529.* Cambridge: Cambridge University Press, 1921.

VILLARI, PASQUALE. *Niccolò Machiavelli e i suoi tempi.* 2 vols. Fourth posthumous edition. Edited by Michele Scherillo. Milan: Hoepli, 1927.

WAILLE, VICTOR. *Machiavel en France.* Paris: A. Ghio, 1884.

WALKER, LESLIE J. *The Discourses of Niccolò Machiavelli.* 2 vols. Translated and edited. New Haven: Yale University Press, 1950.

WEBER, MAX. *From Max Weber: Essays in Sociology.* Translated and edited by H. H. Gerth and C. Wright Mills. New York: Oxford University Press, 1946.

XENOPHON. *Cyropaedia.* 2 vols. Translated by Walter Miller. Loeb Classical Library. Cambridge, Mass.: Harvard University Press; London: W. Heinemann, 1953.

NOTE ON THE TEXT

There have been only three different English translations of the *Arte della guerra*, all made before the nineteenth century.[1] The translation of Peter Whitehorne, or Whithorn, was published in 1560, 1573, and 1588, more printings at the time than of any other translation of a foreign military work. Appended to each of the editions was the translator's own important technical manual, *Certain Waies for the orderyng of Souldiers in battelray*. . . . The editions of 1573 and 1588 also include a translation by H. G. (probably Henry Grantham) of Giralamo Cataneo's *Most brief tables to knowe redily howe manye ranckes of footemen armed with Corslettes, as vnarmed, go to the making of a iust battayle, from an hundred vnto twentye thousande*, first published in Brescia in 1563. Unfortunately, most of the facts about the life of this interesting Elizabethan personage have been erased by time. He describes himself as both a student and a fellow of Gray's Inn, but his name is not to be found in the register of that institution. According to his account he served ten years campaigning against the Moors in North Africa with the imperial forces of another Machiavelli fancier, Charles V. The translation of *The Art of War* was made in Africa some years before publication. In 1563 Whitehorne also published his translation of Fabio Cotta's Italian rendering of Onasander's *Strategicus*. Little else is known, except that in his memoirs, Sir Thomas Hoby, diplomat and translator of Castiglione, mentions his acquaintance with Whitehorne in Italy during 1549 and 1550.

A reprint of Whitehorne's translation of *The Art of War* was published in 1905 (London: David Nutt), with an introduction by Henry Cust, as volume 39 of the Tudor Translations.

A translation by Henry Neville (1620–1694), or Nevill, was

[1] Since this book has gone to press, a new translation has appeared in Niccolò Machiavelli, *The Chief Works and Others*, tr. Allan Gilbert (3 vols.; Durham, N.C.: Duke University Press, 1965).

included in his single volume, folio edition (London, 1675), *The Works of the Famous Nicholas Machiavel*. Subsequent editions of the work appeared in 1680, 1694, and 1720. Neville was of a well-known, propertied Berkshire family. He left Oxford University without a degree, after having studied at Merton College and University College, and toured the continent, visiting Italy. Upon his return in 1645, he plunged into republican activity, and became closely associated with James Harrington, the author of the *Commonwealth of Oceana* (1656). He was returned to parliament for Reading in December 1658. During 1659 he was one of Harrington's close collaborators in the Rota, and acted as a kind of parliamentary agent for that interesting society of republicanism which included John Milton, Andrew Marvell, Christopher Wren, John Aubrey, William Petty, and Samuel Pepys. In October of 1663 Neville was charged with being involved in the Yorkshire uprising and imprisoned in the Tower. After a year he was cleared of the charge and released. The remainder of his life was spent in retirement and study. He expounded his views on the nature of a republican government for England in his *Plato Redivivus, or a Dialogue concerning Government* (London, 1681), which is a dialogue between an Englishman and a Venetian. Neville refers to Machiavelli as "the Divine Machiavel," the "best and the most honest of the modern Politicians."

Ellis Farneworth (d. 1763) included *The Art of War* in his translation, *The Works of Nicholas Machiavel*, published in two volumes in London in 1762. A second corrected edition in four volumes came out in 1775. Farneworth was an Anglican minister who had attended Eton and Jesus College, Cambridge. While caring for his flock in various parishes in Cheshire and Derbyshire, he found the leisure to translate several works from the Italian, including Leti's *Life of Pope Sixtus the Fifth* (London, 1754), and Davila's *History of the Civil Wars of France* (London, 1758).

The translation used here is that of the 1775 Farneworth

edition, in the slightly modified form of the single reprint of 1815, printed in Albany, New York, by Henry C. Southwick. The title of the volume is: *The | Art of War. | In Seven Books. | Written | by Nicholas Machiavel, | Secretary of State, | to the Republic of Florence. | To which is added, | Hints Relative to Warfare, | by a Gentleman | of the State of New York.* The "hints," which form an appendix on torpedo warfare, have not been included. The identity of "a Gentleman of the State of New York" is unknown. No indication is given in the volume as to who is responsible for the slight textual alterations of the Farneworth translation. Peter Whitehorne's dedication to Queen Elizabeth I, included in the Farneworth edition and the 1815 reprint, has been retained, see below, pp. 231–238. The detailed book headings, which Farneworth evidently adapted from those by Whitehorne, have been revised and incorporated into the table of contents. Farneworth's footnotes have been omitted, and new ones designed for today's reader have been added. The primary purpose of the new footnotes is to indicate the sources used by Machiavelli, to identify persons, places, and events, and to refer to relevant passages in the other works of the author.

Machiavelli is a superb prose stylist. Macaulay in 1827 maintained that his prose was clear and unaffected: "The judicious and candid mind of Machiavelli shows itself in his luminous, manly, and polished language." In the eleventh edition of the *Encyclopedia Britannica* John Addington Symonds aptly termed it "an athlete's style, all bone and sinew, without superfluous flesh or ornament." On the quincentennial of the Florentine's death, T. S. Eliot praised his literary skill, deeming it superior to that of Montaigne and Hobbes. In view of such a consensus, the Farneworth translation presents something of a problem. It is a leisurely paced and very readable paraphrase, often elegant, and sometimes lively, with a rather picturesque quality of expression. But the "bone and sinew" of the original has been padded generously with the flesh and ornament of pleonasm and interpolation. Moreover, there are frequent inaccuracies and omissions. The goal of the present revision, however short it may fall, has been to correct these inaccuracies and omissions, and to give some indication of the stylistic merits both in Machiavelli and in Farneworth. Occasionally, readability has been sacrificed for the literal, as when *virtù* and *fortuna* have been left untranslated.

The text followed is that of the *Arte della guerra e scritti politici minori* (Milan: Feltrinelli Editore, 1961) edited by Sergio Bertelli. Signor Bertelli's notes have been indispensable in both editing and revising the translation. Machiavelli's sources have often been consulted. And ever within reach of the editor's table has been Burd's classic guide to the sources, and Father Walker's splendid critical edition of *The Discourses*.

N. W.

THE ART OF WAR

PREFACE

OF NICCOLÒ MACHIAVELLI

CITIZEN AND SECRETARY OF FLORENCE

TO HIS BOOK ABOUT

THE ART OF WAR

ADDRESSED TO

LORENZO DI FILIPPO STROZZI

FLORENTINE NOBLEMAN

MANY ARE now of the opinion, my dear Lorenzo, that no two things are more discordant and incongruous than a civil and a military life. Hence we daily see that when a man goes into the army, he immediately changes not only his dress, but his behavior, his company, his air, his manner of speaking, and that he affects to throw off all appearances of anything that may look like ordinary life and conversation. For a man wanting to be ready-equipped for any sort of violence despises the formal dress of a civilian and thinks no dress fit for his purpose but a suit of armor. And as to civility and politeness, how can we expect to find them in one who imagines that such things would make him look effeminate and that they would be a hindrance to his work, especially when he thinks it his duty, instead of talking and looking like other men, to frighten everyone he meets with a volley of oaths and a terrible pair of whiskers? This indeed gives some countenance to such an opinion and makes people look upon a soldier as a creature different from all other men.

But if we consider the institutions of the ancients, we shall find that there is a very close, intimate relation between these two conditions, and that they are not only compatible and consistent with each other, but necessarily connected and inter-related. For all the arts that have been introduced into society for the common benefit of mankind, and all the ordinances that have been established to make them live in fear of God and in obedience to human laws, would be vain and insignificant if they were not supported and defended by a military force; this force, when properly led and applied, will maintain those ordinances and keep up their authority, although they perhaps may not be perfect or flawless. But the best ordinances in the world will be despised and trampled under foot when they are not supported, as they ought to be, by a military power; they are like a magnificent, roofless palace which, though full of jewels and costly furniture, must soon moulder into ruin since it has nothing but its splendor and riches to defend it from the ravages of the weather.

The ancient lawgivers and governors of kingdoms and republics took great care, therefore, to inspire all their subjects—but particularly their soldiers—with fidelity, love of peace, and fear of God. For who ought to be more faithful than a man entrusted with the safety of his country and sworn to defend it with the last drop of his blood? Who ought to be fonder of peace than those suffering from nothing but war? Who are under greater obligations to worship God than soldiers, daily exposed to innumerable dangers, men who have the most occasion for his protection? This necessity—well considered by those who governed states and modeled armies in former times and strongly enforced upon others under their command—had such an effect upon their conduct and behavior that the life of a soldier was edifying and served as a pattern for others. But since our discipline is now depraved to such a degree that it is totally different from what it was in ancient times, it is no wonder that other men have so bad an opinion of military life and that they endeavor, as much as they can, to avoid the company and conversation of all those following the profession of arms.

Since I am of the opinion, therefore, from what I have both seen and read, that it would not be impossible to revive the discipline of our ancestors and, in some measure, to retrieve our lost *virtù*,[1] I have written the following treatise concerning the art of war, as much for the improvement of others desiring to imitate the ancients in warlike exploits, as for my own private satisfaction, and for avoiding the imputation of spending my leisure in idleness. Although treating an art which I never professed may perhaps seem a presumptuous undertaking, I cannot help thinking myself more excusable than some other people who have taken its actual exercise upon themselves. For an error in my writings may easily be corrected without harming anybody, but an error in their practice may ruin a whole state.

Consider the nature of this work, then, good Lorenzo, and freely bestow either your censure or commendation upon it, as you think it justly deserves. I inscribe it to you not only as a testimony of my gratitude, although conscious how small a return it is for the favors I have received from you, but because it is usual to address things of this nature to persons who are distinguished by their nobility, riches, great talent, and generosity; I know very well that in birth and wealth you have not many equals, still fewer in talent, and in generosity, none at all.

---

[1] In most instances *virtù* has been left untranslated. See the Introduction, pp. liv–lvi, for a brief discussion of Machiavelli's use of the word.

BOOK ONE

SINCE IT is legitimate, I think, to speak well of any man after he is dead, because then there can no longer be any imputation or suspicion of flattery in it, I willingly take this opportunity of doing justice to the memory of my dear, deceased friend Cosimo Rucellai, whose name I never remember without tears in my eyes, as I knew him to possess every quality that his friends and country could wish for in a worthy man and a good citizen. I am very certain that he would cheerfully have sacrificed all he had in the world, and even life itself, for his friends, and that there was no enterprise, however difficult and dangerous, which he would not have undertaken for the good of his country. And I must readily acknowledge that, among all the men I ever knew or with whom I associated, I never met anyone whose heart was more disposed to great and generous actions. As he died, he told his friends the only thing he regretted was that it should be his fate to die so young, and at home, too, without having achieved glory or the satisfaction of having served any man as effectively as he had passionately desired to have done, and to know that nothing more could be said of him after he was dead than that they had lost a good friend. Many others, however, besides myself, can give sufficient testimony not only of his virtues but of the many amiable and gentlemanly accomplishments he possessed, although there are now only a few traces of them left. *Fortuna* [1] has indeed spared some small specimens of the

---

[1] As in the case of *virtù*, the Italian *fortuna* has been retained in most instances. Usually Machiavelli identifies *fortuna* with the incalculable and fortuitous; sometimes, with a cosmic force like destiny. In both usages he often personifies it. Throughout *The Art of War*, he employs the word primarily in the former sense. Human life is conceived in terms of a struggle between *fortuna* and *virtù*. *Fortuna* may place us in particular circumstances, but whether we exert some control over our lives, instead

sprightliness of his genius, consisting chiefly of short essays and love sonnets, which (although he was not of an amorous turn) he composed at free moments during his youth, to avoid being altogether idle until he should find it necessary to employ his thoughts upon subjects of a higher and more serious nature. But even these little samples indicate how happy he was in expressing his ideas, and what honor he might have won in poetry had he thought it worth his while to give himself over to it entirely.

However, since *fortuna* has deprived us of so valuable a friend, the only remedy we have left is to console ourselves as well as we can with the memory of his company and the recollection of such things, whether of a pleasant or serious cast, as we have often admired in him while he lived. And because the conversation that occurred not long ago in his gardens between him and Fabrizio Colonna concerning the art of war (at which I and some other friends were present) is the freshest in my memory, I shall endeavor to recollect what I can of it and commit it to writing. Since on the one hand Fabrizio laid open the mysteries of that art with great perspicuity, and since on the other hand several pertinent questions were proposed, many objections stated, and various arguments supported with no less strength of reason chiefly by Cosimo—a summary account of that conference may serve to revive the memory of his abilities in the minds of such friends as were then gathered together, to make some of those absent regret they had not been there too, and to recapitulate to others the substance of various topics (useful both in civilian and in military life) that were masterfully discussed by another great and experienced man. But to our purpose.

Returning from the wars in Lombardy, where he had commanded his Catholic Majesty's [2] forces for a considerable time and with great reknown, Fabrizio Colonna passed by way of

---

of becoming the plaything of chance, depends upon our *virtù*. Also see the Introduction, pp. liv–lvi.

[2] The Hapsburg Charles I of Spain (1500–1558). In 1519 he became Emperor Charles V of the Holy Roman Empire.

Florence to rest himself a few days in that city and to visit the duke [3] and some other gentlemen there, with whom he was acquainted. Cosimo Rucellai, therefore, invited him to spend a day in his gardens, not merely to gratify his natural turn to hospitality and politeness, but also in hopes of being able to indulge in a long conversation with him concerning several things he wanted to know and about which he thought he could not have a better opportunity of being informed than from so great a man. Fabrizio freely accepted the invitation and came to the gardens, at the appointed time, where he was received by Cosimo, and some of his most intimate friends—among whom were Zanobi Buondelmonti, Battista della Palla and Luigi Alamanni.[4] These young men—whose virtues and good qualities are so well known to everybody that it would be altogether unnecessary to say anything here in praise of them—were very dear to Cosimo, were of the same disposition, and were engaged in the same studies.

To be as brief as I can, then, Fabrizio was regaled there with every possible demonstration of honor and respect. But after the end of the entertainment and usual formalities, which generally are few and short among men of sense who are more desirous of gratifying the rational appetite, and since the days were long and the weather intensely hot, Cosimo, under a pretext of avoiding the heat, took his guests into the most retired and shady part of the gardens. Then, when they had all sat down—some upon the grass, which is very green and pleasant there, and some upon seats placed under the loftiest trees—Fabrizio said it was a most delightful garden and, looking earnestly at some of the trees, seemed not to know their names. Cosimo, being aware of it, immediately said, "Perhaps you do not know some of these trees, but you should not be at all surprised at it, for they are very old ones

---

[3] The Florentine ruler, Lorenzo de' Medici (1492–1519), duke of Urbino, grandson of Lorenzo the Magnificent and nephew of Pope Leo X, to whom Machiavelli dedicated *The Prince*.

[4] See the Introduction and notes, pp. xviii–xix. both for these men and for Bernardo Rucellai, mentioned below.

and were much more in vogue among our ancestors than they are at present." He then told him their names and said that they were planted by his grandfather Bernardo, who was fond of growing such trees. "I thought so," replied Fabrizio, "and both the place and the trees put me in mind of some princes in the kingdom of Naples, who take much delight in planting groves and shady arbors, in the ancient manner." Here he stopped short, and after he had paused a little while, proceeded in this manner: "If I were not afraid of giving offense," he said, "I would give you my opinion of these things. And yet I think none of you will be affronted at what is said among friends in free conversation, and said not with any design to vilify or deprecate such a taste, but for the sake of a little innocent argumentation. How much better, then, would those princes have done (I mention it without intending to reflect upon their memories) if they had endeavored to imitate the ancients in bearing hardships and inconveniences, instead of giving themselves up to ease and indolence, in performing such exploits as were done in the sunshine and not in the shade, in following their example while they continued honest and wholesome, and not when they became dishonest and corrupt. For once these pleasures had distracted my fellow Romans, our country soon fell into ruin." Cosimo then replied (but to avoid the frequent and tiresome repetition of *this one said, and that one replied,* I shall hereafter prefix only the names of the speakers to what they said in the course of this conversation):

Cosimo. You have now introduced a subject which I have long wished to hear thoroughly discussed and I should therefore take it as a particular favor if you would speak your sentiments about it freely and without reserve or fear of offending anyone here. For my own part, I shall take the liberty of proposing some questions and doubts to you in which I should be glad to be satisfied; if I shall seem to impeach or excuse anyone's conduct in my questions or replies, it will not be merely for the sake of blaming or defending them, but for better information.

Fabrizio. It will be a great pleasure to give you all the satisfaction I can in such questions as you shall think fit to propose to me, but I shall not pretend to obtrude my opinions upon you as decisive and infallible. When you have heard them, you may judge for yourself. Perhaps I, in turn, may now and then ask you a question, and have no doubts but that I shall receive at least as much satisfaction in your answers as you will in mine; it often happens that a pertinent question sets a man to considering many things, and gives him light into many others which he would otherwise never have thought of or known.

Cosimo. Let us return, then, if you please, to what you said of my grandfather and the others, who you think would have done better to have imitated the ancients in their hardy and active way of life, than in their ease and luxury. As for my grandfather, I shall make some sort of apology for him, and leave the others to be dealt with as you please, for I do not believe there was any man of his time who detested a soft and delicate way of life more than he did, or who loved more the austere life you have praised. Nevertheless, he found it impossible either for himself or for his sons to practice what he most approved. For such was the corruption of the age in which he lived that if anyone had spirit enough to deviate in the slightest from the common customs and manners of living in those times, he would have been laughed at and ridiculed by everybody—so that if a man should have exposed himself naked upon a sandy beach to the heat of a noonday sun in the middle of summer, or rolled himself in snow in the depth of winter, as Diogenes did,[5] he would have been thought a madman. If anyone had brought up his children, as the Spartans did, in cottages or farmhouses and had accustomed them to sleep in the open air, to go bareheaded and barefoot, to bathe in the coldest streams, in order to teach them not only to bear hardships better, but even to despise both life and death, he

---

[5] Diogenes (*ca.* 400–325 B.C.), founder of the Cynic school of philosophy. See Diogenes Laertius, *Lives of Eminent Philosophers* VI. 2.

would have been accounted a beast rather than a man. If, moreover, he had lived on pulse and roots and had scorned money—like Fabricius of old [6]—he might perhaps have been admired by some few, but he would have been followed by no one at all. My grandfather, therefore, was discouraged by the general practice of the times from imitating the example of the ancients in those things, and he was forced to content himself with doing it in others, which did not lay him open to the charge of attracting attention.

Fabrizio. You have made a very handsome apology for your grandfather in that particular, sir, and there is indeed much truth and reason in it. But when I was talking about imitating the ancients in their austere manner of living, I did not mean to carry matters to such extremities as you seem to think, but to propose some other things of a gentler and more practicable nature, such as would be more suitable to the present times, and which I think might very well be established if they were introduced and countenanced by some men of authority in a government. And if we consider the practice and institutions observed by the old Romans (whose example I am always fond of recommending), we shall find many things worthy of imitation; these may easily be introduced into any other state, if it has not become totally corrupt.

Cosimo. What are these things you would introduce in imitation of the ancients?

Fabrizio. To honor and reward *virtù;* not to scorn poverty; to value good order and discipline in their armies; to oblige citizens to love one another, to decline faction, and to prefer the good of the public to any private interest; and other such principles which would be compatible enough with these times. These principles might easily be introduced if due means were taken for that purpose because they appear so reasonable in themselves, and because their expediency is so

[6] C. Fabricius Luscinus, consul in 282 and 278 B.C. and censor in 275; noted for his uprightness. See *Discourses on the First Ten Books of Livy,* III, 1 and 20.

obvious to common sense that nobody could gainsay or oppose them. He that takes this course plants trees under the shade of which he may enjoy himself with greater pleasure, and more security, than we do here.

Cosimo. What you have said of this matter admits of no contradiction, and I shall therefore leave it to the consideration and best judgment of our present company. But I should like to know why you, who blame others for not imitating the ancients in other weighty and important concerns, have yourself in no way seen fit to copy them in their military discipline and the art of war, which is your profession, and in which you have gained so much reputation.

Fabrizio. You have now come to the point I expected; what I said must naturally lead you to ask such a question, and I shall most willingly give you what satisfaction I can. Although I could make a short and ready excuse for my conduct in this respect, since we have so much leisure and so convenient a place for it, I shall discuss the matter at length—especially since it will give me great pleasure to delve more deeply into what you seem so anxious to know.

Men who have any great undertaking in mind must first make all necessary preparations for it, so that, when an opportunity arises, they may be ready to put it in execution according to their design. Now when these preparations are made cautiously and privately, they are not known or discussed by others; a man cannot be blamed for negligence or omission in that respect, unless something happens which shows either that he has not made due preparations for the execution of his design, or that he never thought of it at all. And therefore, since I have never had any such opportunity of showing what preparations I have made to revive among us the military discipline of the ancients, nobody can reasonably blame me for not doing so. This might serve as a sufficient answer to your charge.

Cosimo. So indeed it might, if I were sure you never had such an opportunity.

Fabrizio. Since you seem to doubt that, I shall show you at length—if you will have the patience to hear me—what preparations are necessary for that purpose; what sort of an opportunity is requisite; what impediments may obstruct the preparations and prevent those opportunities from happening; and lastly (which seems a contradiction in terms), that it is at the same time the easiest and most difficult thing in the world to accomplish such a purpose.

Cosimo. You could not give us more pleasure, and if you are not tired of talking, you may rest assured that we shall never be tired of listening to you. But since the subject is copious and there is much to be said about it, I must beg leave to call in the assistance of these friends now and then. All of us hope you will not be offended if we should happen to interrupt you from time to time with any question that may seem unnecessary or unreasonable.

Fabrizio. You are all heartily welcome to ask whatever questions you think fit; for I see that the ardor and ingenuity of youth incline you to have a favorable opinion of my profession and to listen to what I have to say concerning its duties. But when men are grown gray-headed and their blood is frozen in their veins, they generally either hate the very name of a soldier or become so positive that they can never be argued out of their opinions. Ask freely, then, and without reserve; for that will give me an opportunity of breathing a little sometimes, as well as the satisfaction of answering your questions in such a way that no doubt will remain in your minds.

To begin, then, with what you yourself said, that in the art of war, which is my profession, I have not imitated the ancients in any respect whatsoever, I reply that since war is not an occupation by which a man can at all times make an honorable living, it ought not to be followed as a business by anyone but a prince or a governor of a commonwealth; and if he is a wise man, he will not allow any of his subjects or citizens to make that his only profession—indeed, no good man ever did, for surely no one can be called a good man who, in order to support himself, takes up a profession that obliges him at all times to be rapacious, fraudulent, and cruel, as of course must be all of those—no matter what their rank—who make a trade of war. War will not maintain them in time of peace, and thus they are under a necessity either of endeavoring to prevent a peace or of taking all means to make such provisions for themselves in time of war so that they may not lack sustenance when it is over. But neither of these courses is consistent with the common good; whoever resolves to amass enough in time of war to support him forever must be guilty of robbery, murder, and many other acts of violence toward his friends as well as his enemies; and in endeavoring to prevent a peace, commanders must have recourse to many mean tricks and artifices to deceive those who employ them. But if these commanders fail in their designs, and find they cannot prevent a peace, it often happens that, once their pay is stopped and they can no longer make a living, they illegally set themselves up as soldiers of fortune and have no scruples about plundering a whole province unmercifully.

You must recall that when the late wars were over in Italy, the country was full of disbanded soldiers who formed themselves into a number of bands—calling themselves "companies" [7]—that went about plundering some towns and laying others under contribution. You also must have read how the Carthaginian soldiers (after the end of the first war they had been fighting with the Romans) assembled under the banners of Matho and Spendius (two officers whom they had chosen in a tumultuous manner to command them) and fought a more dangerous war with their own country than that which had just been concluded.[8] In the days of our ancestors. Fran-

[7] Reference is evidently to the mercenary companies in operation during the Hundred Years' War (1337–1453).

[8] This mutiny touched off the so-called Libyan War against Carthage (241–238 B.C.). A detailed account is found in Polybius, I. 65–88. For Machiavelli's reference to the episode, see *Prince*, 12; *Discourses*, III, 32.

cesco Sforza,[9] in order to support himself in splendor and magnificence in peacetime, not only betrayed the Milanese who had employed him in their service, but also deprived them of their liberties and made himself their sovereign.

All the rest of our Italian soldiers who made war their only occupation played a similar part in those times; and even if they did not manage to become dukes of Milan by their villainies, they were no less reprehensible than Sforza; for if we consider their actions and conduct, we shall find their designs were altogether as iniquitous as his. Sforza,[10] the father of Francesco, obliged Giovanna, queen of Naples,[11] to throw herself into the arms of the King of Aragon by suddenly quitting her service and leaving her disarmed, as it were, in the midst of her enemies, simply because he wanted to deprive her of her kingdom, or at least to extort a great sum of money from her. Braccio da Montone [12] endeavored to have himself made king of Naples by using the same means; if he had not been routed and killed at Aquila,[13] he would certainly have accomplished his design.

Such evils are caused by men who make mercenary warfare their sole occupation. You must know the proverb, "War makes thieves, and peace hangs them." When those who do not know how to get their bread any other way find no one who has occasion for their service, and do not themselves have sufficient *virtù* to suffer honorably in poverty and obscurity, they are forced to resort to ways of supporting themselves that generally bring them to the gallows.

[9] Francesco Sforza (1401–1466), a famous condottiere who seized power in the city he served, becoming duke of Milan in 1450. Lauded by Machiavelli; see *Prince*, 7.

[10] Muzio Attendolo Sforza (1369–1424), also a noted condottiere.

[11] Giovanna II (1414–1435).

[12] Andrea Fortebracci (1368–1424).

[13] June 2, 1424. See *Prince*, 12 for a passing reference to these events. A detailed account of the developments in Naples is given by Machiavelli in his *History of Florence*, I, 39.

Cosimo. I had thought the profession of a soldier the most excellent and the most honorable in all the world; but you have set it in such a light, and I now have so poor an opinion of it, that if you have not a great deal more to say in favor of it, you will leave a doubt upon my mind. For if what you have said be true, how does it come about that the memories of Caesar, Pompey, Scipio, Marcellus,[14] and many other Roman generals are immortalized?

Fabrizio. I have not yet finished what I proposed to say concerning the two points I mentioned a little while ago, namely, that a good man could not make war his only profession, and that no wise prince or governor of a commonwealth would allow any of his subjects or citizens to do it. As to the first point, I have said all that has occurred to me; I shall now proceed to the discussion of the second, in which I shall take the opportunity of answering your last question.

I say, then, that Caesar and Pompey, and almost all the Roman generals who lived after the Second Punic War,[15] acquired their reputation as skillful men, not as good citizens; but those who lived before that time won glory by being both civic-minded and skillful. Now the reason for this was that the former made war their sole occupation and the latter did not. And as long as the Roman republic continued incorrupt, no citizen, however powerful, ever presumed to avail himself of that profession in peacetime so as to trample upon the laws, to plunder provinces, or to turn tyrant and enslave his country; nor did any private soldier dare to violate his oath, to enter into faction and cabals, to throw off his allegiance to the senate, or to support any tyrannical attempt upon the liberties of the commonwealth in order to enable himself to live by the profession of arms at all times. The commanders, on the contrary, contenting themselves with the honor of a triumph, returned with eagerness to their former manner of

---

14 M. Claudius Marcellus, who conquered Syracuse in 212 B.C.
15 218–201 B.C.

living; and the common soldiers laid down their arms with much more pleasure than they had taken them up. Each resumed the calling by which he had gotten his bread before, and none had any hopes of advancing himself by plunder and rapine.

Of this we have a remarkable and evident proof in the example of Atilius Regulus,[16] who, being commander in chief of the Roman armies in Africa and having in a manner subdued the Carthaginians, requested the senate's permission to return home and put his little farm in order again, since it had been neglected by his servants. It plainly appears from this that if war had been his only occupation, and he had designed to make his fortune by it, he would not have requested permission to return to the care of his little estate, when he had so many provinces at his mercy and might daily have gained more by plundering them than his whole patrimony was worth. But just as good men who do not make war their sole occupation expect no other reward but toil, danger, and glory for their services, so, when they have obtained that, they cheerfully return to their former way of life.

As for the common soldiers, we see that they also were of the same disposition; although they entered voluntarily into the service, they were no less glad to return to their families when they were no longer wanted. The truth of this is manifest from many circumstances, particularly from the important privilege accorded Roman citizens of not being forced into the army against their will. At any rate, as long as Rome continued to be well governed (which was until the time of the Gracchi) [17] there was never any soldier who made war his only occupation; and so it happened that few of them were dissolute or licentious—and those few were severely punished.

16 M. Atilius Regulus in 256 B.C. The source is probably Valerius Maximus, IV. 4. See *Discourses*, I, 1; III, 25.

17 The reference is to the brothers C. Sempronius Gracchus (153?–121 B.C.) and Tiberius Gracchus (163?–133 B.C.), reformers and leaders of the Roman populace. From their period on, social unrest and class conflict increased. See *Discourses*, I, 4 and 37.

Every well-governed commonwealth, therefore, should take care that this art of war should be practiced in time of peace only as an exercise, and in time of war, only out of necessity and for the acquisition of glory, and that it should be practiced, as in Rome, by the state alone. For if any citizen has another end or design in following this profession, he is not a good man; if any commonwealth acts otherwise, it is not well governed.

Cosimo. I am thoroughly satisfied with the reasonableness of what you have hitherto said concerning this matter. I admit that the conclusion you have drawn is very just, insofar as it relates to a commonwealth, but I cannot tell whether it will hold good with regard to princes—for I should think a prince would want to have some persons around him who make arms their only profession.

Fabrizio. A kingdom that is well governed and constituted ought to be all the more afraid of such persons, because only they corrupt its princes and become the ministers of tyranny. It is useless to urge any current monarchy as an instance to the contrary, for not one is well governed and constituted. A well-governed kingdom never gives absolute power to its prince in anything but the command of its armies, because sudden resolutions are often necessary in this one sphere, so that there must be a supreme command. In other matters, the prince should do nothing without his council. Therefore, his councilors should take particular care not to let men be too near his person who would be continually advising him to make war because they cannot support themselves without war.

But I shall enlarge a little further upon this subject and not insist merely upon a kingdom that is perfectly well governed and constituted, but content myself (for argument's sake) with such kingdoms as we see today. I say, then, that even such governments should fear those persons who make war their only business; and this is because the strength of all armies, without a doubt, consists in their infantry.[18] And if a prince has not enough power over his infantry to make them disband and return cheerfully to their former occupations when a war is over, he is on the road to being ruined. For no infantry can be so dangerous as that which is composed of men who make war their only calling, because a prince either must keep them continually engaged in war, or must constantly keep them paid in peacetime, or must run the risk of their stripping him of his kingdom. But it is impossible to keep them forever engaged in war, or forever paid when war is over; therefore, a prince must run no small risk of losing his kingdom. While the Romans were still wise and good, they never permitted any of their citizens to make war their only employment—as I said before—although they would have been able to keep them in constant pay, because they were continually at war. But, in order to avoid the inconveniences which might have ensued from the toleration of such a custom, they changed their forces (since the times did not change) so that at the end of every fifteen years their legions were filled with new men who were in the flower of their youth—between eighteen and thirty-five years of age, in full health and vigor—and who were never retained after they had grown old and infirm, as the same people did later, in more corrupt times.

For Augustus, and after him Tiberius, more interested in establishing and increasing their own power than in promoting the public good, began to disarm the Roman people (in order to make them more passive under their tyranny) and to keep the same armies continually on foot within the confines of the Empire. But thinking those armies insufficient to keep the senate and people in due awe, they raised another force, called the Praetorian Guard, which was always quartered in or near the city, and served not only to guard the emperor's person but to bridle the people. Afterward, however, when the emperors permitted the men who composed this guard to lay aside all other occupations and to make war their sole profession, they soon became insolent and formid-

[18] A point stressed by Machiavelli in *Discourses*, II, 18.

able, not only to the senate but to the emperors themselves. The Praetorian Guard put many emperors to death and then disposed of the Empire as it pleased, taking the Empire from some, and giving it to others. It frequently happened that different emperors were elected by different armies at the same time, which soon occasioned the division of the Empire, and at last its utter ruin.

A prince, therefore, who would reign in security, ought to select only such men for his infantry as will cheerfully serve him in war when it is necessary, and be as glad to return home after it is over. This will always be the case with those who have other occupations and employments by which to live. To this end, when a peace is concluded, he should order his generals and great officers to return to the government of their provinces, the gentlemen to return to the care of their estates, and the common soldiers to return to their particular callings, so that everyone may be ready to enter into a war to procure a good peace, but no man might presume to disturb the peace in order to stir up a war.

Cosimo. Indeed, sir, I think there is much truth and reason in what you have said. However, since the substance of it is so very different from the judgment I myself had previously formed about these matters, I cannot say that I am altogether satisfied in some respects; for I know several lords and gentlemen who are supported in peacetime by the profession of arms alone—such as yourself, for instance, and others of your rank and quality who receive pensions from princes and other states. I also see many soldiers, especially cavalry and men-at-arms, still kept in pay for the security of fortresses and other cities, so that it appears to me that there is sufficient employment and occasion for all of them in time of peace.

Fabrizio. Surely you cannot be of that opinion, for were there no other reason to convince you of the contrary, the small number of men held in reserve to garrison those places ought to be a sufficient answer to your objection. What proportion is there between a few infantry regiments necessary to defend some strongholds in time of peace and those that are to be kept in pay for the prosecution of war? In time of war are not many more needed to reinforce those garrisons, besides the numbers that are to be employed in the field, and who are always disbanded as soon as peace is concluded? As to the common standing guards that are requisite to any state (but which need not be many), Pope Julius II and your own republic have sufficiently shown the world how dangerous they thought those people who made war their only occupation by dismissing them for their insolence and hiring, in their place, Swiss guards who were not only born and brought up in strict obedience to laws, but picked and chosen from their various vocations in a prudent and regular manner. Your objection, therefore, that soldiers of every kind are necessary and may find adequate employment in peacetime as well as war must naturally fall to the ground.

But the reason why men-at-arms should be kept in pay during peacetime may perhaps not be so obvious. Nevertheless, if we consider the matter thoroughly, it may easily be accounted for; it is a bad custom introduced by men who make a trade of war, and it would be attended with many dangerous consequences to a state in which any considerable number of them was kept in pay. However, since there are seldom enough to make up an army by themselves, they can do no great mischief at present, although they have done so in the past, as I have already shown in the cases of Francesco Sforza, his father, and Braccio da Montone. It is a bad custom, however, and one that can lead to much trouble.

Cosimo. Would you have none at all, then? Or, if you would have any, how would you raise and employ them?

Fabrizio. As a militia; not like the men-at-arms of France, who are as insolent and dangerous as our own, but after the manner of the ancients, who always raised their cavalry from their own subjects and, after a war ended, sent them home again to support themselves by their respective occupations—

as I shall show at greater length before I have finished with this subject.

So that if the cavalry is kept together, receives pay, and lives entirely on it even in times of peace, it is a result of corruption and bad government. And although I myself and some other commanders receive pensions and stipends in peacetime, I must confess I think it a very corrupt custom. A wise and well-governed republic ought never to keep such commanders in constant pay; rather, it should employ its own citizens in time of war and subsequently dismiss them to pursue their former occupations.

So also should an intelligent prince not allow anyone a pension or stipend in peacetime except as a reward for outstanding service, or in order to avail himself of some able man in peacetime as well as in war. And since you have selected me as an example of this kind, I shall take up the charge and make the best apology I can for it. I say, then, that I never made war my sole business and occupation. My profession is to govern my subjects well and to defend and protect them; to this purpose, I study the arts both of peace and of war. And if I am rewarded and esteemed by the prince whom I have the honor to serve, it is not so much because I am experienced in military affairs as because he is pleased to retain me as one of his counselors in time of peace. A prince, therefore, should admit no other sort of persons into his confidence, if he would govern wisely; for if his counselors are too fond of either peace or war, they will lead him into errors and inconveniences.

This much I felt myself obliged to say as a consequence of what I first proposed; and if it is not satisfactory, there is no doubt that you will be able to find others who can give you better information concerning the things you seemed so anxious to know. I dare say, however, that you are beginning to be aware of how difficult it must be to revive the military discipline of the ancients at present, of what preparations are necessary for that purpose, and of what occasions and opportunities are lacking to accomplish it. But if what I have said has not already tired you, I could throw a little more light upon this subject by comparing the particulars of our modern practice and institutions with the discipline of the ancients.

Cosimo. If at first we were anxious to hear you enter into a discussion of these things, we can assure you that what you have just said has now redoubled our desire. We therefore thank you most heartily for the satisfaction you have given us, and we earnestly beg you not to deprive us of the rest.

Fabrizio. Since it is your pleasure, then, I shall deduce this matter from the fountainhead, so that I can explain myself with more perspicuity, and so that you can understand me better.

Whoever engages in a war must use every means to put himself in a position of facing his enemy in the field, and beating him there if possible. For this purpose, it is necessary to form an army. To form an army, he must not only raise men, but arm, discipline, and exercise them frequently—both in large and small battle formations; he must teach them to encamp and decamp; and he must make the enemy familiar to them gradually, sometimes by marching near them, and sometimes by taking a post in a location where they may have a full view of them. These preparations are absolutely necessary in a field war, which is the most necessary and honorable of all wars; a general who knows how to conduct such a war, in order to form and draw up an army, and to give battle to an enemy in a proper and soldier-like manner, cannot err much in other respects; but if he is deficient in this aspect of his profession—though he be ever so able a man in other respects—he will never bring a war to a happy conclusion; besides, if he wins a battle, it cancels all other errors and miscarriages, but if he loses one, it effaces the memory of all his former merits and services.

To form an army, therefore, it is first necessary to choose the proper men for that purpose. The ancients termed this choice a *delectus*,[19] but we call it a military conscription. Those, then, who have prescribed the rules for the art of war [20] unanimously agree that such men should be selected from temperate climates, so that they may be both brave and cautious. It has been generally observed that hot countries produce men who are quick and sharp-witted, but not courageous; on the other hand, that the inhabitants of cold countries are for the most part hardy and brave, but dull and slow to understand. Indeed, this rule might be followed by a prince who had the whole world at his command and could select his men from wherever he pleased. But, to give a rule which may be observed by any state, I say that every prince or republic should select his men from his own dominions, whether hot, cold, or temperate; for we see by ancient examples that good discipline and exercise will make good soldiers in any country, and that the defects of nature may be supplied by art and industry—which in this case is more effective than nature itself.[21] Besides, selecting men from another country cannot properly be called a *delectus,* or a military conscription, because that term signifies picking and culling the best men in a province and implies a power to choose those who are unwilling, as well as those who are willing, to serve in the wars. And this cannot be done in any country but your own, for in territories that are subject to another state, you must be content with those men who are willing to serve you, and not expect to pick and choose whom you please.

Cosimo. But you may either take or refuse whom you think fit from those willing to serve you; therefore, that may be called *delectus.*

[19] *Delectus,* from the Latin *deligo,* to choose, select; the context in Machiavelli refers primarily to the selecting of recruits, and is analogous to our Selective Service System.

[20] Vegetius, *De re militari* I. 2.

[21] An expression of Machiavelli's belief that the quality of a people depends largely upon art—i.e., upon education and conditioning—rather than upon nature, inborn traits. Man is raw material to be molded. Cf. similar remarks below, pp. 61, 64, 151, 169, 202, 209–210, and *Discourses,* III, 36.

Fabrizio. In one respect you are right, but consider the defects to which such a choice is subject, and you will find that in effect it is no choice at all. In the first place, those who are not your own subjects, but yet are willing to enter into your pay, are so far from being the best men that they are generally the worst in any state. For if there be any scandalous, idle, incorrigible, irreligious wretches; any who are runaways from their parents, blasphemers, common cheats, or fellows who have been initiated into every kind of villainy—those are the people who commonly enlist under your banners. What sort of soldiers they are likely to make, I leave everyone to judge for himself. Now when there are more of these honest gentry offering their service than you want, you may indeed pick and choose among them, but you can never make a good choice because they are all so bad. It often happens, however, that there are not so many, even of these, as you need in order to fill up your regiments, so that you are obliged to take them all—then surely you cannot quite so properly be said to be making a *delectus,* a choice, but recruiting foot soldiers. Our Italian armies and those of most other nations, except Germany, are today composed of such disorderly people because our princes do not have it in their power to make a man serve in their wars unless he is willing. Consider among yourselves, therefore, whether it is possible to revive the discipline of the ancients in armies which are selected in such a manner.

Cosimo. What other method would you use, then, to raise them?

Fabrizio. The one I recommended before. A prince should choose his army from his own subjects, and exert his authority in such a choice.

Cosimo. Do you think any form of the ancient discipline might be revived in an army thus chosen?

Fabrizio. Without a doubt it might, if such an army were commanded by its natural sovereign in a principality, or, in a commonwealth, by one of the governing citizens, who should be appointed commander in chief during the time of his authority—otherwise it would be a very difficult matter.

Cosimo. Why?

Fabrizio. I will explain that to you at greater length when it is the proper time. Let it suffice at present to say that no good can be done in any other way.

Cosimo. Well, then, since these conscriptions are to be made in your own dominions, is it better to draw the men from rural areas or from towns?

Fabrizio. All authors who have written upon this subject agree [22] that it is better to take them from rural areas, because such men are accustomed to bearing up under hardships and fatigues, enduring all sorts of weather, handling a spade, digging ditches, carrying heavy burdens—these men are, generally speaking, more temperate and incorrupt than others. But since both a cavalry and an infantry are necessary to an army, I would advise that the cavalry be chosen from towns, and the infantry from rural areas.

Cosimo. At what age would you take them?

Fabrizio. If I were to conscript a new army, I would choose men from seventeen to forty years old; but, if I were to recruit only an old one, I would have no one more than seventeen.

Cosimo. I do not understand this distinction clearly.

Fabrizio. Then I shall tell you its meaning. If I were to conscript an army or establish a militia in a state where none had previously existed, it would be necessary to take the best and most qualified men I could find of all ages—provided they were neither too young nor too old to carry arms—in order to discipline them in a manner about which I shall inform you in its proper place. But if I were to choose men to recruit only for an army that had long been on foot, I would take none

22 Vegetius, I. 3.

more than seventeen, because there would already be men enough of riper age for my purpose in such an army.

Cosimo. Then you would have a militia ordinance similar to our city's? [23]

Fabrizio. Yes; but I would arm, officer, exercise, and discipline them in a manner that I imagine is unknown in your country.

Cosimo. Do you recommend a militia ordinance?

Fabrizio. Why not, sir?

Cosimo. Because many wise men have always disapproved of it.

Fabrizio. You contradict yourself when you say that wise men disapprove of the ordinance. Some men may appear to be wise and able, although they really are not so.

Cosimo. Our unfortunate experience with the ordinance seems to justify that opinion.

Fabrizio. Are you sure that it is not you who are at fault, rather than the ordinance? Perhaps I may convince you that it is, before we part.

Cosimo. We shall be much obliged to you for doing so. But in the first place I shall tell you why the militia ordinance is criticized, so that you may better refute the objections made to it. It is said, then, that a citizens' militia as instituted by the ordinance is of little or no service and, consequently, that if any prince or state depends upon it, he is sure to be undone; or, that if the militia consists of soldiers of *virtù*, the commander may very well use it to seize governmental power. To confirm this, people cite the example of the Romans, who lost their liberties by maintaining a citizens' militia. The examples of the Venetians and the French king are also cited for the same purpose: the former use only foreign troops, so as to prevent any of their own citizens from staging a coup; while

[23] A reference to Machiavelli's militia ordinance of 1506.

the latter has disarmed all his subjects in order to rule them more easily. But, it is urged, there is much more to be learned from the unserviceability of a citizens' militia, for which two reasons are assigned. First, that they are raw and inexperienced; secondly, that they are compelled to serve by force; when people are grown up to years of maturity, they seldom learn anything perfectly, and surely no material service can be expected from men who are forced into the army whether they will or not.

Fabrizio. All these objections seem to be made by very shortsighted people, as I shall show presently. For as to the unserviceableness of a citizens' militia, I say that no troops can be of more service than those chosen from one's own subjects, nor can those subjects be selected in a better or more proper manner. But since this elicits no argument, I shall not waste any more time endeavoring to prove it, especially since there is sufficient evidence for it in the histories of all nations. What has been said concerning inexperience and compulsion, I consider just and reasonable; for inexperience is the mother of cowardice, and compulsion makes men mutinous and discontented; but both experience and courage are acquired by arming, exercising, and disciplining men properly, as I shall plainly demonstrate to you. As to the matter of compulsion, I reply that men selected by their prince's command should be neither all volunteers nor forcibly compelled into the service, for if they were all volunteers, the mischiefs which I just now mentioned would ensue, it could not properly be called a *delectus,* and few would be willing to serve. Compulsion, on the other hand, would be accompanied by no fewer inconveniences; therefore, a middle course ought to be taken whereby—without either using men with outright violence or depending entirely upon their own voluntary offers—they may be motivated by the obedience they think due to their governors to expose themselves to a little immediate hardship, rather than incur their displeasure; and by these means (since their own will seems to cooperate with a gentle sort of compulsion), you will easily prevent those evils that might otherwise result from a spirit of licentiousness or discontent.

I shall not venture, however, to assert that an army composed of such men is invincible, for even the Roman legions were often routed, and Hannibal himself was at last conquered. So you see, it is impossible to model any army so as to prevent it from ever being defeated. Therefore, the wise and able men of whom you speak should not be so peremptory in pronouncing such forces altogether unserviceable because they lost one battle; [24] although they may happen to be defeated once or twice, they may be victorious when they have discovered the causes that contributed to their defeat and provided future remedies for them. When the causes of the defeat are looked into, they may probably be a result of the commanders' bad conduct, rather than of any defect in the order or institution itself. Your acquaintances, therefore, instead of condemning one, should endeavor to correct the other, and I shall show you how that is to be done as we proceed.

In the meantime, I shall convince you how little foundation there is for your objection that such a citizens' militia, under the command of an aspiring subject or citizen, may deprive a prince or republic of his authority and dominions; for it is certain that no subjects or citizens, when legally armed and kept in due order by their masters, ever did the least mischief to any state. On the contrary, they have always been of the highest service to all governments and have kept them free and incorrupt longer than they would have been without them. Rome remained free for four hundred years and Sparta eight hundred, although their citizens were armed all that time; but many other states that have been disarmed have lost their liberties in less than forty years. No state, therefore, can support itself without an army. If a state has no soldiers of its own, it must be forced to hire foreign troops; this will be much more dangerous because they are more likely to be cor-

[24] An allusion to the inglorious defeat of the Florentine militia by the Spanish professionals at Prato on August 29, 1512. See the Introduction, pp. xxvii–xxviii.

rupted and become subservient to the ambition of a powerful citizen who—when he has nobody to deal with but an unarmed and defenseless multitude—may easily avail himself of its assistance to overturn the established government. Besides, every state must naturally be more afraid of two enemies than of one; and the one taking foreign troops into its pay must be apprehensive of them, as well as of its own forces—indeed, you will see there is sufficient reason for this if you remember what I said just now concerning Francesco Sforza. Whereas, a state employing no troops except those composed of its own subjects has only one enemy to fear. But to omit all other proofs which might be adduced to support this point, I shall only lay it down as a certain truth that no man has ever founded a monarchy or a republic, without being well assured that if his subjects were armed, they would always be ready and willing to defend the monarchy or republic. If the Venetians had acted as wisely in this respect as in others, they might have erected a new universal monarchy; they are all the more reprehensible for neglecting this since they had arms put into their hands by their first legislators. But since they did not possess much territory on land, they employed their strength chiefly at sea, where they carried on their wars with great spirit, and made considerable acquisitions. At last, however, when they were obliged to engage in a war on land for the relief of Vicenza, instead of trusting some citizens of their own with the command of their forces, they took the Marquis of Mantua into their pay for that purpose.[25] Now if this false step, which clipped the wings of their ambition and put a stop to their further aggrandizement, resulted from a belief

25 Gianfrancesco Gonzaga I (1366–1407), a Mantuan captain general who developed a pro-Venice policy to free Mantua from the domination of the Milanese Visconti. This policy subsequently involved commanding the Venetian forces against Francesco Novello da Carrara, who had taken over Verona, Brescia, and Vicenza at the death of Gian Galeazzo Visconti in 1402. The war resulted in Vincenza becoming a part of Venice in 1404. Although he did not use the title of marquis, it was conferred upon him in 1403; he is not to be confused with Gianfrancesco Gonzaga II (1407–1444), who was made marquis of Mantua by Emperor Sigismund in 1433.

that although they knew how to make war at sea, they did not know how to on land, it was an ill-founded caution: for a naval officer used to fighting the winds and waves as well as the enemy, will sooner make a good officer ashore, where he has nothing to deal with but men, than a military officer will make a good naval commander. Nevertheless, the Romans, who were most expert in land wars but knew little of naval affairs, once they were engaged in a quarrel with the Carthaginians—who were very powerful at sea—did not take either Greek or Spanish forces into their service, although they were the best seamen in the world at that time; rather, they let that expedition be led by their own military officers, who landed on the enemy's coast and subdued the whole country. But if the Venetians acted in that manner, out of an apprehension that if they did otherwise, some one of their own citizens might seize the government itself, it was an ill-considered fear; for (not to repeat what has been already said) if none of their naval commanders ever made himself master of any town upon their coasts, much less occasion had they to fear that any of their citizens who commanded their armies should use them for such a purpose. If they had considered this, they would have been convinced that tyranny and usurpation are not a result of arming the citizens, but of leading a government weakly, and that while a state is well led, it has nothing to fear from its subjects' arms. The resolution, therefore, which they took upon that occasion was a very imprudent one, and brought great disgrace and many misfortunes upon them. As to the error of which the King of France is guilty in disarming his subjects instead of keeping them well disciplined and ready for war (an example which you urge against me), every impartial man must admit that it indicates a great lack of judgment and has much weakened that kingdom.[26]

But I have made too long a digression, and may perhaps seem to have forgotten my subject; yet I was in some measure obliged to do it, so as to answer your objections and show

[26] Evidently reference is to the French use of Swiss mercenaries, a practice begun by Louis XI (1423–1483). See *Prince*, 13.

you: that a state ought to depend upon only those troops composed of its own subjects; that those subjects cannot be better raised than by a citizens' militia; and that there can be no better method devised to form an army or to introduce good order and discipline among soldiers. If you ever read the institutions established by the first kings of Rome, particularly by Servius Tullius,[27] you must remember that the *classi* he formed were the basis of a citizens' militia which might be quickly raised at any sudden emergency for the defense of the state. But to return to our levies, I again say that if I were to recruit an old army, I would take men about seventeen years old; but if I were to raise a new one and make it fit for service in a short time, I would take them of all ages between seventeen and forty.

Cosimo. Would you pay any attention to their respective trades or occupations?

Fabrizio. Some authors who have written about this subject,[28] will not take fowlers, fishermen, cooks, bawdyhouse keepers, or any other sort of people who make an occupation of pleasure or sport; they prefer plowmen, smiths, farriers, carpenters, butchers, hunters, and such occupations. For my own part, I should not so much consider the nature of their profession as the moral virtue of the men, and which of them could perform the most services. For this reason, I should prefer to choose husbandmen and men who have been accustomed to work in the fields as men more useful in an army than any other kind of person; next to these, I would take smiths, carpenters, farriers, and stonecutters, of whom it is

[27] Traditionally the sixth king of Rome, who reigned from 578 to 534 B.C. According to Livy, I. 42–43, Servius instituted a census that divided the Romans into six classes based upon their property holdings. The class to which a citizen belonged determined the kind of weapons he would furnish, and hence his particular military role. See *Discourses*, I, 49 and II, 3.

[28] Vegetius, I. 7. Machiavelli follows Vegetius in believing that recruits should be selected for moral uprightness rather than for military skill alone.

necessary to have many, because they are very often needed, and it is a good thing to have soldiers who can turn their hands to more services than one.

Cosimo. But how can one distinguish those men who are fit for war from those who are not?

Fabrizio. I shall first inform you of the method I would use to raise the levies to form a new army, because I shall have an opportunity of simultaneously mentioning several things necessary in recruiting men for an old one. I say, then, we must judge the moral virtue of a man who has already served, either from the experience we have had of his former behavior or from probable conjecture. But as for men who are all raw recruits and have never served before—of whom we must suppose all new levies chiefly, if not entirely, to consist— we can have no experience of their *virtù,* and we must resort to such conjectures as we may be able to form from their age, occupation, and appearance. Of the first two we have already spoken; it remains, therefore, to say something of the last. Some, like Pyrrhus, would have their soldiers tall; others, like Julius Caesar, prefer men who are active and vigorous, about which they form a conjecture from the symmetry of their limbs, and the grace of their appearance. Some men who have treated this subject [29] accordingly recommend those who have quick and lively eyes, muscular necks, wide chests, brawny arms, long fingers, small bellies, round sides, spare legs, and little feet—which, for the most part, are signs of strength and agility, two qualities that are principally necessary in a soldier. But above all, we ought to have strict regard to their morals and behavior; otherwise we shall choose men who have neither modesty nor honesty, who will be a scandal to an army, and who not only become mutinous and ungovernable themselves, but sow the seeds of corruption among others. Is it to be expected that any kind of *virtù* or praiseworthy quality can be found in such men?

At this point, perhaps it may not appear impertinent—nay,

[29] Vegetius, I. 6–7.

indeed, it seems absolutely necessary, I think—to remind you of the method used by the Roman consuls, as soon as they entered upon their office, to raise the forces needed for the service of that year; thus you may be more fully convinced of the importance of such a choice. Upon these occasions, then, since their republic was almost continually engaged in war—and obliged to choose some men who had served before, and others who were altogether raw—they had an opportunity, in one case, of deciding upon men who they knew by experience were fit for their purpose, and were forced, in the other case, to use men they had to assume were fit. Similarly, it should be observed that such levies are made either for immediate service, or for discipline so that they can be used later, when occasion shall require. But as I have hitherto spoken only of those who are to be raised and disciplined for future service in countries where there was no previous army, and consequently no proper choice can be made from any experience of those men who are fit for soldiers, I shall continue that subject, because it is easy either to raise good recruits or to form armies for immediate service in places where a military force has once been established—especially if the rulers of the state have sufficient authority to enforce it, as did the Romans of old, and as do the Swiss today. Although there must certainly be many new men in this sort of levy, yet there also will be so many veterans that together they will soon make a very good army. The Roman emperors, however, when they began to put up garrisons and standing armies around the confines of the Empire, thought fit to appoint certain masters or instructors to teach and discipline the *tirones*,[30] or new recruits in warlike arts and exercises, as we may see from the life of the Emperor Maximinus.[31] Only while Rome remained free was such an in-

---

[30] *Tirones*, from the Latin *tiro*, a recruit or novice; the origin of our word "tyro."

[31] C. Julius Verus Maximinus, twenty-sixth Emperor of Rome (A.D. 235–238). The source may be his life in Herodian, VI. 17. See Burd, "le Fonti letterarie di Machiavelli nell' *Arte della guerra*," *Atti della Reale Accademia dei Lincei*, Series V, Vol. IV (1896), Pt. I, 191, n. 1. For Machiavelli's views about the emperors, see *Prince*, 19; *Discourses*, I, 10.

stitution observed at home and not in the camps; and since it was there that the young Romans were trained and inured to this sort of discipline, they made excellent soldiers when a *delectus* was necessary and they were called out into the service of their country. But later, when this custom of training the youth at home was stopped by the emperors, they were forced to make use of the means I just now mentioned.

But, let us return to the method observed by the Romans in making their levies.[32] As soon as the consuls, who always conducted their wars, had begun their office, they began to raise armies—each consul having allotted him two legions, which consisted of Roman citizens only, and were the main strength and flower of their armies. For this purpose they first appointed twenty-four military tribunes, six to each legion, whose function resembled that of our lieutenant colonels, or battalion commanders. Once this was done, they called together all the people able to bear arms and placed the tribunes of each legion apart; then, those officers cast lots to see out of which tribe or class they should begin their choice; upon whichever tribe the lot fell, they took out four of the best men, one of whom was chosen by the tribunes of the first legion, another by those of the second, another by those of the third, and the last fell to the share of the fourth. After this, they picked four more, out of whom the first was chosen by the tribunes of the second legion, the second by those of the third, the third by those of the fourth, and the fourth by those of the first. When these were thus disposed of, four others were drawn out, the first of whom was taken by the third legion, the second by the fourth, the third by the first, and the fourth by the second; thus they varied the turns of their choice among all the tribes, until the four legions were all equal and complete. These levies might be employed in immediate service, as I said before; since they consisted of men—many of whom had previously been tried in the wars, and the rest of whom were well exercised and disciplined at home—such a choice might be made partly from experience, and partly from con-

[32] Polybius, VI. 19–20.

jecture. But when the men are totally raw and untried and must be exercised and disciplined from the beginning to make them fit for future service, the choice must be made by conjecture alone, and can be based upon their age and appearance alone.

Cosimo. What you have said appears to be very just, but before you proceed any further, I wish you would be so good as to gratify my curiosity about a point of which you have reminded me by saying that where the levies that are to be made have not previously been used to military service, they must be chosen by conjecture. I have heard great fault found with our militia in many respects, especially with regard to their number. Some are of the opinion that if they were fewer, they might be better chosen; that it would not be so troublesome and inconvenient for the country, nor for the men themselves; and that they might have more pay, which would make them happier and readier to obey your commands. I should like to know, therefore, whether you would have a large or small number of such men, and how you would go about choosing them in either case.

Fabrizio. Without a doubt, it is much better to have a large number of them than a small one; indeed, where there is not a great number, it is impossible ever to have a good militia. As to the objections which you say some others have made to it, I shall presently show you their futility. In the first place, then, I say that the smallness of the number does not ever make them better soldiers in a country where there are plenty of men, as in Tuscany, for example. If you are to choose them from experience, you will find very few in that country who have had any trial—since not many have been in battle; and of those few, there are hardly any who have given the least indication of worth, or deserve to be preferred to others; so, whoever wants to raise men in that country can have no assistance from experience, but must depend wholly upon conjecture. Since this is the case, then, I should like to know what I am to do, and what rules I must use to choose a certain number, if twenty fine-looking young men should be brought before me. Surely everybody must admit that it would be best to arm and exercise all the men since it will be impossible to judge at first sight which of them will prove to be the best, and defer your choice until they have all had the same exercise and instruction; then you will easily perceive which of them are the most spirited and active and likely to be of the most service. On the whole, therefore, the maxim of choosing only a few, so that they may be much better, is simple and ill-grounded.

As for a large number being troublesome and inconvenient, both to the country and to the men themselves, I reply that no number of such men, whether great or small, can be troublesome or inconvenient to anyone. For nobody, by being a militiaman, is prevented from pursuing his usual occupation or following his necessary affairs, since the militia is only obliged to meet and hold maneuvers on holidays; this cannot be inconvenient either to the country or to the men; on the contrary, it would be a great recreation to both, for instead of being idle at those times, or perhaps spending their leisure in something worse than idleness, the young men would attend these exercises with pleasure, and others would be greatly entertained by such a spectacle.[33]

In answer to the objection that a small number may be better paid, and will consequently be better satisfied and more obedient to command, let it be considered that no number of militia, however small, can be kept in continual pay so as to be always satisfied with it. Let us suppose, for example, a militia to consist of 5,000 men whose pay, if they are to be paid to their satisfaction, will amount to at least 10,000 ducats per month. In the first place, 5,000 infantrymen are not sufficient to make up an army; in the second place, a monthly payment of 10,000 ducats would be an insupportable burden upon most states, and yet not enough to keep their soldiers content

[33] The idleness or indolence (*ozio*) that arises in times of peace and prosperity saps a people of their *virtù* and leads to civic corruption. See the Introduction, p. lv.

and obedient. So, although the expense would be extravagant, your army would be so inconsiderable that it would not be able to defend your own dominions, much less to take the offensive. If you increase their pay or their number, it will be even more difficult to pay them; if you diminish either, they will become dissatisfied and useless. Those who talk of raising a militia, therefore, and of paying them when they have nothing for them to do, talk of things that either are impossible or will serve no purpose; but it is highly necessary, I admit, to pay them—and well too—when they are called out to serve their country. However, if such a regulation should happen to cause the community some inconvenience during peacetime— which can hardly be—surely that must be greatly counterbalanced by the conveniences and advantages resulting from it, for without a regular and well-ordered militia people cannot live in security.

I conclude, then, that those who are for maintaining only a small militia so that they may be able to pay them better, or for any of the other reasons you have alleged, are mistaken in their politics; for (this still confirms my opinion) any number, no matter how large, will be continually diminishing upon your hands because of many unavoidable accidents, and therefore a small one would soon dwindle away to nothing. Besides, when your militia is numerous, you may, if you see the opportunity, employ a considerable force at once; this force must always be more effective than a small one and increase your reputation much more. I might add, that if you raise only a small number of militiamen in a large country and seek to have them well drilled, they must of course be at such a distance from each other that they cannot all be assembled on the days and at the places appointed for that purpose without great trouble and inconvenience; and if they do not hold proper maneuvers they will be no good at all, as I shall show you in due course.

Cosimo. You have fully refuted the objections I have made, I must confess; but I have another problem which I should like to have solved. The persons I mentioned before seem to think that a great number of armed men must naturally occasion much confusion and disorder, and frequent tumults in a country.

Fabrizio. I hope I shall be able to convince you that this notion is as altogether ill-grounded as those already discussed. Any disorder that a militia can bring about must be either among themselves or among others; yet this may easily be prevented, if such an establishment is not so badly constituted and regulated itself as to defeat the end of its institution. For if it is properly conducted, it naturally suppresses all disturbances—rather than fomenting them—among its own constituents because they are under the command of superiors; if the inhabitants of the country where you raise a militia are either so little used to war that they are unarmed, or so united among themselves that they have no factions among them, it will protect them against the fear of foreign enemies, but cannot in any way contribute to dividing them. For men who are well disciplined will always be as cautious of violating the laws when they have arms in the hands as when they have not; and so they will continue, if they are not corrupted by their commanders. As I shall show you presently, that will be no difficult matter to prevent. But if the people are warlike and yet given to faction, such an establishment is most likely to reunite them,[34] because—although they may have arms and leaders of their own—their arms are such as will be of no service to their country, and their leaders serve only to foment divisions and animosities, instead of promoting union and tranquillity; whereas this institution furnishes them with arms that will be of service to their country and with leaders to suppress their differences. For when any man in a divided country thinks himself injured or offended, he immediately applies to the head of his faction. In order to keep up his own interest

[34] The following is the only full and explicit statement of one of Machiavelli's fundamental theses, that a citizens' militia is an important instrument of civic education. By the establishment of a militia, an unruly people may be disciplined, imbued with a respect for law and authority, and given a sense of dedication to the common good. See *Discourses*, I, 4.

and reputation, this leader is obliged to assist the man in taking revenge, instead of discouraging violence. But a leader appointed by public authority acts in a quite different manner. So that by establishing a good and well-ordered militia, divisions are extinguished, peace restored, and some people who were unarmed and dispirited, but united, continue in union and become warlike and courageous; others who were brave and had arms in their hands, but were previously given to faction and discord, become united and turn against the enemies of their country those arms and that courage which they used to exert against each other.

But to prevent a militia from injuring others or overturning the laws and liberties of its country (which can only be effected by the power and iniquity of the commanders), it is necessary to take care that the commanders do not acquire too great an authority over their men. Now, authority of this kind is either natural or accidental: to guard against the one, provision should be made that an officer ought not have any command over the men raised in the district where he was born, but ought to command only those men who were selected from places other than where he has any natural interest or connections; to guard against the other, it may for the most part be prevented by changing the officers and sending them to commands in different parts every year—for a long continuation of command over the same people is apt to create too strict a union between them—one that may be easily converted to the prejudice of the government. How useful this method has been to those who have followed it, and how fatal the neglect of it to others, plainly appears from the histories of the Assyrian and Roman empires; we find that the former continued for more than a thousand years without any sedition or civil war. The whole reason for this was a custom which the government observed of changing the commanders of their armies every year and sending them into different provinces. On the contrary, after the time of Julius Caesar, the omission of this custom in the Roman Empire occasioned all the civil wars between the commanders of different armies and all the conspiracies which those commanders later formed against the emperors. But if any of the early emperors, especially those who gained a reputation—such as Hadrian, Marcus Aurelius, Severus,[35] or others like them—had been provident enough to have changed their generals at certain times, that empire would have enjoyed more tranquillity and lived longer; for then, those commanders could not have had an opportunity to rebel; the emperors would have lived in greater security; and the Senate, when the throne became vacant, would have had more authority and, consequently, would have acted with more judgment in the choice of a successor. But—whether it proceeds from mankind's ignorance, inattention, or indolence, I know not—it is certain that bad customs are seldom changed, no matter who is at the helm or whatever example may be brought either to discredit such customs or to recommend their contraries.

Cosimo. I am afraid that by asking impertinent questions I have broken in upon the order you proposed for yourself and led you away from your subject. For behold, from talking of conscription, we have gotten onto another topic, so that if I had not asked you to excuse my liberties when we began this conversation, I should have thought myself obliged to ask your pardon for it.

Fabrizio. You need not apologize for that, sir, since what has been said is nothing more than was necessary to show the nature of a militia; and since this is an institution condemned by many, I have taken it upon myself to defend and explain it, desiring at the same time to point out the best manner of

[35] Hadrian reigned from A.D. 117 to 138; Marcus Aurelius from 161 to 180. Severus is probably Septimius Severus, the exceptionally cruel and ruthless general who seized power in 193 and ruled until his death from natural causes in 211. Another member of the Severan dynasty, Alexander, a good and just if somewhat feeble emperor (A.D. 222–235), is also mentioned by Machiavelli, but as "Alexander" rather than as "Severus," as Septimius is always called. Machiavelli specifically applies the term *virtù* to only two Roman emperors: Marcus Aurelius and Septimius Severus, the one good, the other wicked. Hadrian is referred to only as good. See *Prince,* 19; *Discourses,* I, 10.

raising one. But before I proceed to other particulars, I should say something concerning the choice of cavalry.[36] The ancients used to choose these troops from among the richest citizens, with due regard, however, for their age and other qualifications—there were only 300 of them in a legion, so that the Romans never had more than 600 cavalrymen in a consular army.

Cosimo. Would you also have these troops trained and disciplined at home, in order to employ them when needed?

Fabrizio. Most certainly; it is absolutely necessary to do so if you would have cavalry of your own, and not be obliged to resort to those who make a trade of hiring themselves out to anybody wanting them.

Cosimo. In what manner would you choose them?

Fabrizio. I would imitate the Romans: I would take the richest from among the people; I would give them officers the way we do at present, and I would have them well armed and well trained.

Cosimo. Would it be proper to allow them any pay?

Fabrizio. To be sure; but only as much as would be sufficient to maintain their horses; if you gave them any more, it would be so burdensome to your subjects that they would complain.

Cosimo. What number would you have, and how would you arm them?

Fabrizio. That is another matter. But I shall answer your question after I have told you how the infantry ought to be armed and prepared for battle.

---

[36] Polybius, VI. 20. For Machiavelli's view of cavalry in modern warfare, see *Discourses*, II, 18.

BOOK TWO

FABRIZIO. Now that we are provided with men, it is time to arm them, I think. Let us therefore see what arms were chiefly used by the ancients; then we shall choose the best. The Romans divided their infantry into heavy- and light-armed companies. The light-armed were called *velites*.[1] Under this name were included all those using slings, bows, and darts; for their defense, the greater part of them wore helmets on their heads, and a sort of buckler on their left arm. They fought outside of the ranks and at a distance from the heavy-armed infantry,[2] who had helmets extending down to their shoulders, cuirasses, and brigandines covering their bodies and thighs, greaves and gauntlets upon their legs and arms, a shield about four feet long and two wide, plated with an iron rim at the top to defend it against the edge of sharp weapons and another at the bottom to keep it from being damaged by frequent rubbing against the ground. Their offensive weapons consisted of a sword, about a yard long, on their left side, a dagger on the right, and a dart in their hand, called a *pilum*, which they threw at the enemy at the first charge. Such were the arms with which the Romans conquered the world.

Some ancient writers say that besides these they had a spear, like a spontoon, or half-pike; but I cannot see how so troublesome a weapon could be used by those carrying shields, since shields would prevent them from using both hands at once, and it would be too unwieldy for one hand. Besides, such weapons could be of no service, except in the front lines of an army where there is room to handle them—something which would be impossible in the other ranks; for those, as I shall show you, must be drawn up close together since that is the

1 Polybius, VI. 22.
2 Polybius, VI. 23.

best way of forming an army, although it may be attended with some inconveniences. Therefore, those weapons more than four feet long are of little or no use in close fighting; for if you have one of those spears and are obliged to use both hands on it, assuming your shield did not encumber you, you could not attack an enemy assaulting you from the rear with it; but if you use only one hand, in order to avail yourself of your shield with the other, you must grab hold of it by the middle of the staff—then there will be so much of it behind you that those in the next rank will prevent you from using it. To convince you, then, that the Romans never had any such spears, or, that if they had, they were of little or no use, read the account which Livy gives of their most remarkable battles. You will find that he very seldom mentions any spears, but tells us that as soon as they had thrown their darts, they fell upon the enemy with their swords. I would have nothing at all to do with these spears, then, but trust to the sword and buckler and other such weapons as the Romans used.

The armor of the Greeks was not as heavy as that of the Romans,[3] but for offensive weapons, they depended more upon the spear than the sword; especially the Macedonian phalanx, which was armed with spears more than 20 feet long, called *sarissae,* with which they broke in upon the enemy, and yet kept good order in their ranks. Although some authors say they had shields too, yet I cannot see, for the above mentioned reasons, how they could manage them and the spears at the same time. Besides, in the battle between Aemilius Paullus and Perseus, king of Macedonia,[4] I do not remember any mention made of shields, but only of the *sarissae,* which were very troublesome to the Romans; so that I imagine the Macedonian phalanx was like the Swiss regiments of today, whose strength lies wholly in their pikes.

3 Polybius, XVIII. 12–16.

4 At Pydna, 168 B.C.; as a result of the Roman victory, Macedonia was divided into four leagues. Thus Perseus was the last king of Macedonia. Consequently L. Aemilius Paullus, who typified the Hellenized Roman, ended the Third Macedonian War; see *Discourses,* III, 16, 25, 35.

The Roman infantry, besides their armor, also had crests and plumes on their helmets, which afforded an agreeable spectacle to their friends and served to strike a terror into their enemies. As to the armor of their cavalry, it consisted at first of a round shield and helmet; the rest of their bodies were uncovered. Their arms were a sword and a long thin javelin with an iron head, so that being encumbered with a shield and a lance at the same time, they could use neither of them properly; moreover, since their bodies were to a large extent uncovered, they were greatly exposed to the enemy. But later on, they were armed like the infantry, except that they still carried a small, square shield and a thicker lance armed at both ends, so that if one should be broken off, they might avail themselves of the other. With these weapons, and this sort of armor for their cavalry and infantry, the Romans subdued the whole world; it is reasonable to suppose from their success that they were the best armed of all the armies that ever existed. Livy himself, when he is comparing their strength with that of various enemies, often tells us that in their *virtù*, arms, and discipline, they were much superior.[5] For this reason, I have chosen to speak more particularly of the arms and armor of the conquerors than of the conquered.

It now remains for me to say something of those that are in present use. The infantry cover their body with a demicuirass, or iron breastplate, which reaches down to their waist; they have a spear 18 feet long, called a pike, and a broadsword by their side. This is their common way of arming themselves, for very few of them have backplates, greaves, or gauntlets, and none at all have helmets; those few carry, instead of pikes, halberds, about six feet long, with sharp points and heads something like a battle-ax; they also have harquebusiers [6]

[5] Livy, IX. 17, 19.

[6] Although Farneworth translated *scoppietto* as "musket," Machiavelli apparently had in mind the harquebus. The two terms have always been employed in a rather imprecise and confused fashion. The harquebus, probably of German origin, differed from the crude hand guns that had been used since the latter part of the fourteenth century in that it had a curved stock and matchlock. The new firearm was first used widely in

among them, instead of the slingers and bowmen employed by the ancients.

These arms and this sort of armor were invented and are still used by the Germans, particularly by the Swiss; since they are poor, yet anxious to defend their liberties against the ambition of the German princes—who are rich and can afford to keep cavalry, which the poverty of the Swiss will not allow them to do—the Swiss are obliged to engage an enemy on foot, and therefore find it necessary to continue their ancient manner of fighting in order to make headway against the fury of the enemy's cavalry. This necessity forces them still to use the pike, a weapon enabling them not only to hold the cavalry off, but also very often to break and defeat them; without the principles adopted from the ancients, men of the greatest experience in military affairs say that the infantry is good for little or nothing. The Germans accordingly put so much confidence in this sort of infantry that they will attack any number of cavalry with 15,000 or 20,000 of them. We have had many recent examples of this. And such is the general opinion of the excellence of these principles, from the many remarkable services they have done, that ever since the expedition of Charles VIII into Italy,[7] all the other nations in Europe have adopted the same weapons and manner of fighting—the Spaniards in particular have obtained a very great reputation from them.

Cosimo. Which method of arming would you recommend, the German or the ancient Roman one?

Fabrizio. The Roman, without a doubt; and I shall show you the advantages and disadvantages of both. The German infantry is not only able to sustain a cavalry shock, but to

---

military operations during the Italian Wars, 1494–1525. Technically speaking, the musket is a much heavier and longer weapon, having greater range and requiring a rest. Most authorities agree that the musket first saw service with the Spanish just prior to 1550; some refer to a Spanish musket dating from the early 1520's. However, the dates given tend to vary.

[7] Charles VIII (1483–1498) of France invaded Italy in 1494.

break it; they are more expeditious on a march and in forming themselves, because they are not overloaded with arms. On the other hand, because they are so slightly armed, they are exposed to every kind of wound, when they fight at a distance and when they are closely engaged; they are of no great use where they meet with a vigorous resistance—in storming a town, or even in a field battle. But the Roman, as well as the German, infantry knew how to deal with cavalry: their armor was such that they were not so liable to be wounded in either close or distant fighting; they both attacked and sustained an attack much better because of their shields; they did more damage with their swords when they fought an enemy hand to hand than the Germans can do with their pikes; and although the latter also have swords, they are not able to do much with them because they have no shields—but the Romans were so well armed and so secure under the shelter of their shields that they were very useful in storming a breach. Therefore they labored under no other inconvenience but the weight of their armor, and they got the better of that by accustoming themselves to carry heavy burdens and to endure all other sorts of hardship and fatigue, which made that matter easy and familiar to them.

You must also consider that infantrymen are often obliged to engage other infantry and cavalry together, and that if they cannot sustain the shock of cavalary—or even if they can, and yet are afraid of facing another body of infantry that is better armed and disciplined than themselves—they are of little account. If, then, you will compare the German infantrymen with the Roman, you will find that the former are very fit to oppose cavalry, as I said before, but that they would certainly be at a disadvantage were they to engage other infantry that were no better than themselves, if these were armed and organized like the Romans; thus, one is to be preferred to the other because the Germans are fit to cope only with cavalry, but the Romans knew how to deal with both cavalry and infantry.

Cosimo. I should take it as a favor if, by way of illustration, you would give us some particular instance of this.

Fabrizio. You will find many in our history, where the Roman infantry has beaten infinite numbers of cavalry; none, where it was defeated by other infantry, either through any deficiency in its own arms or advantage in an enemy's. For had there been any deficiency in their own and had they met with other people who armed their soldiers better than they did, the Romans could not have made such enormous conquests, without setting aside their own method and arming themselves in the same or some better manner; but since they never did this, we may fairly conclude that they never found any other people who excelled them in this respect.

But such cannot be said of the German infantry, for it has always been defeated when it has been engaged by other infantrymen as obstinate and well led as itself—this must be a result of the advantage the enemy had over them in their arms. Filippo Visconti, duke of Milan, invaded by an army of 18,000 Swiss, sent against them Count Carmagnola, who was at that time commander in chief of his forces. But Carmagnola had no more than 6,000 cavalrymen and a small body of infantry in his army; when he came to an engagement with them, he was immediately defeated with great loss. However, since he was an able soldier, he saw what advantage such an enemy had over cavalry; so he raised another army and went to look for the Swiss a second time; but when he came near them, he ordered all his men-at-arms to dismount and fight on foot. They did so with such success that they killed 15,000 of the enemy; the rest, seeing no possibility of escape, threw down their arms and surrendered.[8]

Cosimo. How is this to be accounted for?

Fabrizio. I told you a little while ago; but since you seem either to have forgotten or not to have understood what I

[8] In this battle of Arbedo, June 30, 1422, Carmagnola's forces actually outnumbered the Swiss. Francesco Bussone (1390–1432), count of Carmagnola, served Milan and then Venice as a distinguished condottiere. Machiavelli praises him as a soldier in *Prince*, 12; he describes the battle in *Discourses*, I, 18.

said, I shall repeat it. When the German infantrymen, who, as I said before, are but indifferently provided with defensive armor and use the sword and the pike for their offensive weapons, come to engage an enemy that is well armed at all points—as were the men-at-arms whom Carmagnola caused to dismount—they are easily dealt with; for the enemy has nothing to do but to receive their pikes upon his shields and to rush in upon them sword in hand. After this the danger is chiefly over, for the German pikes are so long that they cannot avail themselves of them in close fighting, nor will their swords stand them in any great stead, since they themselves have little or no armor and are engaged with enemies who are completely covered with armor from head to foot. Hence, whoever considers the advantages and disadvantages on each side will see that those who are so poorly armed have no remedy against an enemy in full armor when he charges home and has sustained the first onslaught of the pikes. For when two armies are resolved to engage and advance upon one other, they must of necessity soon come close together; although some of the men in the first ranks on one side may be either killed or overthrown by the pikes from the other side, there will be enough left to carry the day. Hence it turned out that Carmagnola, with little or no loss on his own side, slaughtered so many among the Swiss.

Cosimo. It must be considered that Carmagnola's troops, though they were on foot, were men-at-arms and covered with armor; thus, they were enabled to do what they did. I should think it would be a good thing, therefore, to arm infantry in the same manner.

Fabrizio. If you would recollect what I said concerning the armor the Roman infantry used, you would be of another opinion; men who have their heads protected by helmets, their bodies defended by shields and breastplates, and their legs and arms covered with greaves and gauntlets, are better able to defend themselves against pikes and to break in upon them than men-at-arms on foot. I shall give you a modern example or two. A body of Spanish infantry was transported from Sicily into the kingdom of Naples to relieve Gonzalo de Córdoba,[9] who was beseiged in Barletta by the French; Monsieur d'Aubigny,[10] was sent to oppose their march with some men-at-arms and about 4,000 Swiss infantry. When they engaged the fight, the Swiss pressed so hard upon the enemy with their pikes that they soon opened their ranks; but the Spaniards, under the cover of their bucklers, nimbly rushed in with their swords, and fought them so furiously that they slaughtered the Swiss and gained a complete victory. Everyone knows what numbers of Swiss infantry were similarly cut to pieces at the battle of Ravenna; [11] for once the Spanish infantry closed with the Swiss, they made such good use of their swords that not one of the enemy would have been left alive if a body of French cavalry had not come up to rescue them; thereupon, however, the Spaniards drew up close together and made a handsome retreat with little or no loss. I conclude, therefore, that a good infantry must be able not only to withstand cavalry but also to confront any other sort of infantry fearlessly; and this, as I have often said before, must be entirely a result of their discipline and arms.

Cosimo. How, then, would you have them armed?

Fabrizio. I would take some of the Roman arms and armor, and some of the German; half of my men would be armed with one and half with the other; for if out of every 6,000 infantrymen, 3,000 were provided with swords and shields like the Romans, and 2,000 with pikes and 1,000 with harquebuses like the Germans, it would be sufficient for my purpose—as I shall show you presently.[12] For I would place my pikemen either in the front ranks, or where I thought the enemy's cavalry

---

[9] Gonzalo de Córdoba (1453–1515) was the great general whose skill in defeating the French made possible the Spanish annexation of Naples. See *Discourses*, I, 29.

[10] Robert Stuart d'Aubigny (1470–1544), Marshal of France.

[11] April 11, 1512. See *Prince*, 13, 26; *Discourses*, II, 16, 17.

[12] Cf. Machiavelli's recommendation in *Prince*, 26.

was most likely to make an impression; I would post the others so as to support the pikemen and push forward when a way was opened for them. I think this would be a better method of arming and drawing up an infantry troop than any other that is currently used.

Cosimo. So much for infantry. I should now be glad to know whether you would recommend the ancient or modern way of arming cavalry.

Fabrizio. Considering the war saddles and stirrups now in use and not known to the ancients, I think men today must sit more firmly on horseback than they formerly did. Similarly I think our way of arming is more secure and our men-at-arms are capable of making a greater impression than any sort of cavalry the ancients ever had. I am not of the opinion, however, that we ought to depend any more upon cavalry than they did in former times; for, as I said before, lately we have seen them often shamefully beaten by infantry. Indeed, they must always come off badly when they engage an infantry armed and appointed in the above-mentioned manner. Tigranes, king of Armenia,[13] brought an army of 150,000 cavalrymen into the field, many of whom were armed like our men-at-arms and called *cataphracti*,[14] against the Roman general Lucullus, whose army consisted of only 6,000 cavalrymen and 25,000 infantrymen.[15] When Tigranes saw the enemy

[13] Tigranes (94–55 B.C.) had given asylum to his father-in-law, Mithridates VI, the Great, and thereby associated himself with the latter's test of Roman strength. This particular battle was fought at the Armenian capital of Tigranocerta; it occurred in 69 B.C., and was a part of the Third Mithridatic War, 74–63 B.C.

[14] A transliteration derived from the Greek καταφράκτης, a breastplate of iron mail; the word thus refers to soldiers clad in mail.

[15] L. Licinus Lucullus (110–56 B.C.) had driven Mithridates into Armenia in 72 B.C.; until his enemy Pompey began fomenting dissension in his ranks, Lucullus had been reforming provincial finances. The battle at Tigranocerta culminated his military career. Machiavelli's source for this passage is Plutarch's *Life of Lucullus*, XXVI, ff. Plutarch's figures are: for Tigranes—150,000 infantry, 5,500 cavalry; for Lucullus—24 cohorts with

army, he said, "These are enough for an ambassador's train." [16] Nevertheless, when they engaged, the king was routed; and the historian imputes the defeat entirely to the little service done by the *cataphracti,* whose faces were covered in such a manner that they could hardly see—much less annoy—the enemy and whose limbs were so overloaded with heavy armor, that when any of them fell from their horses, they could hardly get up again or use their arms.

I therefore assert that such states depending more upon cavalry than infantry will always be weak and exposed to ruin, as Italy has been in our time; we have seen her overrun from one end to the other and plundered by foreigners merely because her princes have taken infantry into little or no account at all and have trusted solely to cavalry. It is right, however, to have some cavalry to support and assist infantry; it is not right to look upon them as the main strength of an army. They are highly necessary for reconnoitering a region, scouring roads, making incursions, laying waste to an enemy's country, tracking down their quarters, keeping them in a continual state of alarm, and cutting off their convoys; but in field battles—which generally decide the fate of nations, and for which armies are chiefly designed—since they are more useful for pursuing an enemy that is routed than anything else, they are consequently much inferior to infantry.[17]

Cosimo. Two difficulties occur to me at this point. In the first place, everybody knows the Parthians never used any other force but cavalry in their wars, and yet they shared the world with the Romans. Next, I should like you to tell me how cavalry may be sustained by infantry, and how the latter comes to have its *virtù* and the former its weakness.

---

no more than 11,000 infantry and a combined total of 1,000 cavalry, slingers, and archers. See also *Discourses,* II, 19.

[16] Bernadotte Perrin's translation of Tigranes' remark in the Loeb edition of Plutarch's *Life of Lucullus* maintains the original's epigrammatic quality: "If they are come as ambassadors, they are too many; if as soldiers, too few."

[17] See *Discourses,* II, 18.

Fabrizio. I either told you before, or meant to, that what I intended to say concerning the art of war should be limited to Europe. Therefore I think myself excused from accounting for the conduct of Asiatic nations. I cannot help observing, however, that the discipline of the Parthians was quite different from that of the Romans. The Parthians all fought on horseback in a loose and irregular manner, which, as a mode of combat, was unsteady and full of uncertainty; the Romans, one might say, fought chiefly as infantrymen in close and regular order—their success varied according to the nature of the countries in which they happened to fight. In enclosed places the Romans generally got the better, whereas the Parthians had the advantage in large open plains, and indeed the nature of the country they had to defend was very favorable to their manner of fighting; it was flat and open, a thousand miles from any seacoast, with so few rivers in it, that they might sometimes march two or three days without seeing any, and with very few towns and inhabitants; thus the Roman armies, slowed down by the heaviness of their arms and armor and the good order they observed, were much annoyed by an active and light-armed, mounted enemy who was at one place one day and 50 miles off by the next. In this manner the Parthians availed themselves of their cavalry with so much success that they ruined the army led by Crassus and reduced the one under the command of Mark Antony to the utmost distress.[18] But, as I said before, I shall confine myself to Europe in what I have to say about these matters and quote only the examples of the Greeks and Romans in former times and of the Germans at present.

Let us now come to the other point, if you please: namely,

18 M. Licinius Crassus Dives was to some degree successful in Mesopotamia against the Parthians in 54 B.C., but his infantry was overwhelmed by their cavalry in 53, and he was treacherously slain. Throughout his career, Mark Antony had suffered reverses at the hands of the Parthians, although they were defeated in 39–38 by the general whom he had sent against them, Ventidius Bassus. See *Discourses*, II, 18; III, 12. Machiavelli's references are probably derived from Plutarch's *Crassus* and *Mark Antony*.

what it is that makes infantry superior to cavalry. In the first place, I say that cavalry cannot march through all roads as infantry can, and they are slower in their motions when it is necessary to change their order; if there should be an occasion for a retreat when they are advancing or for an advance when they are retreating, for wheeling off to the right or left, for moving when they are halting or halting when they are in motion—it is certain they cannot do it as quickly as infantry can; and if they are thrown into confusion by some sudden shock, they cannot rally so easily even when the shock is over. Besides, it often happens that a brave and spirited fellow is put upon a pitiful horse and a coward upon one that is unruly and ungovernable, and in either of these cases some disorder must ensue.

Why then should it seem wonderful that a firm and compact body of infantry should be able to sustain a cavalry attack, especially since horses are prudent animals and when they are apprehensive of danger cannot easily be brought to rush into it? You should also compare the force that impels them to advance with that which makes them retreat; you will then find that the latter is much more powerful than the former. In the one case, they feel nothing but the prick of a spur, but in the other they see a rank of pikes and other sharp weapons presented to them. So, you can see from both ancient and modern examples that good infantry will always be able not only to make headway against cavalry but generally to get the better of them. But if you argue that the fury with which the horses are driven to charge an enemy makes them consider a pike no more than a spur, I answer that even though a horse has begun to charge, he will slow down when he draws near the pikes and, when he begins to feel their points, will either stand stock still or wheel off to the right or left. To convince yourself of this, see if you can ride a horse against a wall; I fancy you will find very few, if any—however spirited they may be—that can be made to do that. Julius Caesar, before an engagement with the Helvetii in Gaul not only dismounted himself but made all his cavalrymen dismount too; he sent the horses to a place at some distance from the field of battle—a place fitter for flight than for fighting.[19]

Notwithstanding these natural impediments to which cavalry are subject, a general who commands an army consisting chiefly of infantry should always lead them, when they march, along roads where he cannot be attacked by cavalry without great trouble and inconvenience—such roads may easily be found in most countries. If he marches over hills, these will protect him from the fury of the cavalry charge, which you seem to think irresistible. If he marches through flat country, hedges, ditches, and woods will generally give him security; every little bank or thicket, no matter how inconsiderable, and every vineyard or plantation is sufficient to impede cavalry and prevent its acting with any material effect; if they engage, it is probable they may encounter the same impediments in a battlefield as on a march, for the least obstruction spoils their charge and dampens their ardor. The Roman armies, I must tell you, put such confidence in their armor and manner of fighting that if it was in their power to choose between a quite rough and confined place—in order to shelter them from the fury of the enemy's cavalry and to prevent the enemy from extending its lines—or a place where cavalry might act with the greatest advantage, they always chose the latter.

But now that we have armed our infantry according to ancient and modern usage, it is time to move on to maneuvers. Let us therefore examine the exercises the Romans used to drill their infantry before they were allowed to engage an enemy. Although soldiers may be well chosen and well armed, they will never be good for anything if they are not diligently drilled. Now these maneuvers ought to be of three types: in the first place, the soldiers must be taught to endure all sorts of hardship and fatigue and to be dexterous and agile; in the second place, the soldiers must be taught to handle their arms well; and lastly, they must be taught to obey orders and to keep their ranks and stations whether in marching, in battle,

[19] Caesar, *Gallic War* I. 25.

or in encamping. These are the three principal operations in an army; if they are well executed, a general will maintain his honor even when he loses a battle.

The ancients, therefore, had very strict laws and ordinances to enforce the constant practice of their exercises in every particular. Their youth were accustomed to run races, to leap, to pitch the bar, and to wrestle,[20] all of which result in very necessary qualifications for soldiers: if they are agile, they can anticipate the enemy in seizing an advantageous post, in coming upon him suddenly, and in overtaking him when he is retreating; if they are nimble, they will know how to avoid a blow, and they will find no difficulty in jumping over a fosse or scaling a breastwork; and if they are strong, they will be able to carry their arms more easily, to attack the enemy, or to sustain an attack better. But above all, they should be inured to heavy burdens. This is very necessary,[21] for on some great and pressing occasions they may be obliged to carry with them, in addition to their weapons, provisions for several days, which they could not do if they were not accustomed to such things; by these means great dangers are often avoided, and sometimes glorious victories obtained.

To accustom their young men to their armor and to teach them how to handle their arms with dexterity, the ancients used to clothe them in armor twice as heavy as that which they were to wear in battle; instead of a sword, they put into their hands a thick cudgel that was loaded with lead and much heavier than a sword; after this, they fixed posts in the earth about six feet high, which were so firm that no blows could move them. On these the young men used to drill with their cudgel and buckler as if they had been real enemies; sometimes they stroked at the top—as if it had been the head or face of a man—sometimes at the right or left side, and sometimes at the lower part; sometimes they used to advance briskly upon it, and at other times, retreat a step or two. By these means they became expert not only at defending themselves but at

20 Vegetius, I. 9.
21 Vegetius, I. 18.

annoying an enemy, and the weight of their false armor made their real ones seem light and easy to wield. The Romans taught their soldiers to thrust rather than cut with their swords,[22] because thrusts are more dangerous and are harder to ward off; he who thrusts does not expose his own body as much, and is readier to redouble than he is to repeat a full stroke.

Do not think it strange, however, that the ancients were so exact and particular in things which to you may perhaps seem trifling and ridiculous, but consider that when men fight hand to hand, the slightest advantage is of great importance; and I must beg leave to tell you that several good authors have entered into much more minute and circumstantial detail of these matters than I have done.[23] The ancients thought that nothing was more conducive to the welfare and security of their country than having a great number of well-disciplined and drilled men ready for war; they well knew that neither riches nor magnificence, but only the reputation of their arms could keep their enemies in awe and subjection; they well knew that defects in other things may sometimes be remedied, but that in war, where their fatal consequences are immediately felt, they admit of no remedy. Besides, expertness in these drills makes men bold and courageous in battle, for instead of being afraid, everyone is eager to distinguish himself in what he knows he excels in. The ancients, therefore, took great care to make their youth perfect in all military exercises; they also accustomed them to throw darts—ones that were much heavier than those they carried in war—at the posts I mentioned before; this taught them to be very expert in the use of that weapon and made their arms strong and muscular. They were also taught how to use the crossbow, the longbow, and the sling; in all these things there were masters appointed for the purpose of instructing them. Thus, when they were called out to serve in the wars, they were so well prepared that they lacked nothing to make them excellent soldiers except

[22] Vegetius, I. 12.
[23] Vegetius, I. 13.

being taught how to keep their ranks on a march or in a battle and how to obey orders; they quickly learned these things by being incorporated with others who had served a long time and were thoroughly experienced in that aspect of discipline.

Cosimo. What exercises would you recommend for those who are to compose our infantry at present?

Fabrizio. Most of the ones I have already mentioned, such as running, wrestling, leaping, carrying heavy arms, and using the crossbow, longbow, and harquebus—the last, you know, is a new, but a very useful weapon. To these exercises I would accustom all the youth in the country, but particularly those destined to be soldiers; for this purpose, I would set aside all holidays and idle periods. I would also have them taught to swim. This is very necessary [24] since not all rivers have bridges over them, nor can boats always be expected to be found ready to transport the men; so, if your soldiers cannot swim, you will lose many advantages and opportunities of doing great things. The reason why the Romans exercised their youth in the Campus Martius was that the Tiber ran close by it, so that when they were fatigued, they might refresh themselves in the river and learn to swim. Like the ancients, I should also choose to have those who are to serve in the cavalry properly exercised. It is very necessary because it teaches them not only to ride well but to avail themselves of their strength in a better manner. For this purpose the Romans had wooden horses upon which they exercised [25] by mounting them sometimes with armor on and sometimes without it, by mounting them without any assistance, and by mounting them on either side; also, upon a signal or word of command from their instructors, they were all either mounted or dismounted in a moment.

Now since these cavalry and infantry drills were practiced then without any difficulty or inconvenience, they might easily be introduced again among the youth of any present state, if its governors so pleased; in fact, they have been introduced

24 Vegetius, I. 10.
25 Vegetius, I. 18.

into some of the nations in the West where they divide the inhabitants into classes. These classes take their respective names from the different types of arms they use in battle; since they consist of pikes, halberds, harquebuses, and bows, the men carrying those weapons are called pikemen, halberdeers, harquebusiers, bowmen, or archers. Every inhabitant is also obliged to declare in which of these classes he chooses to be enrolled. Since some of them are not fit to bear arms, because of their age or some other impediment, they make a *delectus,* or choice, out of each class and call those who are thus chosen *jurati* because they make them take an oath of fidelity and obedience.[26] These *jurati,* then, are called together on holidays and drilled in the use of such arms as they take their name from; each class has the particular place where it is to meet and drill assigned to it by the governors of the state. Every man belonging to a class, as well as to the *jurati,* is to appear and bring his share of money with him to defray the expenses occasioned by those meetings. What, therefore, is actually done by others I should think might be done by our countrymen, but they are grown so lazy and degenerate that they will not imitate anything that is good. It was entirely as a result of these exercises that the ancients had such excellent infantry and that the aforementioned states in the West have a much better infantry at present than we have; for the Romans drilled them either at home under the Republic, or abroad, during the reign of their emperors, as I have said before. But the Italian states are unwilling to drill them at home and unable to do so abroad because they are not their own subjects and will therefore do nothing but just what pleases them. Hence it comes about that these military exercises are now completely neglected, and all discipline is at an end; this is the real reason why many states, especially in this country, have become so weak and contemptible.

[26] *Jurati,* bound by an oath, from *juro,* to swear or take an oath. Machiavelli feels that this oath, sanctioned as it is by religion, is of the utmost importance in maintaining good discipline and respect for authority. See *Discourses,* I, 11; and below pp. 128, 165.

But, let us resume our subject. To make a good army it is not enough that the soldiers are inured to hardships and fatigue, strong, swift, and expert in the use of their weapons; they must also learn to keep their ranks, to obey words of command and signals by drum or trumpet, and to observe good order, whether they halt, advance, retreat, march, or engage the enemy; for without strict attention to these points, an army will never be good for anything. It is certain that a parcel of disorderly and ill-disciplined men, although extremely brave, is not to be depended upon as much as others who are not so courageous by nature, but orderly and well disciplined—good order makes men bold; confusion makes them cowardly. But for you to understand better what I am going to say, it is necessary to know that every nation has had particular bodies of soldiers in its armies and militias which differed in their names but varied little in the number of men they were composed of, since they generally consisted of 6,000 or at most, 8,000 men. Thus the Romans had their legions, the Greeks their phalanxes, the Gauls their *catervae*,[27] and currently the Swiss (who are the only people with any trace of the ancient military institutions left among them) had what we should call regiments in our country; but they all divided them into battalions or smaller bodies, as best suited their purposes. Let us then call them by the most familiar name to us, and form them according to the best dispositions that have been made by either the ancients or the moderns.

Since the Romans divided their legion, which consisted of between 5,000 and 6,000 men, into 10 cohorts, we too divide our regiment, which is to consist of 6,000 infantrymen, into 10 battalions of 450 men each—of these, 400 should be heavy-armed, and the other 50 light-armed. Of the heavy-armed, let 300 have swords and shields, and be called shieldbearers; another 100 should have pikes, and be called ordinary pikemen; the other 50 light-armed men must carry harquebuses, crossbows, halberds, and shields, and be called by the old name of ordinary velites; so, in the 10 battalions there will be 3,000

27 Vegetius, II. 2.

shieldbearers, 1,000 ordinary pikemen, and 500 ordinary velites; that is to say, 4,500. But since our regiment is to consist of 6,000 men, we must add 1,500 more; of whom 1,000 must have pikes, and be called pikemen extraordinary; the other 500 should be light-armed, and called velites extraordinary; thus one half of our infantry would be composed of shieldbearers, and the other of pikemen and other men armed in a different manner. Every battalion should have a lieutenant colonel, or particular commander of its own; 4 captains and 40 corporals, besides a captain and 5 corporals of the ordinary velites. Over the 1,000 pikemen extraordinary, there should be 3 commanders or lieutenant colonels, 10 captains, and 100 corporals; in the velites extraordinary, 2 lieutenant colonels, 5 captains and 50 corporals. For the entire regiment I would then appoint a colonel or commander, with his drums and colors; every one of the aforementioned commanders should also have them. So, the whole would consist of 10 battalions, composed of 3,000 shieldbearers, 1,000 ordinary pikemen, 1,000 pikemen extraordinary, 500 ordinary velites, and 500 more velites extraordinary—in all, 6,000 men. Among these, there would be 600 corporals, 15 lieutenant colonels, 15 drums and colors, 65 captains, and the colonel with his colors and drums.

You see, I have been guilty of some repetition, but it is so that you will understand me better, and so that you may not be puzzled or perplexed when I speak of drawing up an army in battle order. I say, then, that all princes and governors of republics should arm their militia in this manner, should form them into such regiments, and should raise as many regiments as their dominions will admit. When they have been divided into battalions according to the directions I have just now given, in order to make their discipline perfect, it will be sufficient to drill them battalion by battalion; although one battalion has not enough men in it to form a competent army by itself, yet every man may thus learn to do his own duty. For two things must be observed in all armies: first, that the men be taught what they are to do in their respective battalions; next, that every battalion be taught how it is to act when it is joined with other battalions to form an army. Those ready and expert in the first will soon learn the second; but those who are not perfect in one can never be taught the other. Every battalion, then, must first be taught separately to keep good order in its own ranks upon all occasions and in all places; afterward, it must be taught how to act in conjunction with the rest, how to attend to the drums and other instruments by which all orders are regulated and directed in time of battle, and how to understand from the different sounds whether it is to hold its ground, advance, retreat, wheel to the side, or do an about face. So, when the men know how to keep their ranks so that no sort of ground or no sort of maneuver can throw them into disorder, when they understand what they have to do by the beat of the drum or sound of the trumpet, and when they know where to take their station, they will soon learn how to act in concert with the other battalions of their regiment when they are assembled to form an army.

But since it is sometimes necessary to drill all of them together, the whole regiment should be assembled once or twice a year in peacetime to be formed like an army—with front and rear flanks in their proper places—and to be drilled for some days as if they were preparing to engage an enemy. Now, since a commander draws up his forces for battle either upon sight of an enemy or in apprehension of one that is not far off, his army should hold maneuvers according to the occasion; it should be shown in what order it is to march and to engage, if the need should arise, and it should be given particular instructions about how to act if it should be attacked on one side or the other. But when he would prepare his men to attack an enemy that is in sight, a commander should show them how and where to begin the attack, to what point they are to retreat if they should be repulsed, who are to take their places, and what signals, sounds, and words of command they are to observe. A commander inures his men to sham fights in such a manner that they may be desirous, rather than afraid, to enter into a real one. For it is not the natural courage of men that make an army bold, but order and good discipline; because, when the first ranks know both where to retreat and who are to advance in their place if they should be defeated, they will always fight with spirit since relief is so near at hand; nor will the next ranks be daunted at the first's misfortune since they are prepared for such an event—and perhaps they are not sorry for it because they may think it will give them the glory of a victory which others could not obtain.

These exercises are particularly necessary in a newly raised army, and they ought not to be neglected in one that is composed of veterans; although the Romans were trained to the use of arms from their youth, nevertheless their generals always drilled them in this manner with great assiduity for some time before they expected an engagement. And Josephus [28] tells us in his *History* that even the sutlers that used to follow their armies often did good service in battle because they had frequently seen the soldiers drilled, and had learned to handle their arms and hold their ranks firm. But armies composed of new men who have been raised either for present service or for formation into a militia to be used when the occasion arises will be good for nothing at all if the battalions are not first drilled separately, and later as a whole. Since good order and discipline are absolutely necessary, great care ought to be taken to maintain them among those who know their duty, and still greater care, surely, ought to be taken to instruct those who are entirely ignorant of them. To effect these qualities, a wise and able commander will spare no pain or endeavor.

Cosimo. You seem to have deviated a little from your point since before you have told us how a single battalion ought to be drilled, you have described the drilling and preparing of an entire army for battle.

Fabrizio. You are right. Indeed I confess that my zeal for those exercises and institutions and my concern for their being

[28] Josephus Flavius, *Judaic War* III. 4.

so much neglected now have led me a little out of the way and occasioned me to break in upon the order I had proposed. But I shall return to it.

You may remember I told you that in disciplining a battalion it is of the utmost importance to make the men hold their ranks firm. To achieve this, it is necessary to drill them in what the ancients called the "snail fashion." [29] Since I have said there should be 400 heavy-armed infantry in a battalion, I shall keep to that number. These 400 men must be formed into 80 ranks of 5 per rank; they should learn how both to extend themselves and to reduce themselves into closer order, whether they are moving slowly or briskly forward. But how this is to be done is easier to understand by seeing it actually performed than from any description. However, that is not absolutely necessary here because everyone who has the slightest experience in military affairs knows its method, and knows that its chief use is in habituating men to holding their ranks.

But now let us proceed to draw up a battalion. There are three principal ways then of doing so: the first and best is to draw it up closely and compactly in the form of an oblong square; the second is to form it in a square with two wings in the front; and the third is to throw it into a square with an area or vacancy in the middle—commonly called a hollow square. The first way can be effected by two means: one, by doubling the ranks, that is, by receiving the second rank into the first, the fourth into the third, the sixth into the fifth, and so on; so that where there were 80 ranks before, with 5 men in every rank, they may be reduced to 40 with 10 in a rank, and by doubling them a second time, they may be reduced to 20 with 20 in a rank. This will make an oblong square; although there will be as many men in the files as in the ranks, and since the men in the ranks must stand close together so as to touch each other while those in the files must be at least four feet apart from one another, the square will be no longer from front to rear than from the end of the right flank to the end

[29] Evidently to drill them in precise contraction and extension—like a snail.

of the left—that is, the files will be longer than the ranks. The battalion's 50 ordinary velites must not be mixed with the other ranks, but posted on each flank and in the rear when it is formed.

The other way of drawing up a battalion closely and compactly in the form of an oblong square is better than the preceding way, and I shall therefore be more particular in describing it. I take it for granted you remember the number of men and what officers it contains, and how these men are to be armed. Without further repetition, then, I say that the battalion must be formed into 20 ranks, with 20 men in each rank; that is to say, 5 ranks of pikemen in the front, and 15 ranks of shieldbearers in the rear. There must be 2 captains in the front and 2 in the rear. The battalion lieutenant colonel or commander, with his colors and drum, must take a post in the interval between the 5 ranks of pikemen and the 15 of shieldbearers. The corporals are to be placed on the 2 flanks, one at the extremity of each rank, so that everyone may have his men by his side—those on the right will have them on their left; those on the left will have them on their right. The 50 ordinary velites should be posted on the flanks and in the rear of the battalion. Now, in order to throw it into this form, you must draw it up into 80 ranks with 5 men in every rank and place the velites by themselves either in the front or the rear; every captain must put himself at the head of his company—100 men, or 20 ranks of 5 men each—whose 5 front ranks, or those immediately behind him, must be pikemen and the rest shieldbearers. The battalion lieutenant colonel or commander with his drum and colors are to be placed in the interval between the second company's pikemen and shieldbearers, and are to take up the position of 3 shieldbearers. There must be 20 corporals placed on the left flanks of the ranks commanded by the first captain, and 20 more placed on the right flanks of the ranks commanded by the last captain; it is necessary that the corporals of the pikemen carry pikes themselves, and those of the shieldbearers have shields and swords. When your ranks are thus disposed, if you desire to form them in battle order to face an enemy, you must make the captain of the first 20 ranks halt with his men; the captain of the second 20 continues to advance but obliques a little to the right, close to the flank of the first 20, until he comes abreast of their captain and halts there; the third captain then similarly advances with his men along the right flank of the two other companies until he is aligned with the first two captains, and halts there as they do; then the fourth captain and his company also move forward along the right flank of those already joined, and halts when he has advanced as far as the other three. When all of these movements have been executed, two of those captains must immediately quit the front rank and take a post in the rear; then the battalion will be formed in an oblong square, as it was by the other method. The velites must also be posted on each flank as they were before.

One of these ways is called doubling the ranks in a right line, the other, doubling them by the flanks; the former is the easier of the two, the latter the more convenient—it may be better adapted to answer different occasions. In the former, you must conform to the number because five, ten, and twenty doubled make ten, twenty, and forty; so that if you double your ranks in a right line, you cannot make a front of fifteen, or twenty-five, or thirty, or thirty-five, but must be governed in doubling by the number in your first rank. And since it is often necessary to form a front of 600 or 800 infantrymen, doubling your ranks in a right line would throw the men into confusion. Therefore I like the latter method best; although there may perhaps be more difficulty in it, yet that will soon be surmounted by frequent practice and drilling.[30]

I say, then, that having soldiers who know how to take their proper stations in a moment is a matter of the utmost importance. It is therefore necessary to form them into such battalions, to drill them as a whole, to teach them to march quickly or slowly in all directions, and to keep such order in them that no matter how rough or difficult the pass or

[30] See Figure I, diagrams 1 and 2, pp. 216–217.

defile, they will not break their ranks. For if soldiers can do this, they are good soldiers and may be called veterans. If these men have been in a thousand battles and do not know how to maintain good order, they are no better than raw recruits. What has been said relates only to drawing up a battalion in closer order when it is marching in small ranks.

The main difficulty arises if the battalion should happen to be thrown into disorder, after closer order has been made, either by the nature of the country through which it is obliged to march, by an enemy, or by any other accident, and you want to reduce it immediately to its former order. To overcome this requires much drilling, practice, and experience. Therefore, the ancients spared no pains in making their soldiers ready and expert in rallying whenever they were thrown into confusion. For this purpose two things are necessary, namely that there should be several peculiar marks of distinction in every battalion, and that the same men should always be placed in the same ranks. For instance, if at first a man was stationed in the second rank, let him always stay there—not only in the same rank, but in the very same place; and so that he may not be at a loss about how to do it, there must be, as I said just now, several special marks to guide and direct him. In the first place, when several battalions are joined together, the colors should be easily distinguished from those of all the other battalions; next, the lieutenant colonels, captains, and other officers should wear different plumes; and lastly, which is more important, every corporal should be distinguished by some particular mark; [31] The ancients were so remarkably careful and exact that they had their numbers marked upon their helmets in large figures, as the first, second, third, fourth, and so on. But even that was insufficient: each soldier had the number of his rank and his place in that rank engraved on his shield. When men are thus distinguished from one another, and thus accustomed to know and keep their respective stations, it is an easy matter to rally them if they are thrown into confusion; for once the standard

[31] Vegetius, II. 13.

is fixed, the captains and corporals will immediately know their stations and resume them, whether on the right, the left, or at a due distance from it. The soldiers too, guided by their usual marks and the difference in colors, will soon fall into their proper ranks and places; just as when you are to reassemble the staves of a barrel which you have marked before it was taken to pieces, you may easily do so, whereas if the staves have not been marked, you will find it extremely difficult, if not impossible. These things may soon be learned by frequent practice and drill, and they are not easily forgotten; thus a whole province can in time be made into good and experienced soldiers by such drills and by the new recruits being instructed by veterans.

It is also necessary to teach your men to move all at once, where there is occasion, so that either a flank or the rear becomes the front, or the front becomes the rear or one of the flanks; this may be easily done by having every man face toward any particular part in one movement—this part will then become the front. It is true that when they face to either flank there will be some alteration and disproportion in the ranks because the distance which will then be between the front and the rear will not be as great as that between one end of the flanks and the other. This is quite contrary to the form in which a battalion ought to be drawn up; however, it may soon be rectified by well-drilled and experienced soldiers, and it cannot therefore occasion any great disorder. But there is another maneuver of great importance, for which still more readiness and expertness are requisite—when a whole battalion is to move all at once like one solid body. For instance, this occurs when a whole battalion is to wheel to the left about so as to front on that side where the left flank was before; then, those on the left, at the extremity of the front rank, must stand fast and those nearest them on the right must move so slowly that the rest, who are farther from them on the right, and those at the other extremity of that rank, may not be obliged to run—otherwise they will be in great confusion.

Now when a battalion is attacked on its march from one

place to another, it always happens that the companies not posted in the front are forced to fight either on one of the flanks or in the rear, and that the battalion is under the sudden necessity of forming a front where the flank, or perhaps the rear, was before; in order to form those companies in due proportion and order, all the pikemen must be placed in that flank which is to become the front, and the corporals, captains, and lieutenant colonel must take their respective posts—as in the previously described method of forming a battalion. To do this, then, to form the battalion into 80 ranks of 5 men each, you must pull all the pikemen into the first 20 ranks, with 5 of their corporals in the front rank and 5 in the last of that company; and then the other 60 ranks, or 3 companies, will consist wholly of shieldbearers, whose first and last rank must contain 5 of their corporals. The lieutenant colonel, with his standard and drum, must take a post in the center of the first company of shieldbearers, and the 4 captains at the head of their respective companies. When it is thus formed, if you want all the pikemen on the left flank, you must double the companies, one by one, by their right flanks; but if you want them on the right flank, you must double them by the left. Thus, the battalion will have all its pikemen on one flank, its corporals in the front and rear, its captains in the front, and its lieutenant colonel in the center. This is the order it is to observe while marching. But if the enemy approaches, and if you want the battalion's front where one of the flanks was before, you have nothing to do but to order your men to face the flank where the pikemen are; then the whole battalion, with all its ranks and officers, is immediately changed and is in the order I described before—every man will be in his proper station, except the captains, and they will soon take their posts.[32]

But when a battalion is marching forward and apprehensive of a rear attack, the ranks must be disposed so that the pikemen may be posted there; for this purpose, 5 ranks of them should be placed in the rear of every company, instead of the

[32] See Figure II, diagrams 3 and 4, pp. 218–219.

front where they are usually stationed; in all other respects, let the ordinary disposition be observed.

Cosimo. If I remember correctly, you told us that this type of exercise is calculated to reduce all the battalions of a regiment into the form of an army, and that it was sufficient for such a purpose. But were it to happen that this battalion of 450 men should be obliged to fight by itself, how would you draw it up in that case?

Fabrizio. In the first place, the lieutenant colonel should consider where it will be most necessary to place his pikemen, and post them there accordingly. This may easily be done without disturbing the above-mentioned disposition; for though that is the order which should be observed by a battalion when it acts in conjunction with others against an enemy, it may still serve on all other occasions. However, in showing you the other two methods of drawing up a battalion that I promised you a little while ago, I shall answer your question in more particulars; they are used only when a battalion is to act alone and independent of all the others.

In order, then, to form a battalion with two wings in the front, you dispose your 80 ranks of 5 men in a rank in this manner. In the first place, you must post a captain at the head of 25 ranks, consisting of 2 pikemen on the left and 3 shieldbearers on the right. Next to the first 5 ranks, let there be 20 more with 20 corporals posted in them between the pikemen and the shieldbearers, except the 5 carrying pikes who must be placed among the pikemen. After these 25 ranks are thus drawn up, let there be posted another captain at the head of 15 ranks of shieldbearers. In the interval between this company and the third, the lieutenant colonel with his colors and drum is to post himself at the head of the third company, consisting of 15 more ranks of shieldbearers. The third captain is to take a post at the head of the fourth company of 25 ranks, every one of whom is to have 3 shieldbearers on the left and 2 pikemen on the right; after the first five ranks, there must be 20 more with corporals in them posted between the shieldbearers and the pikemen; in the rear of this company, the fourth captain takes his station. If you then want to form these ranks thus drawn up into a battalion with two wings, you must order the first captain to halt with his 25 ranks; you must then order the second captain to make a motion to the right and advance with his 15 ranks of shieldbearers, in order to double the right flank of the 25 ranks that have halted, until he comes abreast of the rank that is the fifteenth from their rear—there he must halt. After this, the lieutenant colonel, with his 15 ranks of shieldbearers, is to do the same thing on the right flank of the first two companies. Lastly, the third captain, with his 25 ranks, and the fourth captain, at their rear, must move to the right and then advance along the right flank of the other 3 companies, but he must not halt until his rearmost rank is on a line with their rearmost rank; when this has all been done, the captain of the first 15 ranks of shieldbearers must quit his station and go to the left of the rearmost rank, and the fourth captain must go to the right of it. In this manner, you will have a battalion of 25 ranks, some consisting of 5 men and others of 20, with two wings—one at each angle of the front—each of which will consist of 10 ranks of 5 men each; and between the wings there is a space large enough to receive 10 men abreast. The lieutenant colonel takes his post in this space—one captain at the front of each wing, and another at each angle in the rear of the battalion; two files of pikemen and 20 corporals are placed on each flank. The wings may serve to protect the carriages and baggage, as well as the artillery, if there be any; the velites may be arranged along the flanks on the outside of the pikemen.[33]

Now in order to reduce this winged battalion into a hollow square, you need to take only 8 of the rearmost of those 15 ranks with 20 men in each, and place them immediately in front of the two wings; these will then become the flanks of the hollow square. The lieutenant colonel is to take his place with his colors and drum in the area left in the middle; the carriages and baggage may go there too, but not the artillery,

[33] See Figure III, diagrams 5 and 6, pp. 220–221.

which is to be stationed either in the front or on the flanks.[34] These are the methods that may be taken to form a single battalion when it is to pass alone through dangerous and suspected places; but the solid battalion, without wings or an area in the middle of it, is certainly the best; nevertheless, either one or the other of those forms may sometimes be necessary to protect the carriages, baggage, etc.

The Swiss also have several forms for drawing up their battalions, one of which is in the shape of a cross: in the spaces between the arms, they place their harquebusiers to shelter them from the enemy's first shock; but since such battalions are fit only to engage separately, and it is my intention to show how several united battalions must fight, I shall not take the trouble of describing the order they observe.

Cosimo. I think I sufficiently comprehend the method to be followed in drilling the men in this battalion; but, if I am not mistaken, you said you would add 1,000 pikemen extraordinary and 500 velites extraordinary to the 10 battalions of your regiment. Would you not also drill them?

Fabrizio. Certainly, and very well too. I would drill the pikemen at least by companies, if not as a whole, in the discipline of the battalion; for I should employ them more than the ordinary pikemen, especially on special operations—in convoys, escorts, plunders, and the like. As for the velites, it may suffice to drill them separately at home in their particular method of fighting without bringing them into the field; since they are to fight in a loose, detached way, there is no need to call them together when the rest of the battalion is assembled to participate in joint maneuvers.

Therefore you must—as I said before, and beg leave to say again—take great care to drill your battalions so that the men are taught to keep their ranks, to know their proper stations, and to rally or alter their disposition quickly when they are either in troublesome defiles, or apprehensive of being attacked, or disordered by an enemy; for when they are perfect

[34] See Figure III, diagrams 5 and 7, pp. 220–221.

in these things, it will be an easy matter to learn where the battalion's station is and what it has to do when it is joined with the others to form an army. So, if any prince or republic would take the trouble to establish this discipline and these exercises, they would always have enough good soldiers in their dominions to make them superior to their neighbors and to enable them to give law to others instead of receiving it from them. But such is the degeneracy of the times we live in that these things are so far from being in any esteem at present; indeed, they are totally neglected and laughed at, which is the reason that our armies are now good for nothing; and if there are still any officers or men among us who are naturally virtuous, they are not able to exhibit it.

Cosimo. How many carriages would you assign to a battalion?

Fabrizio. In the first place, no captain or corporal should be permitted to ride during a march; and if the lieutenant colonel wanted to ride, it should be upon a mule, and not upon a horse. I would, however, allow him two baggage horses, one to every captain, and two between three corporals; because, when they are in camp, I would lodge three of them together— as I shall show in its proper place. Thus every battalion would have 36 horses to carry its tents, kettles, hatchets, mattocks, spades, as well as other such implements and utensils necessary to an encampment; anything else useful or convenient could be added, if there is room for it.

Cosimo. Although I believe all the officers in your battalion may be necessary, nevertheless I should fear so many would create confusion.

Fabrizio. That might be the case, if they were not all under the command of one person; but since they are, they serve to preserve and promote good order; and indeed, it would be impossible to keep order without them. For a wall that is weak and tottering on all sides may be better supported by many props and buttresses, though they are only feeble ones, than by a few, be they ever so substantial; for whatever their strength, it cannot be of much service at any considerable distance. For this reason, there ought to be a corporal over every ten soldiers in all armies; this corporal should be a man of more spirit and courage—at least of greater authority—than the rest in order to inspire them by both his words and his example; he should continually exhort them to hold their ranks firm and conduct themselves like men. How necessary these things are may plainly appear even from the example of our own armies, which all have their corporals, drums and colors, though none of them do their duty. As for corporals, if they would answer the end for which they were first appointed, every one of them should have his particular men under him, should lodge with them, should mount guard with them, and should always march in the same rank with them; for then the corporals might keep the men so regular and compact in their several stations that it would be almost impossible for any enemy to break or disorder them; if that should ever happen, they might presently be rallied; but in these times, corporals are employed in other purposes of a different nature, and do nothing as they should, though their pay is considerable. It is the same with regard to colors, which still serve to make a fine show rather than for any other military use. But the ancients availed themselves of them as guides and rallying standards in case of disorder; for as soon as the colors were fixed, every man knew his post and immediately returned to it. They also knew how and when to move and when to halt by the colors' motion or lack of it; therefore, it is necessary that there should be many different corps in an army, and that every corps should have its particular ensign and marks of distinction; for then it will know what it has to do, and act with spirit.

The soldiers, then, are to observe the motions of their ensigns, and the ensigns are to observe the beat of the drum; for when that beat is rightly managed, it is a direction to the whole army which acts and moves in a certain measure and pace according to the different notes and sounds so that the army may know how to keep due time and order. For this purpose, the ancients had their pipes, fifes, and other sorts of military music perfectly adapted to different occasions; for just as a man dancing keeps time with the music and cannot make a false step, so an army properly observing the beat of its drums cannot be easily disordered. The ancients, therefore, used to vary the sounds and notes of their military music depending upon whether they wanted to excite, abate, or reflect their soldiers' ardor. Since their tunes and marches were different, they gave them different names: the Doric was calculated to inspire men with resolution and firmness, and the Phrygian to excite martial ardor, or rather fury. It is said that one day at dinner Alexander the Great heard a Phrygian march sounded; he was so transported with it that he leaped up from the table and drew his sword as if he had been about to charge an enemy.[35] It would be very useful, then, either to revive these measures or to invent new ones for such purposes; but if that cannot be done, at least those teaching soldiers to obey commands should not be neglected or laid aside; these may be varied and adapted according to the occasion so that by frequent use and drill, they may learn to distinguish them and know their meaning. But at present, our drums are chiefly employed for making noise and parade.

Cosimo. I should be very happy to learn if you have ever considered how it comes to pass that we are so degenerate, and that not only these exercises, but all manner of military discipline, have now fallen into such neglect and disuse among us.

Fabrizio. I shall give you my opinion on the matter very freely, sir.[36] You know, then, that there have been many renowned warriors in Europe—but few in Africa, and fewer still

---

[35] Roberto Valturio, *De re militari*, II, 3.

[36] One of the most significant theoretical statements in all of Machiavelli's works is to be found in Fabrizio's following two speeches. Machiavelli here clarifies and completes several of the discussions about *virtù*— and about the relations between *virtù*, necessity, and religion—from *Discourses*, I, 1, 3, 6; II, Introduction, 2; III, 1 and 36.

in Asia; the reason for this is that the last two mentioned parts of the world have had but one or two monarchies and only a few republics in them, and that Europe, on the contrary, has had several kingdoms, but more republics in it. Now men become excellent and show their *virtù* according to how they are employed and encouraged by their sovereigns, whether these happen to be kings, princes, or heads of republics; so where there are many states, there will be many great men; but where there are few states, there will not be many great men. In Asia, there were Ninus, Cyrus, Artaxerxes, Mithridates, and a few others like them; in Africa (without mentioning the ancient Egyptians), we read of Masinissa, Jugurtha and some Carthaginian commanders of eminent note.[37] The number of these men, however, is very small in comparison with those Europe has produced; for in this part of the world, there have indeed been numbers of excellent men whom we know about, and doubtless many more whose memories are now extinguished by the malevolence of time; because every state is obliged to cherish and encourage men of *virtù*, either out of necessity or for other reasons—where there are more states, there must of course be more men of *virtù*.

Asia, on the contrary, has not produced many men of *virtù* because, to a great extent, that part of the globe is subject to one monarchy alone—to so great an extent that most parts of it languish in indolence and cannot form any considerable number of men for great and glorious enterprises. The same may be said of Africa, although there have indeed been more commanders of *virtù* in that region than in Asia, thanks to the republic of Carthage. There will always be a greater number of excellent men in republics than in monarchies because *virtù* is generally honored in the former, but feared in the latter; hence, it comes to pass that men of *virtù* are cherished

[37] Ninus, a legendary figure whose name is probably a corruption of Ninevah. Artaxerxes II, king of Persia (404?–359 B.C.). Mithridates VI (*ca.* 136–63 B.C.), king of Pontus; see pp. 52–53, notes 13, 15–16. Masinissa (*ca.* 238–149 B.C.), king of Numidia, who fought with Scipio against Hannibal. Jugurtha (156?–104 B.C.), king of Numidia, subject of the *Bellum Jugurthinum* by Sallust.

and encouraged in one, but discountenanced and suppressed in the other.

If we consider Europe next, we shall find that it was always full of principalities, kingdoms, and republics which lived in perpetual jealousy of each other and were obliged to maintain good discipline in their armies and to honor and encourage military merit. In Greece, besides the Macedonian monarchy, there were several republics, and every one produced many excellent men. In Italy there were the Romans, the Samnites, the Etruscans, and the Cisalpine Gauls.[38] France, Germany, and Spain abounded with republics and principalities; and if we do not read of as many excellent men in any of them as among the Romans, that results from the partiality of historians, who generally follow the stream of *fortuna,* and content themselves with praising the conqueror. It is only reasonable to suppose, however, that there were a great many illustrious men among the Samnites and Etruscans since they defended themselves against the Romans for 150 years. The same may be supposed of France and Spain; but the *virtù* which most historians fail to celebrate in particular men, they are forward enough to praise in whole nations, when they tell us with what bravery and resolution these nations exerted themselves in defense of their liberties.

Since it is obvious, then, that where there are many states there will always be many men of *virtù,* it is certain that when the number of those states is diminished, the number of such men will likewise decrease by degrees—just as the effect must cease when the cause is taken away. Thus, when the Roman Empire had swallowed up all the kingdoms and republics in Europe and Africa, and most of those in Asia, *virtù* met with no countenance anywhere but in Rome; so that men of *virtù* began to grow more scarce in Europe, as well as in Asia, until at last there were hardly any to be found. Just as all *virtù* was extinguished, except among the Romans, so when they

[38] The Samnites, an ancient people inhabiting central Italy, were finally subdued by the Romans, 272–268 B.C. The Romans conquered the Etruscans, early inhabitants of modern Tuscany, by 264 B.C.

became corrupt, the whole world was similarly corrupted; and the Scythians [39] poured by swarms into an Empire that, having extinguished the *virtù* of most other nations, was not able to preserve its own.

And although that Empire was afterwards dismembered by those barbarians, yet the several parts into which it was divided never recovered their original *virtù*. In the first place, it is a very difficult matter, and requires a long time, to revive good order and discipline when once it is abolished; in the second place, the Christian religion has wrought such a change in the way of life and values of mankind that they now no longer need to defend themselves as they once did. Then, all who were vanquished in battle were either put to death or carried in perpetual slavery into the enemy's country where they spent the remainder of their lives in labor and misery. If a town was taken, it was demolished or its inhabitants were stripped of their goods, dispersed all over the world, and reduced to the ultimate degree of poverty and wretchedness; so, the dread of these evils obliged them to maintain good discipline in their armies and to honor all those excelling in the art of war.

But at present, those terrible apprehensions are in a great measure dissipated and extinguished; for after an army is defeated, those falling into the conqueror's hands are seldom or never put to death, and the terms of their ransom are made so easy that they do not long continue prisoners. If a town has changed sides a hundred times, it is not demolished nor are its inhabitants dispersed or stripped of their possessions. The worst they have to fear is being forced to pay tribute. So, men now no longer care to submit to the rigor and continual hardships of military discipline to ward off evils which they are but little afraid of. Besides, the provinces of Europe are subject to few rulers at present, in comparison with what they formerly were: all France is under the dominion of one king; all Spain under that of another; and there are not many

[39] The Scythians were the warlike tribesmen in the area north and east of the Black and Caspian Seas.

principalities or republics in Italy; so, the petty states find protection under the wings of the strong, and the more powerful ones are not afraid of utter ruin—even if they should be conquered—for the reasons I have already given.

Cosimo. But, within the last twenty-five years, we have seen many towns sacked and some kingdoms entirely ruined. These are examples which ought to serve as warnings to others to provide for their security by reviving the ancients' military discipline and institutions.

Fabrizio. You are quite right; but consider what towns those were which suffered in that manner, and you will find they were not states themselves, but inferior members of states. If Tortona was sacked, Milan was not; Capua suffered, but Naples escaped; Brescia and Ravenna felt the lash of the conqueror,[40] but Venice and Rome came off with impunity. These examples are not sufficient to make a state change its purpose, but rather to make it determined to persevere in its resolution when it sees that at any time it can redeem itself from destruction by a ransom; for a state will not expose itself and its subjects to the continual anxiety of military discipline and exercises when these anxieties not only seem largely unnecessary, but also attended with much trouble and inconvenience. As for the dependent members which ought to be most affected by these examples, it is not in their power to save themselves; those already ruined states see their error when it is too late to correct it, while others, not yet having shared the same fate, take no pains to prevent it. These states choose to live a lazy, indolent life, free from trouble and inconvenience, and to rely upon *fortuna* rather than their own *virtù;* for seeing that there is now such a proportion of *virtù* left among mankind that it has but little influence in the affairs of the world—and that all things seem to be governed by *fortuna*—they think it is better to follow her train than to contend with her for superiority.

To evince the truth of what I have said, if further proof is

40 Tortona, 1499; Capua, 1501; Brescia, 1512; Ravenna, 1512.

needed, let us consider the state of Germany at present: full of principalities and republics, it abounds with commanders of *virtù;* and indeed, everything worthy of imitation in the military discipline of these times is derived from those states. For, jealous of their neighbors, and abhorring the idea of slavery—a condition not, it seems, much dreaded in some other countries—they take all proper means to defend their liberties, and therefore continue free and respectable.

This, I think, may suffice to show the causes of our degeneracy, and the present neglect of military discipline among us; but I cannot tell whether you are of the same opinion. Perhaps what I have said has not given you the satisfaction you wanted, or not been thoroughly understood; consequently, you may have some doubts left in your mind.

Cosimo. None at all, sir, I assure you. On the contrary, I understand perfectly what you have said, and am very well satisfied with it; but I beg you to resume our subject, and tell us how you would dispose your cavalry in these battalions, how many of them you would have, and how they should be armed and officered.

Fabrizio. Perhaps you thought I had forgotten that, but I have not, although I have but little to say about cavalry for two reasons. In the first place, the main strength of an army lies in its infantry; in the second place, even in these times, the cavalry is much better disciplined than the infantry is; and if it is not superior, it is at least equal to the cavalry of the ancients. I have already shown how they ought to be drilled; as to their arms, I would arm both the men-at-arms and the light cavalry the way they are presently armed; but the light cavalry should consist mostly of crossbowmen, with some harquebusiers among them who, although of little service in other respects, are still very necessary to frighten the country people and drive them from passes which they may perhaps have undertaken to defend; they are more afraid of one harquebusier than of 20 men armed in any other manner.

With regard to their number, since at first I proposed to

take a Roman legion for my model, I should think 300 good horsemen in a regiment would be sufficient; of these, 150 should be men-at-arms, and the rest light cavalry, with a captain, a cornet, 15 corporals, and a drum for each troop. Every 10 men-at-arms should have 5 baggage horses; every 10 light cavalrymen, 2, which, like those belonging to the infantry, should carry their tents, kettles, axes, stakes, and other implements and utensils. Do not think this is out of order, for every one of our men-at-arms has 4 horses allowed him for that purpose; but that is an abuse, for in Germany they have no other horse but the one they are mounted on, and only one carriage to every 20 for their baggage. The Roman heavy-armed cavalry had no more; but indeed, the *triarii*,[41] were always quartered near the cavalry and obliged to assist them to groom and take care of their horses. This is an example which might easily be followed in these times, as I shall show in more particulars when I discuss camps; for surely what was formerly done by the Romans, and is still practiced by the Germans, may be effected at present. Therefore, those that omit or neglect these things are much to be blamed.

Once these squadrons are raised and enrolled in the same manner with the rest of the regiment, they should sometimes be reviewed with the other battalions when they are assembled, and drilled in skirmishes and sham fights with them so as to make them well acquainted with one another and perfect in those exercises. So much for this topic. Let us now proceed to draw up an army into such an order of battle that it is most likely to insure us a victory when we engage an enemy; for this is the end for which all armies are raised, and for which so much care and pain are to be taken in disciplining them.

41 Soldiers of a Roman legion were divided into classes according to their age, experience, and equipment. The *triarii*, from *tres*, three, were the third and oldest class; they were stationed in the third rank behind the *hastati*, in the first rank, and the *principes*, in the second. See below, p. 84 and n. 1.

BOOK THREE

Cosimo. Since we are going to change the subject, I should like to resign my office of interrogator in this conversation; for, as I hate presumption in others, I would not willingly seem guilty of it myself. I therefore lay down the dictatorship and give up my authority to any other person in the company who will be pleased to accept it.

Zanobi. It would have been very pleasant for us all if you would have continued in that office; but since you decline it, at least please tell us whom you deputize to succeed you in it.

Cosimo. I desire to give that responsibility to Signor Fabrizio.

Fabrizio. I freely accept it, and I think we should follow the example of the Venetians, who always appoint the youngest to speak first in their councils and assemblies; and since the art of speaking well is properly the exercise of youth, we may suppose that young men are the best qualified to discuss the duties and exercises of war, as they are the readiest and fittest to put them in execution.

Cosimo. The lot then falls upon you, Luigi; and since I am much pleased with my successor, I am sure he will be equally agreeable to you all. Let us lose no time, however, but return to our subject.

Fabrizio. I know very well that in order to show how an army ought to be drawn up in order of battle that it would be necessary to describe the method in which the Greeks and Romans formed their troops for that purpose; but since this is done by ancient historians, I refer you to them; and, omitting several other particulars, I shall speak only of things that are absolutely necessary to be adopted by those who would improve our present system of military discipline. With this in mind, I shall show you at once how an army of today ought to be formed in order of battle, how it is to be drilled in sham-fights, and how it is to behave in real engagements.

The greatest error, then, that a general can be guilty of, in drawing up an army for battle is giving it only one front, thereby binding it to one conflict and one *fortuna*. This is the effect of having lost the method observed by the ancients of receiving one line into another; for those in the front can neither be supported nor relieved in time of action except by this method so admirably observed by the Romans. Now to point out the method by which these things were effected, I must tell you that the Romans divided each legion into *hastati, principes,* and *triarii* [1]; the first were placed in the front or first line of the army in thick and close array; the *principes* were placed in the second line but in looser order; and the *triarii* in the third, with still larger intervals between the men in their ranks, into which they could admit both the *principes* and *hastati* when the occasion arose. Besides these, they had their slingers, bowmen, and other light-armed soldiers who were not incorporated into these ranks but posted in the front to the right and left between the cavalry and infantry. These light-armed forces used to begin the engagement, and if they overcame the enemy, which seldom happened, they pursued their advantage; but if they were driven back, they retreated either along the flanks of the army, or through certain intervals in it left open for that purpose—to cover the sutlers and servants and other unarmed people that followed the camp. After this, the *hastati* advanced

[1] Here Machiavelli is relying upon Livy, VIII. 8–9, as he specifically states in *Discourses*, II, 16. What follows is an account of Roman military practice that does not take into account the evolution of the legion and the changes that occurred over the ages, or the reasons for the changes. Livy's reference is to the time of the war with the Latins (338 B.C.). Between that day and the period of Polybius, in the second century, and the Empire, numerous modifications of organization and tactics had occurred. Hence Machiavelli's Roman legion is, in fact, one that never actually existed.

against the enemy; if they were repulsed, they retreated leisurely into the spaces left for them among the *principes* and again advanced with them to renew the battle; but if this line too were overpowered, it fell back into the *triarii*, and all three, thus joined together, attacked with greater vigor and strength than ever; if that miscarried, the day was lost, because they had no other resource or means of relief left. The cavalry was stationed on each side of the infantry in the form of two wings. As occasion required, they sometimes engaged the enemy's cavalry and sometimes supported their own infantry. This method of renewing the attack thrice can hardly be withstood, for then *fortuna* must abandon you thrice and the enemy must have enough *virtù* to defeat you thrice.

The Greeks did not have this method of renewing the front of their phalanxes; although these phalanxes consisted of many soldiers and many ranks, they still made only one body, or rather, one front. To relieve each other, one rank did not retire into another, as did the Romans, but one single man advanced into another's place when it was vacant. This was effected as follows: when their phalanx was drawn up into files (which we will suppose to consist of 50 men each) with its front toward the enemy, all the first 6 ranks might engage at once, for their lances, which they called *sarissae*, were so long that those from the sixth rank reached over the shoulders of the men in the first. Therefore, if any man in the first rank were killed or disabled while fighting, the man behind him in the second rank immediately stepped into his place; the person directly behind him in the third rank filled the vacancy in the second, and so on; the ranks in the rear continually filled up the deficiencies of those in the front, so that all the ranks were constantly kept full and entire, except the rearmost, which was exhausted at last, because there was no other to reinforce it. These phalanxes, therefore, might be gradually wasted away and annihilated, but they could seldom be broken, as the close and compact order in their body made them impenetrable.

The Romans at first formed their legions in this manner, in

imitation of the Greek phalanx; but growing displeased with it at last, they divided them into more corps—*cohortes* and *manipuli*—convinced that such corps have more life and vigor in them when they have the more officers to inspire them and when they are so divided that each division can act separately and support itself.

The Swiss regiments at present are also based upon the model of the ancient phalanxes and follow their method both in closing up their order of battle and in relieving their ranks; when they engage, they are placed on each other's flanks, not in a parallel line. They have no method of receiving the first rank, should it be thrown back into the second; in order to relieve each other, they place one regiment in the front and another a little behind it on the right, so that if the first is hard pressed, the second may advance to its assistance; a third is placed behind both these and also on the right, at the distance of an harquebus shot. They have adopted this disposition so that if the other two should be driven back, the third can advance to relieve them, and all of them have sufficient room either to retreat or advance without falling foul of one another; for large groups cannot be received into one another in the same manner as small ones. Therefore the small, distinct groups which composed the Roman legions are the most proper both for receiving and relieving one another; the fact that the method the Swiss observed is not as good as that taken by the ancient Romans appears very plainly from the success of the Roman legions, who always got the better of the Greek phalanxes, whenever they happened to engage, because both their weapons and armor and their way of receiving one rank into another were much better than the arms, the discipline, and the close order of the phalanx.

Now in order to form an army upon the model of both, I would make the Greek phalanx my pattern in some respects, and the Roman legion my pattern in others; therefore, as I told you before, I would have 2,000 pikemen in my regiment, armed like the Macedonian phalanx, and 3,000 men with swords and shields, like the Roman legion. Just as the Romans divided their legion into 10 cohorts, I have divided my regiment into 10 battalions; like them too, I have appointed velites to begin the battle. And since I have retained the arms of both nations, I would also imitate the order and discipline of each, to a certain extent. Thus I have taken care that the first 5 ranks of every battalion should consist of pikemen, and the rest of shieldbearers; this was done so that the rest might be able not only to sustain the shock of the enemy's cavalry in the front and to penetrate into their infantry, but also to open it to the right and left so that the shieldbearers may come in to complete the victory.

Now if you consider the strength of this organization, you will find how well they are calculated for that purpose, because pikes are of admirable service against cavalry and they are also useful before they come to the point of hand-to-hand fighting with the infantry—after that, they are of no use at all. Hence, the Swiss place one rank of halbardiers behind every three ranks of pikemen, so as to give them room to use their pikes; but that room is not sufficient. Therefore, when we place our pikemen in the front and the shieldbearers behind them, they serve both to hold off the enemy's cavalry and to open and disorder his infantry; but after the battle is joined and they become useless, the shieldbearers advance with their swords, weapons that may be managed in the closest fight.

Luigi. We are impatient to hear how you would draw up an army, thus armed and appointed, in order of battle.

Fabrizio. I was just going to do it. You must know, then, that a Roman consular army did not exceed two legions of about 11,000 infantry and 600 cavalry, composed entirely of their own citizens. Besides these, they were supplied with as many more of both sorts by their friends and allies, which they divided into two bodies called the right and left wing and stationed on either flank; but they never permitted the number of these auxiliaries to surpass that of their legions, though there generally was a larger proportion of cavalry among them than in their own forces.[2] With such an army, consisting of about 22,000 infantrymen and 2,000 good cavalrymen, a consul went upon most expeditions; but when the enemy was very formidable, they sent out two consuls with two such armies united.

You must also know that in the three principal operations of an army—the march, the encampment, and the battle [3]—they constantly posted their legions in the center, rightly judging that the forces in which they reposed the greatest confidence should always be compact and united, as I shall show you when I come to speak more particularly of these three operations. But this auxiliary infantry, by their union and daily conversation with the infantry of the legions, soon became as serviceable as they were, for they were drilled and disciplined in the same manner and formed in the same order of battle before an engagement. So, when we know how the Romans drew up one legion for that purpose, we know how they drew up a whole army; as I said, they formed their legion in three lines, so that one line might receive another; I have consequently told you how they drew up their whole army on the day of a battle.

To form an army, then, in an order of battle similar to the Romans, I shall take two regiments, since they had two legions, and you can see by their arrangement how a whole army is to be drawn up; if you would add any more, there is nothing further to be done but to multiply or enlarge the ranks. It will be needless, I suppose, to remind you of how much infantry is in a regiment, of the ten battalions in it, of what sort of arms and armor they have, of how many companies there are, of what officers each has, of how many men ranked as velites and pikemen—both ordinary and extraordinary—of how many shieldbearers, etc.; for when I mentioned these things a little while ago, I desired you to take par-

[2] The infantry of the auxiliaries did in fact exceed the legionary infantry. The customary strength of such an army was 15,000 infantry, 800 cavalry with two legions consisting of about 8,400 infantry and 600 cavalry. See Burd, "Le fonti letterarie," p. 206, n. 1.

[3] Polybius, VI. 26.

ticular notice of them and to remember them as absolutely necessary for giving you a clear idea of the whole arrangement; therefore, without any repetition of that kind, I shall proceed to draw up my army.

For this purpose, I would place the 10 battalions of one regiment on the left, and the 10 of the other on the right. Those on the left are to be formed in this manner: post five battalions on each other's flank in the front with an interval of 8 feet between them, and let the space they occupy be 282 feet wide and 80 feet deep. In the rear of these 5 I would place three others at a distance of 80 feet, the first one should be in a straight line with the battalion on the left flank of those in the front, the second with that on the right flank, and the third with that in the center, so that these three will take up as much ground in both width and depth as the other five; but although the space between every one of those five is only 8 feet, I would have the space between these three to be 66 feet. In the rear of these I would post the two remaining battalions at a distance of 80 feet, one of them in a straight line with that on the left of the last three mentioned, and the other with that on the right with an interval between them of 92 feet. Therefore, the ground which all the battalions thus formed occupies will be 282 feet in width and 400 in depth. I would range the pikemen extraordinary along the left flank of these battalions, at a distance of 40 feet, and I would make 140 ranks of them, with seven men in each rank, so that they would cover the whole left flank of the battalions drawn up in the manner I have described; and, after posting the captains and corporals in their proper places, there would be 40 ranks remaining to guard the baggage, sutlers, and other unarmed people following the camp in the rear of the army. Of the three lieutenant colonels belonging to them, I would place one at the front, another in the center, and another in the rear.

But to return to the front of the army. Next to the pikemen extraordinary, I would place the 500 velites extraordinary and allow them to take up a space of 80 feet. Next to them, on the left, I would place my men-at-arms and allow them a space of 450 feet; and next to them, my light cavalry, whom I would allow the same space. The ordinary velites I would leave with their respective battalions in their proper places—that is, in the intervals between one battalion and another, to be attendants, as it were, upon them—unless I should think it fit to put them under the cover of the pikemen extraordinary; sometimes I would do this and sometimes I would not, depending upon what was most to my advantage. I would place the regimental colonel with his colors and drum either in the center of the space left between the first and second lines of the battalions, or else in front of them in the interval between the last of the first five battalions and the pikemen extraordinary—depending upon which I felt was most convenient. Around him he would have 30 or 40 picked men, who would not only have sense enough to carry his orders properly and distinctly to the different parts of the army, but would also be able to repel the enemy if he should be attacked.

In this manner I would form the regiment on the left; it would be just one-half of the army and occupy a space 572 feet wide and 400 feet deep, exclusive of the space taken up by the 40 ranks of pikemen extraordinary who are to guard the baggage in the rear, which will be 200 feet. The other regiment I would draw up in the same manner on the right of this, with an interval between them of 60 feet. At the head of this interval I would place some pieces of artillery, behind which the general of the army should take post with his standard and drum, and at least 200 picked men, most of them on foot, of whom there should be ten or more fit to carry any orders; he himself should be mounted and armed in such a manner that he could command either on horseback or on foot, as occasion required.

As for the artillery, ten 40 pounders would be sufficient for the reduction of a town, and I would use them in defending my campaign rather than in a field engagement, for my field pieces should be only 12 pounders or so; and these I would place along the front of the whole army, unless the ground was such that I could place them conveniently and safely in the flanks where the enemy could not come at them.[4]

This method of drawing up an army may answer the end both of the Greek phalanx and of the Roman legion; for you have the pikemen in the front, and all the rest of the infantry is so formed in their proper ranks that either in charging an enemy or in sustaining the charge they may, like the phalanx, recruit their front ranks out of those in their rear. On the other hand, if they are so hard pressed that they are obliged to give way, they may retreat into the intervals of the second line and advance again in conjunction with it to face the enemy; if they are repulsed the second time, they may retire into the spaces between the battalions in the third line, and renew the battle with still greater vigor; so that by this method you may reinforce your ranks in either the Greek or the Roman manner. As to the strength of such an army, none can be more compact, for each wing is perfectly well fortified with both officers and men properly armed, and appointed in such a manner that if there is any apparent weakness in it, it must be in the rear, where the carriages and sutlers are stationed—and even those are covered by the pikemen extraordinary. Therefore, since it is so well fortified on all sides, it cannot be attacked anywhere by an enemy without being ready to receive him, for the rear is in no danger; because if the enemy be so strong that he is able to attack you on every side at once, it must have been madness on your part to take the field against him. But supposing he should be

[4] See Figure IV, p. 222. Artillery classification in Machiavelli's time was beginning to be expressed in terms of the weight of a cannon ball, since the charge of the powder depended upon the weight of the ball. The Italian reads *cinquanta* and *quindici libbre di portata*, respectively. Although the weight of the *libbra* varied from town to town, the *Encyclopedia Italiana* says the Florentine *libbra*, at an unspecified date, was equivalent to 339.5 grams, compared with the 453.6 grams to the avoirdupois pound. The figures in the text compensate approximately for this difference, whereas Farneworth's translation reads 36 and 38 pounds respectively.

superior to you in number by one-third, and his army as well armed and drawn up as your own; if he weakens it in order to attack you simultaneously in several areas, and you happen to break in upon him in any one, the day is your own. As for the cavalry, you have nothing to fear from them, for the pikemen who surround you on all sides will secure you sufficiently against their fury, even if your own should be repulsed. Your officers are so conveniently posted that they may easily do their duty; and the spaces between one battalion and another, and between every rank, serve not only to receive the other battalions or ranks when the occasion arises, but also to give the officers enough room to go back and forth with orders from the general.

Now, as I told you before, since the Romans had about 24,000 men in their armies, I would have our army consist of the same number; and since their auxiliaries learned their discipline and order from their legions, I would have our auxiliaries also formed upon the model of our regiments. These things may easily be effected by a little practice; for in adding two other regiments to the army—or as many auxiliary soldiers as there are already, let it be what it will—you have nothing to do but double your ranks by placing 20 battalions on the left, instead of 10, and an equal number on the right; or to extend or contract them, depending upon the nature of the ground and the posture of the enemy.

Luigi. I understand you perfectly, sir. I seem to see your army drawn up for battle, and am impatient to have it begin. For heaven's sake do not turn Fabius Maximus upon us. If you do, I am afraid I shall be tempted to abuse you as the Roman people did him.

Fabrizio. I am ready.[5] The signal is given. Do you not hear our artillery? It has fired but done little damage to the enemy. The velites extraordinary and light cavalry have set up a great shout and begun the attack with the utmost fury. The enemy's

[5] The following imaginary battle is without precedent in previous military literature. See Introduction, p. xxi.

artillery has discharged its volley, but their balls have gone over the heads of our infantry without doing them any harm; but to prevent their artillery from firing a second time, our velites and light cavalry endeavor to make themselves masters of it; a body of the enemy post themselves before it, so that the artillery on both sides is become useless. See with what *virtù* our men charge. The expertness they have acquired by long drilling and discipline inspires them with confidence. The battalions move forward at a regular pace and in good order, with the men-at-arms on their flanks to attack the enemy. Our artillery withdraws through the space left vacant by the velites in order to make room for it. See how the general encourages his men and assures them of victory. Observe our velites and light cavalry returning and extending themselves along the flanks of our army to see if they can do any harm to the enemy through his flank. The two armies are now engaged. See with what *virtù* and silence our men receive the charge. Do you not hear the general giving his men-at-arms orders to hold their ground and not to advance upon the enemy, nor on any account to desert the infantry? See how a party of our light cavalry has now detached itself to charge a body of the enemy's harquebusiers that were coming to take us by the flank, and how the enemy's cavalry is advancing to support them; but the harquebusiers, to avoid being entangled between them, are retiring to their own army. See with what resolution and dexterity our ordinary pikemen handle their weapons; but the infantry on each side have now come so close together that our pikemen can no longer use their pikes; therefore, according to their usual discipline, they gradually retreat until they are received by the shieldbearers. See on the left how a large body of the enemy's men-at-arms have meanwhile pushed back our men-at-arms who retire, as they had previously learned, into the pikemen extraordinary; and, supported by them, not only make headway against the enemy again, but repulse them with great slaughter. Now the ordinary pikemen from the first battalions have retreated among the shieldbearers; they leave them to carry on the battle—behold what havoc they wreak among the enemy; see with what *virtù*, confidence, and coolness they press upon them; see how closely they are engaged with them—they hardly have room to handle their swords. The enemy is embarrassed and falling into confusion; their pikes are too long to do any further work and their swords are of no service against men who are so well protected by their armor. What carnage! How many wounded men! They are beginning to flee. See, they are running away on the right and on the left. The battle is over. We have won a glorious victory. It might have been more complete, however, if we had exerted our whole strength. But you see, we did not need to employ either our second or our third line, since the first was sufficient for doing the job. So, I have nothing more to add on this occasion, except to answer any objection or doubt you may have.

Luigi. You have carried everything before you with such amazing rapidity, that I cannot very easily tell whether I ought to state any objection or not. However, with submission to your superior judgment, I will make so bold as to ask you a free question or two. Therefore, kindly tell me first why you would let your artillery fire no more than once, and why you ordered it to be drawn off so soon without making any use of it afterward. Next, you managed the enemy's artillery just as you pleased and had it aimed so poorly that it could do no damage; I suppose this may indeed be the case sometimes, but if it should happen (as I believe it often does) that the shot should strike home, what remedy would you prescribe? And since I have mentioned artillery, I shall bring up everything I have to say on that subject here so that we shall not have to return to it later. I have heard many people laugh at the arms, armor, and military discipline of the ancients; they say that it would be of little or no service now, since the invention of artillery would break up all their ranks and beat their armor to pieces; they say that it would be folly to draw up a body of forces in an order that cannot be maintained and that undergoes the fatigue of carrying armor that can by no means protect them.

Fabrizio. Your objections are of several kinds; therefore, you must have patience if you expect a particular answer to them all.

It is true, our artillery made but one volley, and I was in some doubt whether I should even permit that one; for it is more important to keep oneself from being hurt than it is to annoy the enemy. Now, in order to protect yourself from artillery, you must either keep out of the reach of its shot or place yourself behind a wall, a bank, or some fence of that kind; there is no other cover that I know of, and again, that cover must be very strong. But when an army is drawn up in order to fight, it cannot skulk behind a wall or a bank, nor even keep at a distance where it will not be annoyed by the enemy's artillery. Since there is no method, then, to shelter oneself from it, the general must resort to such means as will expose him and his men to the least danger; for which purpose, the best, and indeed the only, way is to make themselves masters of it if possible—and as soon as they can. To do this, it is necessary that a body of your men should march up and suddenly rush it; but they must not do so in close order because the suddenness of the attack will prevent the artillery from firing more than once, and when your men are thinly drawn up it cannot do much damage among them. Now, a compact body of regular forces is not at all proper for this service; if it moves fast, it must naturally fall into disorder in and of itself; if it extends and weakens its ranks, it will presently be broken by the enemy.

Given these considerations, I drew up my army in a manner that was most proper for such an attempt: having placed 1,000 velites along its wings, I ordered them to advance, together with the light cavalry, as soon as our artillery had fired, to seize the enemy's. This is the reason why I would not allow our own to discharge a second volley, for fear that the enemy should have time to do the same, as they might easily have done; perhaps they would have done so before our artillery was loaded again, if I had not taken these means to prevent it. So that the only way to render the enemy's artillery useless is to attack it as soon as possible; if they desert it, naturally it falls into your hands; if they defend it, they must place a body of forces in front of it, and then they will not dare to fire again because their own men must be the chief ones to suffer.

These reasons, I think, might be sufficient in themselves without quoting any examples to support them; but since antiquity furnishes us with many, I shall give you one or two. When Ventidius had resolved to fight an engagement with the Parthians,[6] (whose strength lay chiefly in their bows and arrows), he let them advance almost to the very entrenchments of his camp before he drew out his army; and he did this so that he might suddenly fall upon them before they could use their arrows. Caesar tell us[7] that in one battle the Gauls attacked him so suddenly and so furiously that his men did not have time to throw their darts at the enemy—as the Romans always used to do. Now we see from these instances that in order to protect an army in the field from the effects of any weapons disturbing them from a distance, there is no other way but to march up to them as fast as possible, and get possession of them if you can—or at least to prevent their effects.

In addition to these reasons, I had still another which determined me to fire my artillery no more than once; it may perhaps seem trifling to you, but for me it carries much weight. There is nothing that occasions greater confusion and embarrassment among a body of men than having their sight dazzled or obstructed; this is a circumstance that has been the ruin of many gallant armies blinded either by the sun or by clouds of dust; and what can contribute more to that than artillery smoke? It would be more prudent, therefore, to let the enemy blind themselves than to go seeking them blindfolded. Thus, I would either not use any artillery at all, or if I did—to avoid censure now that large guns are in such credit—I

---

6 Publius Ventidius in 38 B.C. Frontinus, *Strategemata* II. 2. 5.
7 Caesar, *Gallic War* I. 52.

would place it along my flanks so that when it was fired, the smoke might not blind my men in front, where I would have the flower of my army. The effects of this may be seen from the conduct of Epaminondas,[8] who, while going to engage the enemy, had all his light cavalry trot back and forth in the front of their army; this raised such a dust that it threw them into disorder and gave him an easy victory over them.

As for my seeming to have aimed the enemy's artillery as I pleased and made the shot fly over the heads of our infantry, I answer that it more often happens that way than otherwise; this is so because infantry stands so low, and because it is no easy matter to manage heavy pieces of cannon well—if you either elevate them or lower them the slightest bit too much, in one case the balls will fly quite over their heads, and in the other they will fall into the ground and never come near them. The least inequality of terrain is also a great boon for them, since any little bank or brake between them and the artillery serves either to hinder the shot or to divert its direction. As for the cavalry and especially the men-at-arms (who, because they are drawn up in a closer order and stand so much higher than light cavalry, are more exposed to danger), they may stay in the rear of the army until the artillery has fired.

It is certain that small pieces of cannon and shot from harquebuses do more damage than heavy artillery. The best remedy against the latter is making a resolute attack upon it as soon as possible; if you lose some of your men in so doing (which must always be the case), surely a partial loss is not so bad as a total defeat. The Swiss are worthy of imitation in this respect; they never decline an engagement out of fear of artillery, but always give the death penalty to those who would stir from their ranks, or those who show the least sign of being frightened by it. I therefore had my artillery drawn off as soon as it had been discharged in order to make room for the battalions to advance; I made no further mention of

8 Epaminondas (*ca.* 418–362 B.C.), great military leader of Thebes. Frontinus, II. 2. 12.

it because it became a thing of no consequence after the two armies had joined battle.

You also say that many people laugh at the arms, armor, and military discipline of the ancients because, since the invention of artillery, these things are useless; hence, one would be apt to imagine that moderns had made effective provision against it. If so, I should be glad to hear what that provision is, for I confess I know of none, nor do I think it possible to make any but what I have already mentioned. Why does our infantry at present wear iron corselets and why are our men-at-arms covered with armor from head to foot? If they despise this manner of arming among the ancients, as being useless against artillery, why do they continue to use it themselves? I should also like to know why the Swiss, like the ancients, form their regiments of 6,000 or 8,000 infantry drawn up in close order; why all the other nations have begun to imitate them, since that method exposes their army to no less danger from the artillery than many other institutions the ancients had as models. These are questions which I fancy the people whom you mention cannot easily answer; but if you should propose them to soldiers of judgment and experience, they would tell you that they arm themselves in that manner not because they think such armor will protect them effectively against cannon balls, but because it will defend them against crossbows, pikes, swords, and many other weapons an enemy may use in an offensive. They will tell you further that the close order observed by the Swiss is necessary to push back the enemy's infantry, to stand up against their cavalry, and to make it harder for the enemy to break in on them. So we see that soldiers have many other things to dread besides artillery, against which this order and this sort of arms and armor serve to protect them. Hence, it follows that the better an army is armed, and the closer and stronger it is drawn up, the less it has to fear; therefore, the persons to whose opinion you referred not long ago must either have had very little experience, or must not have considered the matter in the light they ought to have done. For since we find that only the an-

cients' pikes and close order—still in use among the Swiss—
have done such wonderful service, and have contributed so
much to our armies' current strength, why may we not conclude that the rest of the military institutions observed by the
ancients, but now entirely laid aside and neglected, might be
equally serviceable? Besides, since the fury of artillery does not
make us afraid of drawing up our battalions in close order like
the Swiss, there can certainly be no other disposition contrived
that can make us more apprehensive of its effects.

Furthermore, if we are not terrified by the enemy's artillery
while we lay siege to a town, when it may annoy us with the
greatest security, when we can neither come at it nor prevent
its effects because it is protected by walls, and when we must
endeavor to dismount it with our own cannon, which may
perhaps require much time, and expose us to a continual fire
all the while; then why should we fear it so much in the field
where we can immediately make ourselves masters of it or put
a stop to its firing? Therefore, the invention of artillery is no
reason, in my opinion, why we should not imitate the ancients
in their military discipline and institutions, as well as in their
virtù; and if this matter had not been thoroughly discussed
in a lately published piece, I would have dwelled longer upon
it at present, but for brevity's sake I refer you to that discourse.[9]

Luigi. I have read it, and I generally believe that on the
whole you have sufficiently shown the best remedy against
artillery to be its earliest possible seizure—that is, in a field
battle. But suppose the enemy should place it in the flanks
of their army, where it would still gall you, and yet where
it would be so well protected that you could not make yourself master of it. For in drawing up your army, you may remember that you left an interval of 8 feet between every
battalion and of 40 feet between the battalions and the pikemen extraordinary; now, if the enemy should form their
army in the same order and place their artillery deep in those

9 *Discourses,* II, 17.

intervals, I should think it would disturb you very much—without any risk of being taken—because you could not come at it there.

Fabrizio. Your objection carries much weight with it, and therefore I shall endeavor either to resolve your doubt or to find some remedy. I told you before that when battalions are engaged with an enemy, they are in constant motion and consequently must draw closer and closer to each other; so, if you leave only small intervals between them for the artillery, these will soon be filled up in such a manner that the artillery is useless; but if you make them large, to avoid that inconvenience, you naturally must encounter a much greater one because then you leave room enough for the enemy to rush into them and not only seize your artillery, but throw your whole army into confusion. But you must understand that it is impossible to place your cannon, especially those fixed to carriages, between your battalions; since they are drawn one way and point another, they must all be turned a different direction before they can be fired; to do that would require so large a space that 50 pieces would disorder any army. So they must necessarily be placed somewhere out of the battalions, and then they may be approached in the manner I have already prescribed.

Let us suppose, however, that they could be placed within the battalions and that we could hit upon some medium that would both prevent the battalions from frustrating the effects of the artillery when they drew closer together and not leave such large intervals between them that the enemy might push into these intervals; I say that even then a method might be found to elude the artillery's force: open counter-intervals in the enemy's army to let your shot pass through without doing any damage. For in order to protect your artillery effectively, you should place it at the rear of the intervals between your battalions, and, to avoid harming your forces, it should be aimed so that the shots will always pass straight through the intervals. By so doing, you will open up comparable passages in the enemy's army, and his shots will pass through without inflicting damage upon your men; for it is a general rule always to give way to such things as cannot be opposed—as the ancients used to do when they were attacked by elephants and armed chariots.

You see, I won a victory with an army formed and appointed in the manner I recommended; I must beg leave to repeat (if what I have already said be insufficient), that such an army must at the very first onset necessarily defeat any other army that is armed and drawn up like ours at present. For the most part such an army can make only one front, is entirely unprovided with shields, and is not only armed in such a manner that they cannot defend themselves against an enemy that closes with them, but is also so formed that if they post their battalions flank to flank, they make their lines too thin and feeble; if they place them in the rear of each other, since they have no method for receiving one another, they soon fall into confusion and are easily broken. And indeed, although they are divided into three bodies called the vanguard, the main body, and the rear guard, still this division is of no use except on a march or in an encampment in order to distinguish them; for during an engagement they are combined and, therefore, are all liable to be defeated at once by the first shock.

Luigi. I further observed in your late battle that your cavalry were repulsed and forced to take cover under the pikemen extraordinary, by whose assistance they not only made headway against the enemy a second time, but in their turn, repulsed them. Now, I am persuaded that pikemen can support cavalry in a thick and closely drawn-up body like the Swiss regiments, but in your army there are only five ranks of pikemen in the front and seven on the flanks, so I cannot see how they can keep off a body of cavalry.

Fabrizio. Although I told you before that six ranks of pikemen might charge at a time in the Macedonian phalanx, yet I must now add that if a Swiss regiment consisted of 1,000 ranks, no more than four or five at most could charge at once; for since their pikes were only 18 feet long, and we can imagine that three feet must be taken up between one hand and the other, so, the first rank would have only 15 feet in which to use their pikes. The second, besides the three feet between the men's hands, as many more feet must be taken up by the distance between one rank and another; then there would be only 12 feet of the pike that could be of any service. The third, for the same reasons, would have only nine feet, the fourth six, and the fifth three; the other ranks behind them are useless, since they could make no use at all of their pikes, except serving to recruit and support the first five ranks, as we have shown before. If, then, five of their ranks could keep off the enemy's cavalry, why cannot five of ours do the same thing since they also have other ranks in their rear to support them—although they do not have pikes like the others? And if the ranks of pikemen extraordinary placed on the flanks of our army seem to you too thin, they may be reduced into a square and posted on the flanks of the two battalions in the rear; from this place they may aid either the front or the rear, and occasionally assist the cavalry.

Luigi. Would you, then, always use this form and order of battle whenever you want to engage an enemy?

Fabrizio. No indeed. As I shall show you before we part, I would always suit my order of battle to the nature of my ground and the quality and number of the enemy. But I recommended this order not only as the best, which it certainly is, but as a rule to direct and assist you in forming others—every art has its general rules and principles upon which it is founded. One thing, however, I would have you remember: never on any occasion draw up an army so that the front cannot be relieved by the rear; whoever is guilty of that error prevents the greatest part of his army from doing him any service at all, and will never win a victory over an enemy who has the least degree of either courage or conduct.

Luigi. I confess I have still another objection to the order in which you disposed your army. You made your front consist of five battalions, posted on each other's flank, your second line of three battalions, and your third line of two battalions. Now I should think it would be better to invert that order, for surely it must be more difficult to break the army that is stronger and stronger the farther you penetrate into it, than another army that is weaker and weaker.

Fabrizio. If you will please recollect that the third line in the Roman legions was composed of only 600 *triarii* and that they were placed in the rear, you would drop your objection; for you see according to that model, I have placed only two battalions in the rear, yet it consists of 900 men. So, if I have been guilty of any error in following the example of the Romans in that respect, it is by making my rear stronger than they did. Now although the authority alone of such an example might serve as a sufficient answer to your objection, yet I shall give you my reasons for what I have done. The front ranks of an army ought always to be solid and compact because they are to sustain the enemy's first shock, and they have no friends to receive into them; thus, they should be close and full of men, otherwise they will be loose and feeble. But since the second line is occasionally to receive the first into it before it is to engage, there should be large intervals left in it for that purpose. Therefore, this line must not consist of as many men as the first: if their number were larger or just equal, either you must leave no intervals—which would cause confusion; or you will have a longer line than the first, if you do—which will make it out of proportion and give it a strange appearance.

As to what you say about the enemy's finding our army weaker and weaker the deeper he penetrates into it, this is a manifest error; for the enemy cannot engage the second line until he has received the first into it. So, the enemy will find the second line much stronger than the first was when they are both united, and they will find the third line even stronger than either of the other two because these lines will then have the strength of the whole army to cope with at once; and since the third line is to receive more men than the second, it is necessary for it to have larger intervals in it and consequently to consist of fewer men.

Luigi. I am thoroughly satisfied on this point. But if the five battalions in the front retire into the three that are in the second line, and afterwards those eight retire into the two that are in the rear, it does not seem possible that the eight battalions in the second line—much less the ten in the third—can be contained in the same space of ground that the first five were.

Fabrizio. To this I answer, first, that the space of ground is not the same in that case; there were intervals between the first five battalions which are filled up when they retire into the second line, and when the second retires into the third; there was also an interval between the two regiments, and one between them and the pikemen extraordinary—together they afford them enough room. Besides, the battalions take up different spaces of ground when they keep their ranks and when they are disordered; for in the latter case, the men either get closer together or extend themselves. They extend themselves when they are so hard pressed that they are about to run away; they keep closer together when they are determined to make an obstinate resistance. I might add that when the five ranks of pikemen in the front have done their business, they retire through the intervals between the battalions into the rear to make way for the shieldbearers to advance upon the enemy. There they will be ready for any service for which the general shall think fit to employ them; for in the front, after the two armies were closely engaged, they could be of no further use; thus, the space allotted will be sufficient to contain the whole army. But if it should not, since the flanks are composed of men and not stone walls, they can easily open and extend themselves so as to make enough room.

Luigi. When the five first battalions retire into the three in the second line, would you have the pikemen extraordinary—whom you place in the flanks of your army—stand fast in their ranks and form two wings, as it were, to the army, or would you have them retire with the battalions too? In the latter case, I cannot imagine how they are to retire since they have no battalions in their rear with proper intervals to receive them.

Fabrizio. If the enemy does not attack them at the same time that the battalions are forced to retire, those pikemen may continue firm in their station and take the enemy at his flanks as they are pressing upon the battalions in their retreat; but if they are attacked at the same time, as they most likely will be, they also must retire; they may do this very handily, although they have no battalions in their rear to receive them, by doubling their ranks in a right line to the center and receiving one rank into another, as I showed you a while ago. But to double them in order to retreat, you must observe a different method from the one I spoke of then; in that case, I told you the first rank must receive the second, the third the fourth, and so on; but in this you must begin in the rear instead of the front, so that the ranks may retreat and not advance in doubling each other.

But to answer everything that may be objected to the way in which I conducted the late battle, I must beg leave to say again that I drew the battalion up and caused it to engage first, to show you how an army ought to be formed in order of battle; second, to show you how it ought to be drilled. No doubt you perfectly comprehend the order now; as for drilling, I say that the regiments ought to be joined and drilled in this manner as often as possible, so that the officers may learn to post their battalions in their proper places; for, just as every private should know his own rank and place in that rank, so every lieutenant colonel should know where to station his battalion in the army; all of them should learn to obey their general. They should also know how to join one battalion with another and to take their respective posts instantly; for this purpose, the colors of every battalion should have their number marked upon them so as to be visible to everyone—not only to distinguish the battalions from one another, but also to make it easier for the lieutenant colonel of every battalion, and his men, to know where to find each other. The regiments also ought to be numbered, and their numbers marked upon the colonel's colors. Thus, it would be known which regiment is posted on the right and which on the left, what battalions are placed in the first, second, or third line, etc.

There also should be several steps and gradations to preferment in our army. For instance, the lowest officer should be a corporal, the next above him a captain of fifty ordinary velites; the next, a captain of a company in the battalions; the next, the lieutenant colonel of the tenth battalion; the next, the lieutenant colonel of the ninth; the next, the lieutenant colonel of the eighth, and so on in succession until you come to the lieutenant colonel of the first battalion, who should be next in command to the colonel of the regiment; nobody should be advanced to this post until he has passed through all the subordinate degrees just now mentioned. But since there are also three lieutenant colonels of the pikemen extraordinary and two of the extraordinary velites, I would have them rank with the lieutenant colonel of the tenth battalion; I see nó absurdity in having six officers of equal rank in the same regiment, since it may serve to create emulation among them and inspire each one of them to conduct himself so as to be thought worthy of being preferred to the command of the ninth battalion. When each of these officers knows where his corps is to be posted, and as soon as the general's standard is erected, the whole army will immediately be in proper order. This is the first drill exercise to which an army should be accustomed: to range itself immediately in order of battle; to do this, it should be drawn up and separated again not just every day, but several times a day.

Luigi. What other distinctive marks would you have on the colors besides their particular number?

Fabrizio. The general's standard should have the arms of his prince upon it; the other standards may have the same, with some variation of the field or colors as the prince shall think fit; that is a matter of no great moment, provided they are sufficient to distinguish one corps from another.

But let us now pass on to another sort of exercise in which an army ought to be very ready and expert; that is, learning to move at a due pace and distance, and to keep its ranks when it is marching.

The third kind of exercise is teaching men to act as they should when they are actually engaged with an enemy; to discharge the artillery, to draw it off; to make the velites extraordinary begin the attack, and then retire; to make the first line fall back into the second as if it were hard pressed, and then the second into the third; afterward, to resume their first stations; and to habituate them so frequently to these and other such exercises that each man may know every part of his duty, which will soon become easy and familiar to him by practice.

The next exercise is instructing your men in the nature of signals, and in how to act by the beat of a drum, the sound of a trumpet, or the special motion of the colors; they will easily understand orders given by word of mouth. And since different notes and sounds are of great importance, and since they have various effects, I shall tell you what sorts of military music were used by the ancients. The Lacedaemonians, as Thucydides informs us,[10] used flutes in their armies, as the most proper instrument to make them move regularly and resolutely, but not precipitously. The Carthaginians, for the same reason, used citharas in their first attack.[11] Alyattes, king of Lydia, used both;[12] but Alexander the Great and the Romans used horns and trumpets,[13] which they thought the fittest instruments to rouse the courage of their men and to inspire them with martial ardor. But since we have imitated

10 Thucydides, V. 70.

11 The reference should probably be to the Cretans instead of the Carthaginians. See Burd, "Le fonti letterarie," pp. 208–209.

12 Herodotus, I. 17.

13 For the Romans, Vegetius, II. 22. It is uncertain that Alexander's army used horns. See Burd, p. 209 and n. 2.

both the Greeks and Romans in arming our men, we shall also borrow our military music from each of those nations. The general, then, should have his trumpets about him, since they are the most proper instruments for inspiring his army, and since they can be heard farther than any other. The lieutenant colonels, and other battalion officers, should have small drums and flutes, not to be played upon as they commonly are, but to be played in the same manner that they are sounded at great banquets and other festivities. With these trumpets the general can immediately make his army understand when he would have it halt, advance, or retreat, when he would have the artillery discharged, and when he would have the velites extraordinary move forward; by various notes and sounds he can acquaint them with all the different maneuvers he thinks need to be made; these signals should afterward be repeated by the drums; and the whole army should frequently be drilled in this exercise because it is of the utmost consequence. As for the cavalry, they may have trumpets too, but of a smaller size and of a different sound. This is all that occurs to me at present concerning the forming and exercising of an army.

Luigi. I have only one more question to ask; I hope it will not tire your patience if I ask why in the recent battle the velites extraordinary and light cavalry began the attack with a great shout, whereas there was a dead silence when the rest of the army began to engage? I confess I am at a loss to account for this, and therefore beg you to explain it to us.

Fabrizio. The opinions of ancient authors vary concerning this matter; that is, whether those beginning the battle should rush on with furious shouts and outcries, or march up to the attack with silence and composure. The latter is certainly the most proper means of preserving good order, and of hearing commands more distinctly; the former is certainly the most proper means of inspiring your own men and dismaying the enemy; as I think some regard ought to be had for all these circumstances, I made one part of my army begin with a great shout and the other with deep silence. But I do not think a continual shout can be of any service; quite the contrary, it will prevent the general's orders from being heard—this must be attended with terrible consequences. Nor is it reasonable to suppose that the Romans used any such shouts after the first onset; we read in many parts of their history that when their armies were beginning to give way, they were often prevented by the exhortations and reproaches of their commanders; we also read that their order of battle was sometimes changed, even in the heat of action. These things could not have been done if the voice of the officers had been drowned in the shouts of the soldiers.

BOOK FOUR

LUIGI. SINCE we have gained one glorious victory under my auspices, I do not care to tempt so fickle and inconstant a deity as Fortune any further. Consequently, I desire to give up my post to Zanobi Buondelmonti, the youngest man in the company who has not yet filled it, according to the order agreed upon; I dare say he will accept that honor, or rather trouble, as much out of graciousness to me as out of his natural courage, which is greater than mine; he will not be afraid of risking another battle in which he has a chance to be beaten as well as to be victorious.

Zanobi. Sir, I shall willingly accept whatever you think fit to confer upon me, although I confess I would much rather have continued an auditor; the questions you proposed and the objections you stated while you were in the post you now desire to resign were much more pertinent and necessary than any occurring to me. But so as not to waste any more time in ceremonies that may perhaps be disagreeable to Signor Fabrizio, let us entreat him to proceed, if we have not already trespassed too much upon his patience.

Fabrizio. That I shall do with great pleasure, especially since this change of persons will give me an opportunity of seeing the difference in your respective judgments and dispositions. But I should like to know whether you have any more questions to ask relating to the matter in which we were last engaged.

Zanobi. I could wish to be informed of three things before we leave it. First, is there any other way of forming an army in order of battle that you can think of at present? Next, what precautions are necessary before a general leads his army into an engagement with the enemy, and, if any accident or disorder should happen during the battle, how is it to be remedied?

Fabrizio. I shall endeavor to give you what satisfaction I can on these points. But I shall not answer your questions separately and distinctly; what I shall say in answer to one question may sometimes possibly also serve as an answer to another.

Previously I told you I gave you a general order of battle that you might easily change into any other, as the number and quality of the enemy and the nature of your ground required; you must always act according to those circumstances. But remember that unless your army is very numerous, you cannot be guilty of a greater or more fatal error than making a large, extensive front; if it is not numerous, you ought by all means to form it so that it will be greater in depth than in width. For when your army is not as large as the enemy's, you must resort to other expedients, such as drawing it up so that it may be flanked by some river swamp or securing its flanks by ditches and entrenchments to prevent its being surrounded,[1] as Julius Caesar used to do in his wars with the Gauls.[2]

But in such cases you must make it a general rule to contract or extend your front according to the number of your own men and those of the enemy. When the enemy is less numerous, you should endeavor to draw them into plains and open places, especially if your army is well disciplined, so that you may extend your front and surround them; for in rough and narrow places your numerical superiority will not be of any great advantage to you, because you cannot give your ranks the due extent. This is why the Romans always chose clear, open ground and avoided a rough and confined field of battle. On the contrary, if you have only a small and ill-disciplined army, you must seek out an advantageous location where you can shelter your men and where their inexperience cannot prejudice you much; it will be better still if

1 Vegetius, III. 20.
2 Caesar, *Gallic War* II. 8; VII. 72.

your site is elevated from whence you may fall upon the enemy with greater advantage. You should take care, however, not to draw up your army either on the declivity of a hill or on any place near its base where an enemy may get above you; in that case you will be much annoyed by their artillery, and your men so embarrassed that you cannot annoy the enemy again with your own cannon.

Great attention also should be paid to the wind and sun in forming any army for battle; [3] for if you have them in your face, one will dazzle your sight with its rays, and the other will blind you with dust. Besides, when the wind is against you, it will diminish the force of your blows; as for the sun, you must be careful that it is not in your face when the battle begins, and that it may not afterward be troublesome to you. To do this you should contrive, if possible, to have it full upon your back at first, so that it may be a long time before it comes upon your face—as Hannibal did at Cannae, [4] and as Marius did when he defeated the Cimbri. [5] If you are inferior to the enemy in cavalry, post your army among vineyards, hedges, and other such impediments, when you have an opportunity, as the Spaniards did long ago when they beat the French at Cerignola in the kingdom of Naples. [6] It also has often happened that the same armies beaten by others have beaten them again in their turn, only by changing their order and their ground; the Carthaginians, for instance, defeated several times by Marcus Regulus in rough and narrow defiles, were at last victorious by the conduct of Xanthippus the Lacedaemonian who advised them to come down into the plains where they availed themselves of their elephants and cavalry and defeated the Romans. [7]

I have observed from the conduct of many great generals among the ancients that when they knew where the enemy

3 Vegetius, III. 14.

4 August 2, 216 B.C. Livy, XXII. 43. 10–11.

5 The battle of Campi Raudii in 101 B.C. See *Discourses*, II, 8; III, 37.

6 April 28, 1503. See *Discourses*, II, 17.

7 255 B.C. Polybius, I. 32–35. See *Discourses*, II, 18.

placed the main strength of their army, instead of employing the flower of their own forces, they appointed the worst of their troops to oppose them in that quarter and appointed the best of their troops to oppose the worst of the enemy; afterward when the battle had begun, they ordered their choicest troops not to press the enemy, but only to sustain the charge; they ordered the weakest to retire gradually into the rear of the army; by these means the best part of the enemy's army is surrounded, and while they consider themselves sure of a victory, they are presently thrown into confusion and routed. Thus, when Cornelius Scipio was sent into Spain against Hasdrubal the Carthaginian,[8] he was aware that Hasdrubal thought he would place the legions, his best troops, in the center of his army and that Hasdrubal would therefore do the same; when they engaged, Scipio changed his usual order of battle, placing the legions in the two wings and the worst of his forces in the center of his army. But just before the battle began, Scipio ordered the center to move forward very slowly and the two wings to advance briskly, so that only the wings of both armies were engaged, while the centers of each were at such a distance from one another that they could not come together in due time; since the strongest part of Scipio's army was engaged with the weakest of Hasdrubal's, the latter was entirely defeated.

This method might be practiced in those times, but it cannot be used now that artillery is in use; the distance which must be left between the center of each army would give the artillery time to fire again and again, and this would do as much damage as if they were closely engaged. It is time, therefore, to lay it aside, and resort to the method I prescribed a little while ago; that is, let the whole army engage, and the weakest part of it give way.

If your army is larger than the enemy's and you want to surround it without his discovering your design, let your own be drawn up with a front equal to his, and afterward, when the battle is begun, let your main body retire little by little, and

8 208–206 B.C. Livy, XXVIII. 14; Polybius, XI. 22.

let the wings extend themselves; thus the enemy will find himself surrounded and entangled before he is aware of it.

When a general would fight and secure his army in such a manner that he may be almost certain of not being routed, he should post it in a place from which he may easily and presently retreat into a safe and defensible situation, such as into a swamp, or among mountains, or into a strong fortress—places where the enemy cannot pursue him, although he may pursue them. Such was the means Hannibal used when *fortuna* began to become unfavorable and he began to be afraid of Marcus Marcellus.[9] Some generals, in order to disturb and disconcert the enemy, have ordered their light-armed troops to begin the battle and then to retire into their proper station again; after both armies were warmly engaged, they were ordered to sally out from the flanks again and make a second attack; this attack has sometimes succeeded so well that the enemy has been thrown into disorder and routed by it. If you are inferior to the enemy in cavalry (besides the methods already recommended), you should place a body of pikemen in their rear; in the heat of action, let the cavalry open to the right and left in order to make way for the pikemen to advance upon the enemy—this will certainly give you the advantage over them. Some generals have accustomed part of their light-armed infantry to mingle with their cavalry and to fight in conjunction with them; this has been of very great service to them.

But of all those who have excelled in drawing up armies in order of battle, without a doubt Hannibal and Scipio showed the most consummate skill and abilities in the African wars; [10] since Hannibal's army consisted not only of Carthaginians, but also of auxiliaries from various nations, he placed 80 elephants in his front; next to them, his auxiliaries; behind

[9] M. Claudius Marcellus held Nola and resisted an attack of Hannibal in 216 B.C. Livy, XXIII. 16; XXVII. 12, 14. See *Discourses*, II, 2.

[10] Zama, 202 B.C. Hannibal's last battle, and the end of the Second Punic War. Livy, XXX. 32 ff.; Polybius, XV. 9 ff.; Frontinus, II. 3. 16. See *Discourses*, II, 27.

them, his Carthaginians; and last of all, his Italians, in whom he had but little confidence. He adopted this disposition so that his auxiliaries, with the enemy in their front and the Carthaginians in their rear, would not have an opportunity of running away if they were so inclined; since they were forced to fight, he hoped they might either break or disconcert the Romans in such a manner that when he advanced with a fresh body of his best troops, he might entirely defeat them. Scipio, on the other hand, according to the usual Roman manner, drew up his three lines of *hastati, principes,* and *triarii* into such order that they might easily support or receive one another. In the front ranks of his army, he left several intervals opposite Hannibal's elephants; but to make the army appear close and united, he filled these intervals with velites whom he ordered to give way as soon as the elephants advanced upon them and to retire through the ordinary spaces into the legions in order to leave a free passage for the elephants. He thus evaded the fury of those beasts, and, engaging the enemy, entirely defeated them.

Zanobi. Now that you mention the battle, I remember having read in some account of it that Scipio did not let the *hastati* retire into the line of the *principes,* but had them file off to the right and left and take a post in his army's flanks to make room for the *principes* to advance. Now, I should like to know for what reason he deviated from the usual order and discipline of the Romans upon this occasion.

Fabrizio. I shall tell you. Hannibal had placed the strength of his army in the second line; Scipio, therefore, in order to oppose him with equal force, joined his *principes* and *triarii* together so that the intervals among the *principes* were occupied by the *triarii* and there was no room left to receive the *hastati;* hence, he had them open to the right and left and wheel off to the flanks. But remember that this method of opening the first line to make room for the second to advance cannot be used except when you have the advantage over the enemy—then it can be easily practiced, as it was by Scipio. But if you have the worst of the battle and are repulsed, you cannot do it without exposing yourself to the danger of a total defeat; therefore, it is necessary on these occasions to have intervals in the second and third lines for receiving your men. But to return to our subject.

Among other inventions the ancient Asiatics had for annoying their enemy were chariots with scythes fixed to their axletrees; these scythes served not only to open the enemy's ranks, but to mow them down as they drove through them. Now, their enemies had three ways of guarding against these dangerous machines: they drew up in such close order that the scythes could make no impression upon them; they received them into the intervals between the battalions, as Scipio did the elephants; or they made some strong fences against them. This is the method Sulla used in the battle he fought with Archelaus,[11] who had a great number of these armed chariots; in the ground before his first line he fixed several rows of sharp pointed stakes or palisades which stopped the course of the chariots and prevented the damage they must otherwise have done. The new method which Sulla used in drawing up his army at that time is also noteworthy; he placed his velites and light cavalry in the rear and all his heavy-armed men in the front, leaving several intervals there through which those in the rear might advance when required, and won a complete victory.

In order to throw the enemy into confusion after the battle has begun, it is necessary to resort to some invention that can strike terror into them; you may do this either by spreading a report that you have supplies coming up, or by making a false show of such supplies at a distance—this has often occasioned such consternation in an army that it has been immediately defeated. This stratagem was put into practice by the Roman consuls Minucius Rufus and Acilius Glabrio;[12] Caius

11 Battle of Cheronea, 86 B.C. Frontinus, II. 3. 17.

12 Q. Minucius Rufus defeated the Scordiscans and Dacians by this ruse in 109 B.C. The consul, Manius Acilius Glabrio, repulsed the army of Antiochus III of Syria at the Pass of Thermopylae in Greece in 191 B.C. Frontinus, II. 4. 3–4; Livy, XXXVI. 14 ff.

Sulpicius also mounted a great number of sutlers and servants following his camp upon mules and other beasts that were of no service in battle; having drawn them up and accoutered them like a body of cavalry, he ordered them to appear on a neighboring hill as soon as he was engaged with the Gauls; this had such an effect that he soon routed them.[13] The same was done by Marius in a battle which he fought with the Germans.[14]

If, then, these false alarms have such consequences in the heat of an action, what may not be expected from a real one; especially if the enemy is suddenly and unexpectedly attacked in either the flank or the rear when they are engaged in the front? But this is no easy matter to effect unless you are favored in it by the nature of the country; if it be plain and open, you cannot conceal a part of your forces as would be necessary upon similar occasions; but if it abounds with woods or mountains, you may lie in ambush and, when he least expects it, fall suddenly upon an enemy and be assured of success.

It is also sometimes of great service in time of battle to circulate a report that the enemy's general is killed, or that one part of his army is giving way; it has not been unusual to throw cavalry into disorder by strange noises and uncommon appearances; thus Croesus brought a great number of camels against the enemy's cavalry,[15] and Pyrrhus used elephants against the Romans' cavalry; this occasioned great confusion and disturbance among them.[16] Not long ago, the Grand Turk routed the shah of Persia and the sultan of Syria merely

13 358 B.C. C. Sulpicius Peticus, consul in 364 and 361, was dictator in this year. Frontinus, II. 4. 5; Livy, VII. 12–15. See *Discourses*, III, 10, 14.

14 C. Marius overcame the Teutons at Aquae Sextiae in 102 B.C. Frontinus, II. 4. 6. See *Discourses*, II, 8.

15 Croesus, king of Lydia, in a battle on the plain before Sardis against Cyrus the Great in 546 B.C. See Frontinus, II. 4. 12. The stratagem, however, is usually attributed to Cyrus, who defeated Croesus and then captured Sardis. See Herodotus, I. 80; Xenophon, *Cyropaedia* VII. 1. 27. 48–49.

16 Pyrrhus, king of Epirus, who was fighting for the Tarentines against the Romans at the battle of Heraclea in 280 B.C. Frontinus, II. 4. 13. See *Discourses*, II, 1.

by the use of harquebuses—their explosion struck such terror into his enemies' cavalry that they turned tail and ran away.[17] The Spaniards, in their battles with Hamilcar, used to place ox-drawn carriages full of flax in the front of their armies; they set fire to the flax as soon as the battle began, and the oxen were so frightened that they rushed in among the enemy and opened their ranks.[18]

Where the nature of the terrain is such that you cannot draw the enemy into an ambush easily, you may, however, dig ditches and pitfalls in the plains, cover them over lightly with brushwood and clods, and leave areas of solid ground through which you may retire in the heat of the battle; if the enemy pursues, he is undone.

If you are aware of any accident happening during the action which you think may dispirit your men, it is best either to conceal it, if you can, or to give it such a turn as may serve to produce a quite different effect. This is what Tullus Hostilius[19] and, later, Lucius Sulla[20] did. The latter saw a body of his forces go over to the enemy he was fighting; seeing that the defection had greatly discouraged his own men, he immediately spread a report through his army that it was done for a secret purpose and by his own order; so, instead of being daunted, his men fought with greater courage and beat the enemy. The same commander sent a party of soldiers on an attack in which they were all killed; afraid the rumor might discourage the rest of his army, he said publicly that he had sent them on that errand purposely so that they would be cut off by the enemy since he knew they were a pack of rascals and traitors. Sertorius, in a battle with the Spaniards, killed

[17] In 1514, Selim I, called the Grand Turk by his contemporaries, defeated the shah of Persia, Ismail I, in eastern Anatolia. He overthrew the Mameluke dynasty in 1517 by completing the conquest of Syria and Egypt begun by his father, Bajazet II. See *Discourses*, III, 35.

[18] 229 2.3. Frontinus, II. 4. 17.

[19] Tullus Hostilius, third king of Rome, reigned, according to tradition, from 672 to 642 B.C. This incident occurred in 658 against the Veientians. Frontinus, II. 7. 1; Livy, I. 27. See *Discourses*, I, 22.

[20] Frontinus, II. 7. 2–3 for this and the following anecdote.

one of his men who brought him word that one of his generals was slain, because he feared that any news of the death would dampen the ardor of his army.[21]

It is a very difficult matter to stop an army beginning to run away, and to make it charge again. But here we must make a distinction between an army that is actually running away, when it is impossible to restore them, and one that is only partially in flight, when some remedy may be found. Some of the Roman generals restored order by reproaching their soldiers and upbraiding them about their cowardice, as we may cite in the conduct of Sulla, who, seeing part of his legions begin to flee before the army of Mithridates, rode up to the head of them with a drawn sword in his hand, and cried out, "If anybody should inquire after your general, tell them you left him fighting on the plains of Boeotia."[22] The Roman consul Atilius detached a body of his best troops to stop the flight of some others who were running away; he told them that if they did not turn back, they would be attacked by their own friends as well as by the enemy.[23] Philip of Macedon, finding some of his troops were afraid of the Scythians, posted a body of cavalry—in whom he had much confidence— in the rear of his army with orders to kill any man attempting to quit his rank; when the rest heard this, they chose to hazard their lives in battle rather than to be unmercifully killed if they fled; they fought so manfully that they beat the Scythians.[24] Several of the Roman generals have taken a pair of colors out of the hands of an ensign in the heat of battle and thrown it into the middle of the enemy with a promise of a reward to those retaking it; but this was done not so much to prevent their running away, as to create a rivalry among their soldiers and to encourage them to fight with greater ardor.

[21] 75 B.C. Q. Sertorius turned against Pompey. Frontinus, II. 7. 5. The slain general was Hirtuleius.

[22] Battle of Orchomenus in 86 B.C. Frontinus, II. 8. 12.

[23] M. Atilius Regulus, during the Samnite War in 294 B.C. Frontinus, II. 8. 11; IV. 1. 29; and Livy, X. 36.

[24] Philip II of Macedon in 339 B.C. Frontinus, II. 8. 11.

Having now spoken of things that have to be done not only before a battle but during the period of action, perhaps it may not be amiss to say something about what ought to be done after the battle is over, especially since I shall be very brief on this point; still, it should not be omitted because it is a part of our system. I say, then, that when you have won a victory, you ought by all means to pursue it, and to imitate Julius Caesar rather than Hannibal in this respect; the latter lost the empire of Rome by trifling away his time at Capua, after he had routed the Romans at the battle of Cannae.[25] Caesar, on the other hand, never rested after a victory; he always pursued and harassed the enemy after they were broken and were fleeing, with greater vigor and fury than when he first attacked them.

But when a general happens to lose a battle, he is to consider first how to make the best of his loss, particularly if he has any considerable force left. Perhaps he may reap some advantage from the enemy's neglect, tardiness, or inadvertency. After a victory, soldiers often grow too remiss and secure and give the army they have beaten an opportunity to beat them; this is what L. Marcius did to the Carthaginians who, having slain the two Scipios in battle and defeated their armies, took little account of the forces left under the command of Marcius until he attacked and routed them.[26] Hence we see that nothing is as easy to effect as what the enemy imagines you will never attempt, and we see that men are frequently in the greatest danger when they think themselves most secure.

But if a general can reap no sort of advantage from his first

[25] 216 B.C., during the Second Punic War, when Hannibal's cavalry tactics out-maneuvered, surrounded, and defeated the Roman army led by L. Aemilius Paullus and C. Terentius Varro. The reference to the enervating effect of Hannibal's wintering at Capua—rich, luxurious, lazy—is a standard rhetorical commonplace among moralists.

[26] 212 B.C. Machiavelli is relying upon Frontinus, II. 10. 2, who refers to Titus Marcius. However, in Livy, XXV. 37, the praenomen is Lucius. The two Scipios are Gnaeus Cornelius Scipio Calvus, consul in 222 B.C., and his younger brother, Publius Cornelius Scipio, also consul in the same year, and father of Scipio Africanus the Elder.

loss, he should by all means endeavor at least to make it as light and bearable as he can and to prevent any further damage; he thus ought to use every method either to divide or to retard the enemy if they pursue him. In the first case, when they are aware that they can no longer stand their ground, some generals have ordered their subordinate commanders to separate and retreat with their forces by different routes to some appointed rendezvous; this has made the enemy afraid of dividing his forces and made him let all or most of them escape. In the second case, many generals have thrown their baggage and effects onto the road, so that while the enemy was busy plundering and ransacking, they might have time to save themselves. The artifice made use of by Titus Didius to conceal the loss he had sustained in battle is not unworthy of notice: after he had fought from morning until night and lost a great number of his men, he ordered most of them to be buried during the night, so that the next day, the enemy, seeing so many of his own men—and so few Romans—killed, considered himself worsted and immediately began to retreat.[27]

And now I think, to a great extent, I have answered your questions, although perhaps not as distinctly and particularly as you expected. It is true, I have yet to add something concerning the method of forming armies in order of battle, since some generals have drawn up their forces in the shape of a wedge, with its edge in the front, imagining that form to be the best adapted for penetrating and opening an enemy's ranks.[28] To provide against this, the other side ordinarily drew up their army in the form of a pair of open shears, to receive the wedge in the vacuity, and so to surround and attack it on every side. Let me recommend a general rule to you: *to frustrate any of your enemy's designs, it is best to do of your own volition what he endeavors to force you to do.* Then you may proceed in a cool and orderly manner to turn to your advantage what he intended as the means of your ruin; but if you

[27] Titus Didius, consul in 98 B.C., fought in Spain from 98 to 93. Frontinus, II. 10. 1.

[28] Vegetius, III. 19.

are compelled to do it, you will surely be undone. To confirm the truth of this, it is needless to repeat what I have said before; for when the enemy advances in a wedge—intending to open, and as it were, to cleave your army asunder—if you open it yourself in the above-mentioned form it is certain that you will cut him to pieces and that he cannot much hurt you. Hannibal placed elephants in the front of his army to break in upon Scipio's, but once Scipio opened a way for them himself, he won a complete victory.[29] Hasdrubal also posted the flower of his army in the center of his front for the same purpose; but Scipio, ordering his front to open and file off, disappointed his intention and defeated him.[30] So, when such designs are known, they are generally frustrated and prove the ruin of the contrivers.

I think I also have something left to say relating to the precautions a general should take before he leads his army to battle; in the first place, it is my opinion that he should never engage unless he has an advantage over the enemy, or he is compelled to act. Now the advantage may arise from the terrain or from the order, superiority, or bravery of his army; he may be compelled to engage by a conviction that if he does not, he must inevitably be ruined. Such ruin may occur either when he has no money to pay his troops and they begin to mutiny and talk of disbanding, or when he has no provisions left and must otherwise be starved, or when he knows the enemy expects to be reinforced; in such circumstances he always ought to engage because it is better to try *fortuna* while she is still favorable than to try nothing and allow her surely to destroy you.[31] Therefore, it is as great a fault in a general not to hazard an engagement upon such occasions, as it is if he had a fair opportunity of gaining a victory and neglected it out of either ignorance or cowardice.

Some advantages may result from the enemy's negligence

[29] Battle of Zama, 202 B.C.

[30] Scipio, while driving the Carthaginians out of Spain, defeated Hasdrubal at Becula in 208 B.C.

[31] See *Discourses*, I, 22, 23.

and misconduct, and others from your own vigilance and good conduct: many armies have been routed while fording rivers by an enemy who has waited till one half of them have been transported and then fallen upon them; this is what Caesar did to the Helvetii when he cut off a fourth of their army which was separated from the rest by a river they had forded.[32] Sometimes an enemy is so jaded and fatigued by too rash and hasty a pursuit that if your men have had a little time to rest and refresh themselves, you have nothing to do but to face about and win a victory. If an enemy offers you battle early in the morning, you ought not to draw out your army to fight him immediately; rather, let his men wait under arms for some hours until their ardor is abated and then come out of your entrenchments and engage him, as Scipio and Metellus did in Spain—the former when he had Hasdrubal upon his hands, and the latter, Sertorius.[33] If the enemy has diminished his strength by dividing his army, as the Scipios did in Spain, or for any other reason, by no means ought you to miss that opportunity of fighting him.

Most prudent generals have chosen to receive the enemy rather than to attack him, because the fury of the first shock is easily withstood by men standing firm, resolute, ready, and prepared in their ranks; when that shock is over, their fury commonly subsides into languor and despair. By proceeding in this manner, Fabius routed both the Samnites and the Gauls; but his colleague Decius took the other course, was defeated, and slain.[34] Some generals, who have thought the

32 Caesar, *Gallic War* I. 12.

33 Publius Cornelius Scipio Africanus the Elder defeated Hasdrubal in 208 B.C.; Frontinus, II. 1. 1; Livy, XXVIII. 15. According to Frontinus, the other battle (76 B.C.) was between the forces of Caecilius Metellus Pius and of Hirtuleius, a lieutenant of Sertorius. Machiavelli confuses this incident with the one Frontinus describes in his next paragraph. After the defeat of Hirtuleius, Metellus joined Pompey against Sertorius; Metellus decided to withdraw rather than fight because of the enemy's great spirit and enthusiasm. Frontinus, II. 1. 2–3.

34 Q. Fabius Maximus Rullianus and Publius Decius Mus the Younger at the battle of Sentinum in 295 B.C. Frontinus, II. 1. 8; Livy, X. 28. See *Discourses*, III, 45.

enemy superior to them, have chosen to defer a battle until evening, so that if they should be defeated, they might save themselves under the shelter of night; others who have known that the enemy would not fight at particular times, out of reverence to the laws of their religion, have taken that opportunity to attack and defeat them; Julius Caesar availed himself of this advantage against Ariovistus in Gaul,[35] and Vespasian against the Jews in Syria.[36]

But above all,[37] a general should take care to have men of proven fidelity, wisdom, and long experience in military affairs near his person as a sort of council. From such men a general may learn not only the state of his own army, but also that of the enemy's: which of the armies is superior to the other in number, which is the better armed and disciplined, which is the stronger in cavalry, which of his own troops are fittest to undergo hard service and fatigue, and whether his infantry or his cavalry is likely to be the most serviceable. Let his councilors well consider the nature of the terrain where they are: whether it is more advantageous to the enemy or themselves; which of the two armies can be most conveniently furnished with provisions and other supplies; whether it is better to come to an engagement directly, or to defer it; and what advantage or disadvantage may accrue from time; for it sometimes happens that when soldiers see a war protracted and a battle put off from time to time, they lose their ardor and become so weary of hardships that they grow mutinous and desert their colors. It is also of great importance to know the qualities and disposition of the enemy's general and of those about him, for instance, to know whether he is bold and enterprising, or cautious and timid. A general should next consider to what extent he can have confidence in his auxiliaries. He should be particularly careful not to bring his army to an engagement if he perceives his men are in the least dis-

---

35 58 B.C. Frontinus, II. 1. 16; cf. Caesar, *Gallic War* I. 50.

36 The Emperor Vespasian in A.D. 70. Frontinus, II. 1. 17.

37 Much of the advice in the remainder of the speech follows Vegetius, III. 9.

pirited or diffident about victory, for it is a bad omen indeed when they think an enemy invincible. In such circumstances, either you must endeavor to avoid a battle by following the example of Fabius Maximus,[38] who always took the advantage of situations in which Hannibal dared not attack him, or—if you think the enemy will not attack you, however advantageous your situation may be—you must leave the field entirely and distribute your forces in different towns and fortresses to tire him out with sieges and blockades.

Zanobi. Is there no other way of avoiding an engagement?

Fabrizio. I think I told some of you in a conversation we had once before that an army in the field cannot possibly avoid an engagement if the enemy is absolutely determined to fight, unless it suddenly decamps, moves to a distance of 50 or 60 miles from the enemy, and always keeps retreating as the enemy advances. Fabius Maximus never refused to fight Hannibal, but did not choose to do so without an advantage; and Hannibal, considering the manner in which Fabius always took care to fortify himself, was too wise to force him to it; but if Fabius had been attacked, he would have been forced to fight him at any cost, or to have fled. When Philip of Macedon, the father of Perseus, was at war with the Romans, he encamped on top of a very high hill to avoid an engagement with them, but they attacked and routed him there.[39] Cingetorex, general of the Gauls, retreated to a considerable distance so that he would not be obliged to fight Julius Caesar who, contrary to his expectation, had suddenly forded a river that was between them.[40] The Venetians, in the recent wars, might have avoided a battle with the French if they had marched

[38] Q. Fabius Maximus Cunctator, so called because of his cautious policy in dealing with Hannibal. He is not to be confused with the Q. Fabius Maximus Rullianus of n. 34 above. See *Prince,* 17; *Discourses,* I, 53; III, 9, 10, 40.

[39] For both examples, see *Discourses,* III, 10. Here, and for the remainder of Book IV, Machiavelli is discussing Q. Fabius Maximus Cunctator. The battle Philip of Macedon fought was at Cynocephalae in 197 B.C.

[40] 52 B.C. Not Cingetorex, but Vercingetorix. Caesar, *Gallic War* VII. 35.

away from them, as Cingetorex did from Caesar, instead of waiting until they forded the Adda; but they did not take the opportunity of attacking them while they were fording that river—afterward, they could not retreat, for the French were then so close at their heels that as soon as the Venetians began to decamp, the French fell upon them and defeated them.[41] In short, there is no other way of avoiding a battle, if the enemy is fully determined to bring you to one; therefore, it is to no purpose to cite the example of Fabius Maximus, for in that case Hannibal avoided an engagement as much as Fabius.

It often happens that soldiers are eager to fight; by considering the superiority of the enemy, the nature of the terrain, or some other circumstances, you know that you are at a disadvantage, and therefore would willingly decline a battle. It may also happen that necessity may force you—or opportunity may invite you—to fight, but you find your soldiers dispirited and averse to it; in the one case, it is necessary to repress their ardor, and in the other, to excite it. In the first case, when persuasion and exhortation have no effect, it is best to let some part of them be roughly handled by the enemy, so that both those who have suffered and those who have not may learn to be more tractable and conformable to your will another time. What was the effect of chance in the army of Fabius Maximus may be done deliberately by any other commander upon a similar occasion. It happened that not only his cavalry general, but all the rest of his army, were very impatient to fight Hannibal,[42] though Fabius himself was utterly against it; the dissension grew to such a height that at last they divided the army between them. Fabius, with his troops, kept close in his entrenchments. Minucius went out and engaged the enemy, but he would have been entirely defeated if Fabius had not finally marched out to his aid. From this example, both the general of his cavalry and all the rest of the army were con-

[41] Battle of Agnadello in 1509. See *Prince*, 20, 26; *Discourses*, I, 6; II, 10; III, 31.

[42] 217 B.C. The cavalry general was M. Minucius Rufus. Livy, XXII. 24 ff.

vinced that it would have been wiser to have submitted to the opinion of Fabius.

As for the means of animating your men and inflaming them with a desire to fight, it would be good first to enrage them against the enemy; to tell them they are despised; to insinuate that you have corrupted some enemy officers and hold a private correspondence with them; to camp in a location where you may daily see what they are doing and now and then skirmish with them; for things that are often seen eventually become familiar and are but little regarded.[43] If these measures fail, you should treat them with disdain and harangue them in a weighty and pitiless manner, upbraiding them for cowardice. You should endeavor to make them ashamed of themselves by telling them that if the rest have not courage enough to follow you, you will take such or such a regiment—one you know you can depend upon—and fight the enemy with that regiment alone. But to make your men bolder, more courageous, and more resolute, above all else you ought to take care that they may not send any of their money or plunder away to their own houses, or deposit it in any other safe place until the war is over; so, they may rest assured that if they run away, they may save their lives, perhaps, but they must certainly lose their treasure; the love of money ordinarily operates as strongly upon men as love of their life.

Zanobi. You say that one should inspire soldiers to fight by haranguing them. Would you harangue the whole army, then, or only the officers?

Fabrizio. It is an easy matter to induce a few people either to do or not to do a thing, for if arguments are not sufficient, you may use force and authority; but the great difficulty lies in making a whole army change its resolution when its execution must either prejudice the public, or thwart your own private schemes and designs; in that case, you can avail yourself of nothing but words, which must be heard and considered

43 Vegetius, III. 12. See *Discourses*, III, 37.

by the whole army if you would have the whole army affected by them. For this reason, it is necessary that a general should be an orator as well as a soldier; for if he does not know how to address himself to the whole army, he will sometimes find it no easy task to mold it to his purposes. But there is not the least attention shown to this point at present. Read the life of Alexander the Great,[44] and you will see how often he was obliged to harangue his troops; otherwise he never could have led them—rich and full of spoil as they were—through the deserts of India and Arabia where they underwent every sort of hardship and fatigue. Many things may prove the ruin of an army, if the general does not frequently harangue his men; for by so doing he may dispel their fears, inflame their courage, confirm their resolution, point out the snares laid for them, promise them rewards, inform them of danger and of the way to escape it; he may rebuke, entreat, threaten, praise, reproach, or fill them with hopes, and avail himself of all other arts that can either excite or allay the passions and the appetites of mankind. Therefore, if any prince or republic would make their armies respectable, they should accustom their generals to harangue the men and the men to listen to their generals.

Religion too, and the oath soldiers took when they were enlisted, greatly contributed to making them do their duty in ancient times; for upon any default, they were threatened not only with human punishments, but the vengeance of the gods.[45] They also had several other religious ceremonies that had a very good effect on all their enterprises, and would have still in any place where religion is held in due reverence. Sertorius knew this well; he used to have consultations with a hind that he said was sent by the gods to assure him of victory.[46] Sulla pretended to converse with an image he had taken out of the temple of Apollo,[47] and several generals have given

[44] Plutarch's.

[45] On the oath and religion in general see *Discourses*, I, 11–15; also p. 60 above and p. 165 below.

[46] Frontinus, I. 11. 13.

[47] Frontinus, I. 11. 11.

out that some god or other has appeared to them in dreams and visions and commanded them to fight the enemy. In the days of our ancestors, when Charles VII of France was at war with the English, he pretended to be advised in every thing by a virgin sent from heaven, commonly called the virgin of France,[48] who won him many a victory.

It is also proper to teach your men to hold the enemy in contempt, as Agesilaus the Spartan did when he showed his men some naked Persians so that, having seen their soft, white skins, his men would no longer have cause to fear them.[49]

Some commanders have forced their men to fight by depriving them of all means of saving themselves except victory; this is certainly the best method of making them fight desperately. This resolution is commonly heightened either by the confidence they put in themselves, their arms, armor, discipline, good order, and lately-won victories, or by the esteem they have for their general. Such esteem is a result of the opinion they have of his *virtù*, rather than of any particular favor they have received from him; or it is a result of the love of their country, which is natural to all men. There are various ways of forcing men to fight, but that is the strongest and most operative; it leaves men no other alternative but to conquer or to die.[50]

[48] Joan of Arc (1412–1431).

[49] Agesilaus II of Sparta defeated the Persians at Sardis in 395 B.C. Frontinus, I. 11. 18; Xenophon, *Hellenica* III. 4. 19; Plutarch, *Agesilaus* 9. The incident is most clearly explained by Xenophon. He writes that the Persians had such soft, white skin because they always wore clothes and rode in carriages; hence, seeing them stripped, the Spartans would conclude that their enemies were no better than women.

[50] For Machiavelli's important concept of necessity, see esp. *Discourses,* III, 12; also above, p. 76, n. 36; below, p. 175.

BOOK FIVE

Fabrizio. I have shown you how an army about to engage another ought to be formed, how an enemy may be defeated, and many other circumstances relating to it that may happen through various accidents and occurrences. I think it is now time, therefore, to show you how I would draw up an army that has not an enemy actually in sight but expects to be attacked suddenly, particularly when it is marching through an enemy's country or one suspected of inclining to the enemy.

You must know then, in the first place, that the Roman generals usually sent some cavalry troops ahead of their armies to reconnoiter the country and scour the roads; after them came the right wing with the carriages and baggage belonging to it in its rear; then followed one of the legions with its carriages; next, the other in the same manner; last came the left wing with its baggage, and the rest of the cavalry followed behind everything.[1] This was the order they commonly observed while marching, and if they were attacked in either the front or the rear, they immediately had all the carriages drawn off to the right or left, as best suited their convenience and the nature of the ground; after which, the whole army—freed from that incumbrance—faced about to the enemy. If they were attacked on the right flank, they drew off the carriages to the left, and vice versa, converting the flank attacked into a front. Since in my opinion this is a very good and orderly method, I think it is worthy of imitation; therefore, upon similar occasions, I would always send my light cavalry ahead of the army to reconnoiter the country and scour the roads; the four regiments of which it consists should march next, one after another, each with its own baggage in its rear. And as

1 Polybius, VI. 40.

there are two sorts of baggage, namely, that belonging to individuals and that used by the army in general, I should divide the latter into four parts and assign one-fourth of it to the care of each regiment. The artillery, sutlers, and others who attend the camp should also be distributed among them in the same manner, so that every regiment might have an equal share of the baggage train.

But since it sometimes occurs that you march through a country that is not merely your suspected, but your professed enemy, and where you hourly expect to be attacked, you will then be obliged for greater security to change the form and order of your march, and to draw up your men in such a manner that neither the peasants nor the enemy's army may find you unprepared to receive them on any side if they should suddenly attack you. In such cases, the generals of the ancients used to form their armies into an oblong square so that they might defend themselves on every side and be ready to fight as well as to march. I confess I like that disposition so well that I shall follow their example in drawing up the two regiments I have taken for the model of an army in the same manner upon similar occasions: that is, in an oblong square with a hollow in the middle and 424 feet on every side. My flanks would then be that distance from one another; in each of them I would place five battalions, one behind the other, with an interval of six feet between them, so that these battalions would take up a space 424 feet deep, including the intervals between them and supposing each battalion occupied 80 feet. In the front and rear of the hollow square in the middle, I would place the other ten battalions; that is, five of them in the front of it and five in the rear, in such a manner that four of them abreast of each other should be next to the front of the right flank, and four drawn up in the same manner next to the rear of the left, with an interval of eight feet between them. I would post another next to the front of the left flank, on a line with the first four, and another next to the rear of the right, also on a line with the other four there. Now since the distance from one flank to another is 424 feet and the battalions posted in the front of the square—including the intervals between them—will take up no more than 274 feet, there will remain a vacant space of 150 feet between the four battalions on the right and the single one on the left. There will also be the same room left between the battalions in the rear, without any difference except that the space in the front will be near the left flank and that in the rear near the right. I would place my ordinary velites in the former of these spaces, and my extraordinary in the latter; this would not amount to quite a thousand men in each space. But to arrange it so that the hollow square in the middle of the army should be 424 feet on every side, care must be taken that neither the five battalions posted in the front nor the other five in the rear may take up any part of the space included between the flanks. For this purpose, the last man on the right and left of the first rank of the battalions in the rear should be close—not in a straight line, but rather obliquely—with the innermost man in the last rank of each flank; the last man on the right and left of the last rank of the battalions in the front should be close, in the same manner, with the innermost man in the first rank of each flank; then there will be a space left at every angle of the army large enough to receive a body of 333 pikemen extraordinary. But since there would still be two more corps of pikemen extraordinary left, I would draw them up in a square in the middle of the area within the army; at the head of this square I would post the general himself, together with his staff.

Now, although these battalions thus drawn up all march in one direction, but may be obliged to fight on any side, you must take care to qualify them properly for that purpose; therefore, the first five battalions, protected on all sides but in the front, must be formed with their pikemen in their foremost ranks. The last five battalions are covered on every side except the rear and must therefore be formed with their pikemen in the rearmost ranks. For the same reason, each flank should have its pikemen in the outermost ranks. The corporals and other officers should take their proper posts at the same time, so that when the army engages, every corps and every member of that corps may be in due place, according to the order and method I described before when I was speaking of ranging an army in battle array.

I would distribute the artillery along each flank; the light cavalry should be sent before to reconnoiter the terrain and scour the roads; I would post the men-at-arms in the rear of each flank and at a distance of 80 feet from the battalions. For it should be a general rule in drawing up an army always to post your cavalry either on the flanks or in the rear, because if you post them in the front, you must do it at such a distance from the army that, should they be repulsed by the enemy, they may have time and room enough to wheel off without falling foul of your infantry, or you must leave proper intervals in the front to receive them so as not to disorder the rest of your forces. This is a matter that deserves to be remembered well, for many who have neglected these precautions have been thrown into disorder and routed by their own men.

The carriages, sutlers, and other unarmed people who follow the camp should be placed in the hollow square and arranged so that any person, when the occasion arises, may have a free passage through them, either from the front to the rear, or from one flank to another.

The depth of the whole army, when the battalions are thus disposed, will be 584 feet from front to rear, exclusive of the cavalry and artillery; since it is composed of two regiments, it must be considered how each of them is to be posted. Now since the regiments are distinguished by their respective marks and numbers, and each of them consists of ten battalions and a colonel, the first five battalions of the first regiment should be posted in the front of the army, and the other five in the left flank; the regimental colonel should take his station in the left angle of the front. After this, the first five battalions of the second regiment should be placed in the right flank, and the other five in the rear, with their colonel in the angle they make there, where he fulfills the function of a captain of the rear guard.[2]

When the army is thus formed, you have to put it in motion and to observe this order during your whole march, which will effectively secure you against any attack from the inhabitants of the country. All other provisions for that purpose are unnecessary, unless you shall now and then think it fit to send a troop or two of light cavalry, or a party of velites, to drive them away; for such types of disorderly persons are so afraid of regular forces that they will never come within reach of their pikes, much less of their swords; they may perhaps set up a great shout and make a feint of attacking you, like a parcel of curs barking at a mastiff to whom they dare not venture to come too near. Thus, all the time Hannibal was traversing Gaul to invade Italy, he took little or no account of the country people.[3] For the sake of convenience and speed on a march, you should send pioneers before the army to make a clear passage for it; and these pioneers should be covered by the light cavalry sent forward to reconnoiter the country. An army will march ten miles a day in this order with great ease and still have enough time to camp and refresh itself before dark, for the usual march of an army is about 20 miles a day.

If you should happen to be attacked by a regular army, it cannot be so suddenly that you will have insufficient time to put yourself into a proper defensive posture; for such an army must move in an orderly manner, and you will therefore be able to draw up your forces, either in the form I have been describing or in another of similar nature. For if you are attacked in the front, you have nothing to do but to draw your artillery from the flanks and your cavalry out of the rear, and to post them in the places and at the distances I just now recommended. The 1,000 velites in the front may advance, and —having divided themselves into two bodies with 500 in each

2 See Figure V, p. 224.
3 Polybius, III. 50 ff.

—let them take position between the cavalry and each wing
of the army. The gap they leave may be filled with the two
corps of pikemen extraordinary who were posted in the middle of the hollow square. The velites extraordinary, who were
in the rear, may divide into two bodies and range themselves
along each flank of the battalions to strengthen them; all the
carriages and sutlers may draw off through the opening then
created there into the rear of the battalions. Since the hollow
square is thus left empty, let the five battalions that were in
the rear march up toward the front through the vacancy between the flanks, three of them advancing until they come
within 80 feet of those in front, the other two halting at
the same distance in the rear of those three, with proper
intervals between them all. All this may be done in very
little time, and your order of battle will much resemble the
first and principal of those I recommended earlier; and if
it is in close order in the front, it is also more compact in the
flanks, which will make it so much the stronger. But since
the five battalions in the rear have posted their pikemen in
their last ranks for the reasons I have already mentioned, it
will be necessary upon this occasion to place them in their
foremost ranks, so as to support the front of the army. For
this purpose, they must either wheel to the right or left about
—battalion by battalion, all at once, and like one solid body—
or the pikemen must pass through the ranks of the shieldbearers and place themselves in front of them; this is a much more
expeditious way than the other, and subject to less disorder.
The same must be done during an attack in all parts of the
army where the pikemen are in the rear of the shieldbearers,
as I shall show you.

If the enemy presents himself in the rear, you have nothing
more to do than to make your whole army face about to that
part, and then your rear immediately becomes the front and
your front the rear, whereupon you must observe all the directions I have already given in forming that front. If the
enemy is likely to fall upon your right flank, the whole army
must turn its face that way and—as I said—make the front

there; take care to place your cavalry, velites, and artillery according to that disposition. These changes make very little difference except in the distances between the flanks and between the front and the rear. It is true that in converting the right flank into the front, the velites that are to fill the space between the cavalry and the wings of the army should be those nearest the left flank, and the two corps of pikemen in the area should advance to fill their places; but before they do that, the carriages and unarmed people should quit the area and retire through the opening left by the velites behind the left flank, which will then become the rear of the army. The other velites, those posted in the rear, should keep their place so that no opening may be left there, because what was the rear before will now become the right flank. All the other maneuvers necessary in this case must be conducted in the manner already prescribed.[4] What has been said about making a front of the right flank may be applied to the left, since the same disposition and maneuvers are to be made upon that occasion.

If the enemy is so numerous and drawn up in such a manner that he may attack you on two sides at once, you must strengthen both sides with those men who are not attacked by doubling their ranks and dividing all the artillery, velites, and cavalry between them. But if the enemy attacks you on three or four sides at the same time, either he or you must be very imprudent, for surely no wise general would ever expose himself to attack on so many sides at once by a powerful and well-ordered army; on the other hand, the enemy cannot do that with success, unless his army is so numerous that he can spare almost as many men as your whole army consists of to attack you on every side. If, then, you are so imprudent as to venture into an enemy's country, or any other place where you may be attacked by an army three times as strong and as well-disciplined as your own, you have nobody to blame but yourself if any misfortune happens to you; but if the misfortune is not a result of your own imprudence, but of some

4 See Figure VI, p. 226.

strange and unexpected accident, you may save your reputation although you are totally ruined by it—as was the case with Scipio in Spain, and Hasdrubal in Italy.[5] But if the enemy is not much stronger than you are and attacks you on two or three sides at once in hopes of throwing you into disorder by it, that is his error and your advantage; for in that case he must weaken himself so much that you may easily sustain the charge in one place and attack him vigorously in another; this must consequently lead to his defeat.

Therefore, this method of drawing up an army against an enemy not actually in sight, but one that may attack you suddenly, is very necessary; it is of great importance to accustom your soldiers not only to being formed and marched in this order, but to preparing themselves for battle as if they were going to be attacked in the front, and then to fall into their former order again and move forward. After this, they should be shown how the rear or either of the flanks may be converted into the front and then reduced into their first arrangement; all this must be practiced often if you would have your army ready and expert in these exercises. This is a point which all princes and commanders should carefully attend to, for military discipline consists chiefly in knowing how to command and execute these things; only an army that is perfect in their practice can be called a good and well-disciplined army; and if such a one were now in existence, I do not think it would be possible to find another that could beat it. If it be said that forming an army in these squares is attended with a good deal of trouble and difficulty, I allow it; but since it is very necessary, the difficulty must be overcome by frequent drilling; once that is done, all other parts of military discipline will seem light and easy.

Zanobi. I agree with you that these things are highly necessary, and I think you have explained them so well, that no

[5] Hasdrubal, victor in Spain in 211 B.C., attempted to join his brother Hannibal in Italy and lost his life there during the rout of his army in the Metauro River valley in 207; see p. 163, n. 6.

material has been omitted or can be added. There are two other points, however, about which I should like to be satisfied. In the first place, when you would convert the rear or one of the flanks into the front of your army, and the men are to face about to that part, are they to do so by word of command, by drum beat, or by some other signal? In the second place, should those whom you send ahead of the army to clear the roads and make a free passage for it be soldiers belonging to your battalions, or other sorts of people appointed expressly for that service?

Fabrizio. Your first question is very pertinent; for many armies have been thrown into great confusion when the general's orders have been either not heard or mistaken. Such orders, therefore, should be very clear and intelligible, especially on important occasions; if they are given by drum beat or by the sound of a trumpet, it should be done in so distinct a manner that one note or sound cannot be mistaken for another; but if they are delivered by word of mouth, you should take great care not only to avoid general terms, and use particular ones, but also even in those, not to hazard any that may admit of a double interpretation. Some armies have been ruined by the officers crying out, "give way, give way," instead of "retreat"; this should be a sufficient warning never to use that expression again.[6] If you want to convert the rear of one of the flanks into the front, and would have your men turn and face that way, do not say "turn," but "about face," "right face," "left face," as the occasion requires. Similarly, all other commands should be plain and simple, as "close ranks," "halt," "forward," "retreat"; if orders can be delivered clearly and distinctly by word of mouth, let them be given that way; if not, use a drum or a trumpet.

As for the pioneers, I would delegate some of my own soldiers for that service, not merely because the ancients used to do so, but so that I might have fewer unarmed people, and consequently, fewer incumbrances in my army. For this reason, I

[6] Cf. *Discourses,* III, 14.

would take as many men as I wanted out of every battalion; these men would leave their arms and accouterments in the care of the men in the nearest ranks, and would be furnished with axes, mattocks, spades, and other such necessary implements, so that when the enemy approached, they might immediately return to their respective ranks in the army and take up arms again.

Zanobi. But how are their pioneering implements carried?

Fabrizio. By the carriages appointed for that purpose.

Zanobi. I doubt if you would be able to make your soldiers do that sort of work.

Fabrizio. It is very easy, as I shall convince you before we part. But let us waive that matter at present, if you please, because I shall tell you first how I would supply them with provisions; since we have pretty well fatigued them with so much exercise, I suppose it is now high time to give them a little refreshment. All princes and commanders should take particular care that their armies be as light and little encumbered as possible, so that at all times they may be fit and ready for any enterprise or expedition. Now the difficulties occasioned by the want or the superabundance of provisions may be reckoned among the most considerable incident to an army. The ancients did not trouble themselves much about furnishing their troops with wine, for when they came into countries where there was none to be had, they drank water with a little vinegar in it to give it a taste; so, instead of wine, they always carried vinegar along with them. They did not bake their bread in ovens, as is usual in towns; every soldier had a certain allowance of meal or flour and lard, which, when kneaded together, made a very good, nourishing bread. Also, they used to carry a sufficient quantity of oats and barley for their horses and other cattle, for they had herds of oxen and flocks of sheep and goats that were driven after the army, and therefore did not occasion any great hindrance. As a result of these precautions, their armies would sometimes march for many days through desert countries and rugged defiles without distress or difficulty.

On the contrary, our modern armies, which can neither live without wine, nor eat any bread but that baked and made as it is in towns (and they cannot carry enough to last for any length of time), must often be reduced to great distress, or be obliged to provide themselves with those necessities in a manner that must be very troublesome and expensive. I would, therefore, re-establish this method in my army, and not allow any kind of bread to be eaten by the soldiers except what they made themselves. As for wine, I should not prohibit its use, if any were brought into the camp, but I would not make the slightest effort to procure it for them. In all other things also relating to provisions, I should follow the example of the ancients, by which many difficulties and inconveniences might be avoided, and many great advantages gained in any expedition.

Zanobi. We have beaten the enemy in a field battle, and afterward marched our army into his territories; it is only reasonable that we should now take advantage of it by plundering his country, levying tribute from the towns, and taking prisoners. But I should first like to know how the ancients proceeded upon such occasions.

Fabrizio. I take it for granted, since we had some conversation upon this matter once before, that you will admit that wars, as they are currently conducted, impoverish not only those beaten, but also those conquering; for if one side loses its territories, the other is at an immense expense in gaining them; this was not the case in former times when the conqueror was always enriched by victory. The reason for this is that plunder is not now brought to account, as it used to be formerly, but left entirely to the soldiers' discretion; this occasions two very great disorders, one of which I have already mentioned; the other is, it makes soldiers so greedy for spoil that they lay aside all regard for order and military discipline;

hence it has often happened that the conqueror has had the victory snatched out of his hands again.

The Romans, however, who were very attentive to this point,[7] provided against both these inconveniences by ordering that all the plunder should belong to the public treasury, which should afterward dispose of it as it thought fit. For this purpose they had *quaestors* attending their armies, men whom we should call paymasters and in whose hands all the booty taken in war was deposited; the consul paid the soldiers, defrayed the expenses of the sick and wounded, and provided for all other necessary charges of the army out of this fund. Indeed, the consul had the power to distribute a part of the plunder among the soldiers, and he often did; but this was not attended with any ill consequence, for when the enemy was conquered, all the spoils taken from him were placed in the middle of the army and a certain proportion of it was given to the soldiers according to their rank and merit. This custom made them more intent upon victory than plunder. After the legionary soldiers had defeated the enemy, they never pursued them, nor even so much as stirred out of their ranks —the cavalry and other light-armed forces were employed for that purpose; for if the plunder were to have been the property of the first man who got it, it would have been neither reasonable nor possible to have kept the legions firm and quiet in their ranks; therefore, such a measure would have brought very bad consequences. Hence it came about that the public treasury was enriched by any victory, since every consul, when he entered Rome in triumph on his return from the wars, always brought with him for the common stock the greatest part of the treasure amassed through tribute and plunder of the enemy. The ancients acted very wisely in another point relating to this matter;[8] they ordered the third part of every

---

[7] Polybius, X. 16–17.

[8] Vegetius, II. 20. The *dimidia pars* of Vegetius, however, becomes *la terza parte* in Machiavelli's version, a point noted by Burd, p. 223, n. 1.

man's pay to be deposited in the hands of the standard-bearer of his corps; he was not to be accountable for it until the end of the war. This seems to have been done for two reasons: in the first place, to save their money, which they otherwise might have squandered away in idle and unnecessary expenses —as most young men are apt to do when they have too much in their pockets; and in the second place, to make them more resolute and obstinate in defending their colors, since they must know that if the standard were taken, they would lose all their back pay. A due observation of these institutions, I think, would very much contribute to reviving the ancient military discipline among us.

Zanobi. When an army is marching, it must certainly be exposed to many dangerous accidents; to obviate and avert these, the utmost sagacity and abilities of the general, as well as the most determined bravery of the soldiers, must be exerted. You would much oblige us, sir, if you would point out those occasions.

Fabrizio. I shall very willingly comply with your request, since such knowledge is absolutely necessary to anyone anxious to be perfectly instructed in the art of war. While a general is marching, then, he ought—above all things—to beware of ambushes, into which he may happen to fall by himself, or be cunningly drawn by the enemy before he is aware. To prevent one, he should send out strong parties to reconnoiter the country; he should be particularly circumspect if it abounds with woods and mountains because those are the fittest places for ambushes; these sometimes lead to the destruction of a whole army when the general is not aware of them, but they can do no harm when he is. Flights of birds and clouds of dust have frequently disclosed an enemy, for whenever the enemy approaches they must of course raise a great dust; this should serve you, therefore, as a sufficient warning to prepare for an attack. It has also often happened that when generals have observed a great number of pigeons, or other birds that usually fly together in flocks, suddenly take wing and hover about in the air a great while without lighting again, they have suspected there was an ambush thereabouts; in which case, by sending out parties to discover it, they have sometimes escaped the enemy and sometimes defeated them.

To avoid being drawn into an ambuscade by the enemy, you must be very cautious of trusting to flattering appearances: [9] for instance, if the enemy should leave considerable booty in your way, you should suspect there is a hook in the bait; or if a strong party of the enemy should fly before a few of your men, or a few of his men should attack a strong party of your army; or if the enemy suddenly runs away, without any apparent cause, it is reasonable to imagine there is some artifice in it and that he knows very well what he is doing; so, the weaker and more remiss he seems to be, the more it behooves you to be upon your guard, if you would avoid falling into his snares. For this purpose you are to act a double part. Although you ought not to be without your private apprehensions of the enemy, yet outwardly, in all your words and actions, you should seem to undervalue and despise him: the one will make you more vigilant, and less apt to be surprised; the other will inspire your soldiers with courage and assurance of victory.

Similarly, you should always remember that an army is exposed to more and greater dangers while marching through an enemy's country than on a battlefield; consequently, it concerns a general to be doubly circumspect at such times.[10] The first thing he ought to do is to get an exact map of the whole country through which he is to march so that he may have a perfect knowledge of all the towns and their distance from each other, and of all the roads, mountains, rivers, woods, swamps, and their particular location and nature. For this purpose, it is necessary to procure by various means several persons who are from different parts and who are well ac-

[9] Concerning Machiavelli's doctrine of appearances, see *Prince*, 18; *Discourses*, I, 25.

[10] Most of the remainder of the speech closely follows Vegetius, III. 6.

quainted with those places; he should question them closely and compare their accounts, so that he may be able to form a true judgment of them. In addition to doing this, he should send out cavalry parties under experienced commanders not only to discover the enemy, but to observe the quality of the terrain and to see whether it agrees with his map and the information he has received.[11] He must keep a strict eye over his guides, whom he should encourage to serve him faithfully with promises of great rewards if they do their duty, and threaten with the severest punishment if they deceive him. But above all things, he ought to keep his designs very secret; this is a matter of the utmost importance in all military enterprises. To prevent his army from being thrown into disorder by any sudden attack, he should order his men to be constantly prepared for it; for if a thing of that kind is foreseen and expected, it is neither so terrible nor prejudicial when it happens as it otherwise might have been.

In order to prevent confusion during a march, many generals have placed their carriages and unarmed people near the standard and ordered them to follow it as closely as possible, so that if there should be an occasion either to halt or to retreat, they might do so with greater ease and readiness; I think this is a custom not unworthy of imitation. A general should also be very careful neither to allow one part of his forces to detach itself from the other while they are marching, nor to let any of the corps move faster or slower than the rest; for then his army would become weak and unconnected, and consequently exposed to greater danger. It is necessary, therefore, to post officers along the flanks, and to keep a uniform pace among them by restraining those who march too fast, and quickening others who move too slowly; this cannot be done more properly than by drum beat, or by the sound of some musical instrument. The roads should also be laid open and cleared so that at least one battalion can march through them at a time in order of battle.

[11] On the importance of a knowledge of topography, see *Prince,* 14; *Discourses,* III, 39.

The quality and customs of the enemy are to be considered next: whether they usually attack in the morning, at noon, or in the evening; whether they are more powerful in cavalry or infantry—you are to regulate your own proceedings and preparations according to these circumstances. But let us proceed to a particular case. It sometimes happens that a general is obliged to decamp before the enemy because he is not able to cope with them and because he tries to avoid an engagement; but as soon as the enemy is aware of it, they too decamp, and press so hard upon the general's rear, that the enemy probably comes upon him, and forces him into an enegagement before he can ford a river lying in his way. Now, some who have been in this dangerous situation have encircled the rear of their army with a ditch and filled it with fagots and other combustible matter which they have set afire; thereby, they gained time to ford the river in safety, before the enemy could get over the ditch.

Zanobi. I can hardly think such an expedient could be of much service, because I remember having read that when Hanno the Carthaginian was surrounded by the enemy, he set fire to a parcel of fagots on the side where he intended to make his push; this was so effective, that the enemy, thinking it unnecessary to guard that quarter, drew off its guards to another; as soon as Hanno was aware of that, he ordered his men to throw their shields in front of their faces, so as to protect them from the flames and smoke and to push through the fire; thus he got clear with his whole army.[12]

Fabrizio. Very true, but remember what I said, and compare it with what Hanno did. I told you that the others had a deep ditch dug and filled with combustibles which they set on fire, so that the enemy had not only the fire but the ditch to pass through before they could come at them. Now Hanno had no ditch. Therefore, since he intended to pass through the fire, he made certain that it would not be a very fierce one; otherwise that alone would have stopped him, without any ditch. Do you

12 Hanno, one of Hannibal's generals. Frontinus, I. 5. 27.

not remember that when Nabis was besieged in Sparta by the Romans, he set fire to the part of the town in which he was himself to prevent the enemy, who had already gotten possession of some streets, from advancing any farther? Thus, he not only stopped them where they were, but drove them entirely out of the town again.[13] But to return to our subject.

The Roman Quintus Lutatius, having the Cimbri close at his rear and coming to a river which he wanted to pass, seemed determined to halt there and fight them; for this purpose, he fixed his standard, dug entrenchments, erected tents, and sent out cavalry parties to forage; in short, he acted in such a manner that the Cimbri were fully persuaded he intended to camp there; they too entrenched themselves and sent out several parties into the country as he had done; when Lutatius was aware of this, he immediately struck his tents and forded the river without any impediment.[14]

Some generals have diverted the course of a river, when they had no other means of fording it, and drawn off a part of the stream in another direction until the other has become fordable.[15] When the current is very rapid, the strongest and heaviest horses should be placed higher up the stream than the infantry to break its force and facilitate their passage; the light cavalry should be placed somewhat lower than the infantry to pick up any of them that may happen to be carried away by it. But rivers that are not fordable must be crossed by the help of bridges, pontoons, and other such conveniences; therefore, it is necessary to carry along with the army the proper materials and implements for their construction.

It sometimes happens that you find the enemy posted on the other side to oppose your crossing; in such a case I would recommend an expedient used by Julius Caesar in Gaul; [16] when he came to a river and found Vercingetorix posted with

13 Nabis, king of Sparta, in 195 B.C. Livy, XXXIV. 39.

14 Q. Lutatius Catulus in 101 B.C. Frontinus, I. 5. 3.

15 This and the following recommendations are found in Vegetius, III. 7.

16 Caesar, *Gallic War* VII. 34–35.

an army on the opposite bank, Caesar marched down one side
of it for several days, while Vercingetorix marched down the
other. At last Caesar camped in a woody part of the country
where he could conceal part of his men; he drew three cohorts
out of every legion and left them there with orders to throw
a bridge over the river and to fortify it as soon as they could
when he was gone; he then continued his march. Vercingetorix, in the meantime, observing the number of Caesar's legions was the same, and not suspecting that any part of them
was left behind, followed Caesar's motions as he had done
before, on the other side; but when Caesar thought the bridge
was finished, he made a sudden countermarch and, finding
everything executed according to his orders, immediately
forded the river without any opposition.

Zanobi. What rule or mark is there by which one may discover a ford with any certainty?

Fabrizio. A river is always the shallowest and most fordable
where you see a sort of a ridge or streak across it, between
the place where the water seems to run slowly and where it
seems to run fast, because there is more gravel and sand left
there than in any other place. The truth of this observation
has been confirmed by long experience, and therefore may be
depended upon.

Zanobi. But suppose the bottom should be so rough and
broken, or so soft and full of holes, that cavalry cannot pass
with safety; what remedy is there in that case?

Fabrizio. I would make hurdles and sink them; they might
easily pass over these. But let us proceed.

If a general with his army happens to be enclosed in a pass
between two mountains, out of which there are but two ways
of extricating himself—one in his front, the other in his rear
—and they are both occupied by the enemy, there is still a
method which has been practiced by others with success in
such circumstances, that is: to dig a very deep and wide ditch
in the rear with an intent, so it may seem, to secure himself

effectively on that side, and to use every other method to make the enemy believe he intends to exert all his strength in the front in order to force his way out on that side if possible without apprehending any danger in his rear. In such cases, therefore, the enemy, deceived by these appearances, has naturally turned his whole force from the rear where he thought he had the general safe, to block him up more securely in the front; at this, the general has taken the opportunity of suddenly throwing a drawbridge over the ditch, and thus escaped out of the enemy's hands. Lucius Minucius, the Roman consul, and his army were shut up by the enemy in the mountains of Liguria; since they saw no other means of getting clear, they sent a body of Numidians—whom he had with him—who were very badly armed and mounted upon poor, lean horses, toward the pass blocked up by the enemy; the enemy immediately doubled his guards, and took all necessary measures to defend the pass vigorously on their first appearance; but perceiving, as they came nearer, what a pitiful figure they cut, the enemy drew off part of his guards. As soon as the Numidians were aware of this, they immediately set spurs to their horses and made so furious an attack upon those left, that they broke through them and afterward wreaked such havoc and devastation in the adjacent country, that the enemy was forced to quit his posts and leave the pass open for Minucius and his whole army to come out of the mountains where they had been shut up.[17]

Some generals, when they have been attacked by a much superior force, have drawn up their men very closely together, and let themselves be surrounded by the enemy in order to make their way by one resolute push through that part of their army which they saw was the thinnest and weakest; this method has sometimes succeeded very well. Mark Antony, in his retreat out of Parthia, observed that the enemy attacked

[17] Instead of Lucius Minucius, Machiavelli means Q. Minucius Thermus, consul in 193 B.C. Burd, p. 227, n. 1, sees this mistake as evidence that Machiavelli was following Frontinus, I. 5. 16 rather than Livy, XXXV. 11, since the Frontinus manuscript mistakenly referred to L. Minucius.

him early every morning when he was decamping, and harassed his rear all day long; he then resolved not to decamp until noon. The Parthians, concluding that he would not move at all that day, returned to their own camp, and left him to continue his march all the rest of the day without any disturbance.[18] The same commander, to guard against the Parthians' arrows, ordered that all his men kneel down when the enemy drew near, and that the second rank should cover the heads of the first with their shields, the third of the second, the fourth of the third, and so on; thus the whole army was under a roof, as it were, safe from their arrows.[19] This is all that occurs to me at present concerning the accidents that may happen to an army during a march. If you have no other questions to ask relating to this matter, I shall pass on to another part of our subject.

[18] 36 B.C. Frontinus, II. 13. 7. See *Discourses*, II, 18.
[19] Frontinus, II. 3. 15.

BOOK SIX

ZANOBI. SINCE we are now going to change our subject, I beg your leave to divest myself of my office; I hope Battista della Palla will take it up. In so doing, we shall in some measure imitate the example of experienced commanders, who in time of battle (as Signor Fabrizio has informed us) generally place the best of their men in the front and rear of their armies, so that the former may begin the attack with vigor and the latter may support it with resolution. Cosimo Rucellai, therefore, was wisely hit upon to lead the vanguard (if I may use the expression) in this conversation, and Battista della Palla to bring up the rear: Luigi Alamanni and I took it upon ourselves to lead the second line; since we all readily submitted to the charge assigned us, I dare say Battista will do the same.

Battista. Hitherto I have let myself be governed entirely by the company and shall do so for the future. We entreat you then, Signor Fabrizio, to proceed in your discourse and to excuse this interruption.

Fabrizio. If it is an interruption, it is an agreeable one, I assure you, for this change of officers, as I told you before, refreshes my mind rather than tires it. But let us resume our subject. It is now time to camp and rest our army in security; for all creatures, you know, naturally require due intervals of rest from their labor, and anyone not simultaneously enjoying security cannot properly be said to rest. Perhaps you might expect me to have camped my army first and then shown the order of a march, and, last of all, pointed out how it should be formed to engage an enemy. But I have done quite the contrary; indeed, I was obliged to. Since I was to show what an army marching had to do when it was suddenly forced to prepare for action, it was necessary to tell you first in what order of battle it should be drawn up.

Now, to lodge your men in security, your camp ought to be strong and well governed; the former depends either upon art [1] or upon the nature of its location, the latter upon the commander's care and good discipline. The Greeks used to look for a location that was strong by nature; [2] they would never encamp in any place that was not fortified by a mountain, a river, a wood, or some other similar defense. The Romans, on the contrary, not depending so much upon nature as upon art and good discipline in their camps, constantly chose locations where they could arrange their forces in usual order and exert their whole strength when the need arose. Hence it came to pass that the form of their encampment was always the same because they never swerved from their established discipline, but selected a location which they could make conformable to it; whereas the Greeks were often obliged to vary the form and manner of their encampments because they made their discipline give way to the location of the place, which could not always be the same as or similar to it. Therefore, when the location was indifferent, the Romans used to supply that defect by art and industry. Since I have hitherto proposed the conduct of that people as a model in most cases, I would also recommend their method in the encampment of their armies, not that I would follow it exactly in every particular, but only insofar as it may best suit the circumstances of the present times.

I have already told you more than once that they had two legions of their own citizens in their consular armies, amounting to about 11,000 infantry and 600 cavalry, plus 11,000 more infantry composed of the auxiliaries furnished by their friends and confederates; but the number of auxiliaries in those armies never exceeded the number of their own citizens—except their cavalry, about which they were not so scru-

---

[1] See above, p. 25, n. 21.

[2] The comparison of Greek and Roman encampments relies upon Polybius, VI. 42.

pulous. I told you, too, that they always posted their legions in the center and their auxiliaries in each wing whenever they engaged; they also observed this custom in their encampments, as I dare say you must have read in ancient history. Therefore, I shall not trouble you now with a detailed account of the method they followed upon such occasions, but content myself with telling you how I would choose to encamp an army at present; you will thus easily perceive what I have borrowed from the Romans.

You know that since they had two legions in a consular army, I have similarly composed mine of two regiments, each consisting of 6,000 infantry and 300 cavalry; you remember into how many battalions I divided them, how they are armed, and by what names the different forces of which they consist are distinguished; lastly, you know that in drawing them up for a battle or a march, I have mentioned no other troops, but only shown that when their number is to be doubled, there is nothing more to be done than to double the ranks.

But now that I am to show you the method of encamping, I shall not confine myself to only two regiments, but teach you how a whole army should be disposed of, an army consisting—like those of the Romans—of two regiments of our own forces, and the same number of auxiliaries. I do this to give you a clear idea of a complete encampment; for in the exercises and operations which I have hitherto described and recommended, there was no occasion to bring a whole army into the field at once.[3]

In order, then, to encamp an army of 24,000 infantry and 2,000 cavalry divided into four regiments, two of our own subjects and two of our auxiliaries, I would observe this method.[4] After I had hit upon a convenient location, I would erect my standard in the middle of a square, 200 feet deep on

[3] See Figure VII, p. 228.

[4] Machiavelli's detailed description of the encampment follows Polybius, VI. 27–32, with, perhaps, some reliance upon Vegetius, III. 8. No doubt Machiavelli was also familiar with the account in Xenophon, *Cyropaedia* VIII. 5. 1–15.

every side; one of the sides of this square should face east, another west, another north, and another south, and here in this square the general should fix his quarters. Next, since it was generally the practice of the Romans, and seems worthy of imitation, I would separate the combatants from the non-combatants, and those who should be ready and fit for action from those loaded and encumbered in another manner; for this purpose, I would quarter either all or the greater part of my soldiers on the east side of the camp, and the others on the west, making the east side the front, the west the rear, and the north and south the flanks of my camp.

To distinguish my soldiers' quarters, I would draw, from the general's standard toward the east, two parallel lines 1,360 feet long and 60 feet apart; at the extremity of these lines I would have the eastern gate of my camp. By these means a street 1,260 feet long would be formed directly from that gate to the general's quarters, for the distance from the standard to the end of his quarters is 100 feet on each side; this interval should be called the Main Street. Next, let another street be drawn from the south to the north gate across the head of the Main Street, and ranging close to the east side of the general's quarters; this street should be 2,500 feet long, since it is to extend from one flank of the camp to the other, and 60 feet wide; let this be called the Cross Street. Having thus marked out the general's quarters and drawn these two streets, I would proceed to provide quarters for the two regiments of my own subjects; I would lodge one on the right side of the Main Street, and the other on the left. For this purpose, I would place 32 lodgments on the left, and as many more on the right of that street, leaving a space 60 feet wide between the sixteenth and seventeenth lodgment for a Traverse Street to pass through the middle of the quarters of these two regiments, as you may see it marked out in the plan I shall make. In the front of these two orders of lodgments, on each side of the Main Street where they border upon the Cross Street, I would quarter the commanders of my men-at-arms, and their men in the 15 lodgments adjoining them; for since I have allocated

150 men-at-arms to each regiment, there would be ten men in each one of these compartments. The commanders' tents should be 80 feet wide and 20 feet deep; those of their men, 30 feet deep and 60 feet wide. But I must here ask you to remember once and for all that whenever I use the word "width," I mean the space extending from north to south; when I speak of "depth," I mean the space ranging from east to west. In the next 15 compartments which are to be on each side of the Main Street, and east of the Traverse Street (and to occupy the same space as that occupied by the men-at-arms), I would quarter my light cavalry; since there are 150 in each regiment, it too would amount to ten in every tent; in the remaining sixteenth I would lodge their commanders, assigning them the same room as that taken up by the commanders of the men-at-arms. The cavalry of both regiments, then, are thus provided with quarters on each side of the Main Street; they will direct us how to dispose of our infantry, as I shall show you next.

You have observed how I have quartered the 300 cavalrymen belonging to each regiment, and their officers, in 32 lodgments on each side of the Main Street, beginning from the Cross Street, and that I have left an empty space 60 feet wide between the sixteenth and seventeenth lodgment for a Traverse Street. In order, then, to quarter the 20 battalions, of which the two regiments consist, I would appoint lodgments for two battalions behind the cavalry on both sides of the Main Street; each of these lodgments should be 30 feet long and 60 feet wide, like the others, and so close to those of the cavalrymen that they should join together. In each of the first lodgments, beginning from the Cross Street, I would quarter the battalion lieutenant colonel, who would then be on a line with the commander of the men-at-arms; only this lodgment should be 40 feet wide, and 20 feet deep. In the next 15 lodgments, reaching to the Traverse Street, I would quarter an infantry battalion on each side of the Main Street; since each consists of 450 men, there would be 30 in every lodgment. I would place the other 15 lodgments contiguous with the light cavalry, on each side of the Main Street, and east of the Traverse Street, allowing them the same dimensions as those on the west; in each of these ranges, I would quarter one battalion, assigning the sixteenth lodgment, which should be 20 feet long and 40 feet wide, to the lieutenant colonel of the two battalions; he would then be close abreast with the commanders of the light cavalry. By this disposition, the first two ranges of lodgments would consist partly of cavalry and partly of infantry; but since the cavalry should always be clean and ready for action, and the horsemen should have no servants to assist them in dressing and taking care of their horses, the infantry of the two battalions quartered next to them should be obliged to wait upon them for that purpose; in consideration of which, they should be excused from all other duty in the camp, according to the practice of the Romans.

Leaving an empty space, then, 60 feet wide at the back of the lodgments, on each side of the Main Street, one of which may be called the First Street on the Right, the other, the First Street on the Left, I would mark out another range of 32 double lodgments parallel to the others, with their backs close together; I would allow the same dimensions, with a similar interval between the sixteenth and seventeenth for the Traverse Street; in each of these I would quarter four battalions, with their commanders in the first and last of them. Next, I would leave another space 60 feet wide at the back of these two lodgments for a street which should be called the Second Street on the Right, on one side of the Main Street, and the Second Street on the Left, on the other; close to these, I would have another range of double lodgments on each side of the Main Street, in every respect like the other two; there I would quarter the four remaining battalions and their lieutenant colonels, so that all the cavalry and infantry of our own two regiments would be disposed in six ranks or lines of double lodgments, with the Main Street between them.

As for the two auxiliary battalions, consisting of the same number and sort of forces, I would place them on each side of our own, in an order and number similar to the double lodgments; the two first lines should be partly cavalry and partly infantry, and at a distance of 60 feet from the two third lines of our own on each side of the Main Street to make room for a street between them; this should be called on one side the Third Street on the Right, and on the other, the Third Street on the Left. After this, I would mark out two other lines of lodgments parallel to the first on each side of the Main Street; these lodgments should be divided like those of our own battalions, with spaces of 60 feet between them for other streets, and they should be numbered and named according to their location and distance from the Main Street; then, all this part of the army would be quartered in 12 ranges or lines of double lodgments, with 13 streets between the several divisions, including the Main Street, the Traverse Street, and the Cross Streets. In addition to this, I would have an empty space left 200 feet wide between the lodgments and the fosse which should encompass them; so, computing the whole distance from the center of the general's quarters to the eastern gate, you will find that it amounts to 1,360 feet.

There are still two vacant intervals remaining, one from the general's quarters to the south, and the other from thence to the north gate of the camp; each of these, reckoning from the center, is 1,250 feet long. Deducting, then, from each of these spaces the 100 feet occupied by the general's quarters on each side, and 90 feet on each side for an area or piazza, and 60 for a street to divide the two above-mentioned spaces in the middle, and 200 more for the interval between the lodgments and the fosse—there will be a space left 800 feet wide and 200 feet deep for a line of lodgments on each side; their depth is the same as that of the general's quarters. If these spaces are properly divided, they will make 40 lodgments on both sides of the general's quarters, each of which will be 100 feet long and 40 feet wide; in these I would quarter the colonels of the several regiments, the paymasters, the quartermaster-general, and in short, all those who had any particular charge or business with the army; some lodgments should be left vacant for the reception of strangers or volunteers, and attendants upon the general.

To the rear of the general's quarters, I would make a street from north to south 62 feet wide and call it the Head Street, which should run along the west side of the 80 lodgments just mentioned; then these lodgments and the general's quarters would be included between that street and the Cross Street. From the Head Street I would draw another street directly from the general's quarters to the western gate of the camp; it should be 60 feet wide and the same length as the Main Street, and it should be called the Market Street. When these two passages were drawn, I would make a market place or square, at the beginning of Market Street opposite the general's quarters and adjoining the Head Street, which should be 240 feet on every side. On the right and left of the market place, I would have a row of quarters, each of which should contain 8 double lodgments, which should be 30 feet deep and 60 feet wide; that is, 16 on each side of the market place. In these I would lodge the superfluous cavalry belonging to the auxiliary regiments, and if there should not be room enough for all of them there, I would quarter those that were excluded in some of the 80 lodgments next to the general's quarters, but chiefly in those nearest the fosse.

It now remains for us to quarter our pikemen and velites extraordinary, for you know there are 1,000 of the former, and 500 of the latter in every regiment; so, with our own two regiments having 2,000 pikemen and 1,000 velites extraordinary, and those of the auxiliaries as many more, we have still 6,000 infantrymen to allocate; I would quarter all of them on the three sides of the fosse in the western part of the camp. For this purpose, I would have a row of five double lodgments 150 feet long, and 120 feet wide on the west side of the north end of the Head Street, leaving a vacant space of 200 feet between them and the fosse; if this row consisted of ten single lodgments, and if every lodgment were 300 feet deep and 60 feet wide, it would hold 300 infantrymen, that is, 30 in each one of them. Next to these, but with an interval of 62 feet between them, I would place another row of five double lodgments with the same dimensions; after that, another, and so on until there were five rows of five double lodgments of the same size, and with the same intervals between them, all in a straight line at a distance of 200 feet from the fosse to the west of the Head Street, and on the north side of the camp; so, there would be a total of 50 lodgments containing 1,500 men. Turning then from the left toward the western gate, I would mark out five other rows of double lodgments, with the same contents and proportions, in the space between the last of the other five rows and that gate—but with intervals of only 30 feet between one row and the other; here I would also quarter 1,500 men; in this manner, all the pikemen and velites extraordinary belonging to our own two regiments would be disposed of in 10 rows of double lodgments, that is, 100 single ones, counting 10 in a row, along the range of the fosse from the north to the west gate. Similarly, I would provide for the pikemen and velites extraordinary belonging to the auxiliary regiments by quartering them all in ten rows of double lodgments of the same dimensions and with the same intervals between them along the range of the fosse from the west to the southern gate; I would allow their colonels and other officers to take up such quarters there as should be most convenient for them.

I would plant my artillery along the banks on the inside of the fosse; in the vacant space, which would still be left on the west side of the Head Street, I would lodge all the unarmed people and impediments belonging to the camp. Now you must know by the word "impediments" the ancients meant all the baggage, people, and stores necessary to an army, except the soldiers: men such as carpenters, joiners, smiths, stonecutters, masons, engineers, canoneers (although indeed these may properly be counted as soldiers), cooks, butchers, and herdsmen, oxen and sheep for the army's sustenance; in short, all manner of craftsmen and implements, together with the proper vehicles and beasts of burden to carry the ammunition, provisions, and other requisites. However, I would not assign separate and distinct lodgments for all these, but content myself with ordering some streets to be left entirely clear and unoccupied for them. Of the four empty areas which would be left between these passages, I would assign one to the herdsmen and their cattle, another to the craftsmen of every kind, another to the carriages containing the provisions, and the last to those loaded with arms and ammunition. The streets which I would have left totally unobstructed should be the Market Street, the Head Street, and another called the Middle Street; this street is to be drawn across the camp from north to south; it should cut the Market Street at right angles and answer the same purposes on the western side of the camp as the Traverse Street does on the eastern. In addition to this, I would have still another street drawn behind the lodgments of the pikemen and the velites extraordinary, who are ranged on three sides of the fosse; each one of these streets should be 60 feet wide.

Battista. I confess my ignorance in these matters, yet I think I have no reason to be ashamed of it, since the art of war is not my profession. However, the disposition you made pleases me very much, and I have only two problems, which I beg you to resolve, to raise relating to it. The first is why you make the streets and areas around the lodgments so broad? The second, which perplexes me the most, is how are the areas you allow for the lodgments to be occupied?

Fabrizio. The reason why I make all the passages 60 feet wide is that a whole battalion at a time, drawn up in order of battle, may pass through them, for I told you before, if you remember, that every battalion takes up a space 50 or 60 feet wide. It is also necessary that the interval between the lodgments and the fosse should be 200 feet wide, in order to draw up the battalions there properly, to manage the artillery, to make room for booty or prisoners taken from the enemy, and, when necessary, to have room for digging new banks and ditches. Moreover, it is better to have the lodgments at a good distance from the fosse, so that they may be more out of the reach of the enemy's fire, and other offensive things upon which he might otherwise draw. In answer to your second question, I must tell you that it is not my intention for every space I have laid out as lodgments to be covered entirely by one great tent alone, but for it to be divided and occupied so as to suit best the convenience of those for whose use it is designed; they may have more or fewer tents in it as they please, provided they do not exceed the limits prescribed them.

But in order to lay out these lodgments, there should always be able and experienced engineers, quartermasters, and builders ready to mark out a camp and to distinguish its several streets and divisions with stakes and cordage as soon as the general has fixed upon its proper site; to prevent confusion, the front of the camp should always appear the same, so that every man may know what street he is near and in which quarter he may find his tent. This rule ought to be constantly observed, so that the camp will be a sort of moving town carrying with it the same streets, the same houses, and the same aspect wherever it goes.[5] This is a convenience which those who choose only those naturally strong and advantageous locations may not expect, because they must always change the form of their camp according to the nature of the ground. The Romans, as I said before, made their camps strong in any location by having ditches and ramparts around them, and by leaving a vacant space, generally twelve feet wide and six feet deep, between their lodgments and the ditch; they sometimes made it both wider and deeper, especially if they intended to remain long in the same place, or expected to be attacked. For my own part, I would not fortify a camp with a palisade unless I intended to winter in it; I would content myself with a rampart and a ditch, not of less width or depth than what has been just now mentioned, but greater if occasion required; in addition to these, I would have a half-moon

[5] Cf. Polybius, VI. 31: "The whole camp thus forms a square, and the way in which the streets are laid out and its general arrangements give it the appearance of a town" (trans. W. R. Paton, "Loeb Classical Library").

at every angle of the camp with some pieces of artillery in it to take the enemy in flank, if the trenches should be attacked. The army should be frequently drilled in this exercise of encamping and decamping in order to make the several officers ready and expert in laying out the distinct lodgments properly, and to teach the soldiers to know their respective quarters. There is no great difficulty in this exercise, as I shall show elsewhere. I shall now proceed to say something concerning the guards necessary in a camp, because if that point is not duly attended to, all the rest of our labor and care will be to no purpose.

Battista. Before you do that, I wish you would tell me what is to be done when you would encamp near an enemy; for on such an occasion, there surely cannot be enough time to dispose things in this regular order without exposing yourself to great danger.

Fabrizio. No general will ever encamp very near an enemy, unless he is in a condition to give him battle whenever he pleases; if the enemy is similarly disposed to engage, the danger cannot be more than ordinary, because a general may draw out two-thirds of his army and leave the other to form his camp. The Romans, in such cases, committed the care of digging entrenchments and laying out their camp to the *triarii,* and had only the *principes* and *hastati* to stand to their arms; since the *triarii* were the last line of their army to engage, they might leave their work, if the enemy advanced, and draw up under arms in their proper station. So, if you would imitate the Romans, in a similar instance, you should leave the care of laying out and fortifying your camp to the battalions in the rear of your army—those resembling the Roman *triarii.*

But to return to what I was going to say concerning the guards of a camp. I do not remember having read that the ancients used to keep any guards or sentinels outside their entrenchments at night, the way we now maintain sentries. I take the reason for this to be that they thought their armies were exposed to much danger by using them, since they might perhaps betray or desert them of their own accord, or be surprised or corrupted by the enemy; therefore, they did not think it fit to put any confidence in them. Thus, they trusted wholly to the guards and sentinels stationed within their entrenchments; these were kept with such order and exactness that the least failure in that duty was punished with death. I shall not trouble you, however, with a long, detailed account of the order and method they observed in this matter, because you very likely have read it in their histories; or, if you have not, you may meet with it there whenever you please. For the sake of brevity then, I shall tell you only what I myself would do upon such occasions.

I would have a third of my army continue under arms every night: one fourth of this third would be on guard along the entrenchments and other proper places of the camp, allowing a double guard at every angle of it; one part should constantly remain there, and another patrol all night from that angle to the next, and back again; this method should be observed during the day also, if the enemy is near.

As for giving out a *parole,* or password, changing it every night, and other such arrangements proper to guards and sentinels, I shall say nothing of them because they are known by everyone. But there is one thing of the utmost importance, whose practice will be attended with much advantage, and whose neglect, with great prejudice: strict observation of those who go out of the camp at night and those who come into it for the first time. This observation is a very easy thing to do for those complying with the manner and order of encamping I have recommended, because every lodgment has a certain number of men belonging to it; thus, you may immediately see if there are more or fewer in it than there should be. If any are absent without leave, they should be punished as deserters; if there are more than there ought to be, you should diligently inquire who they are, what business they have there, and what other circumstances there may be relating to them. This precaution will make it very difficult—if not impossible—for the enemy to hold any secret correspondence with your officers, or to be cognizant of your designs. If the Romans had not carefully attended to this point, Claudius Nero could not have left his camp in Lucania, gone secretly into The Marches, and returned to his former quarters while Hannibal knew nothing of the matter, although the two camps lay very near each other.[6]

But it is not sufficient just to give out good orders for this purpose, if their observance is not enforced with the utmost severity; for there is no case whatsoever in which the most exact and implicit obedience is as necessary as in the government of an army; therefore, the laws established for its maintenance ought to be rigorous and severe, and the general who executes them, a man of inflexible resolution in supporting them. The Romans punished with death,[7] not only those who failed in their duty when they were on guard, but all those who abandoned their post in time of battle, carried anything by stealth out of the camp, pretended they had performed some exploit in action which they had not done, fought without the orders of the general, or threw away their arms out of fear. And when it happened that a cohort or a whole legion had behaved poorly, they made them cast lots and put every tenth man to death—this was called "decimation." [8] It was done to avoid shedding too much blood, and although they did not all suffer, every man would be apprehensive that the lot might fall upon him. But where there are severe punishments, there should also be proportionate rewards to excite men to behave themselves well from motives

[6] C. Claudius Nero and M. Livius Salinator were consuls in 207 B.C. Claudius Nero was fighting Hannibal in Apulia near Lucania, while Livius Salinator was trying to prevent Hasdrubal from coming down through Italy with reinforcements for his brother Hannibal. Claudius Nero secretly hastened north with part of his army, defeated and slew Hasdrubal along the Metauro in The Marches, returned to his army, and tossed Hasdrubal's head into Hannibal's camp. Livy, XXVII. 39–50. See *Discourses*, II, 10; III, 17; also, above p. 137, n. 5.

[7] These offenses are in Polybius, VI. 37.

[8] Decimation is described in Polybius, VI. 38.

of both hope and fear; [9] therefore, they always rewarded those who had distinguished themselves by any meritorious action, especially those who had saved the life of a fellow citizen in battle, had been the first in scaling the walls of an enemy's town or storming their camp, or had wounded, killed, or unhorsed an enemy. In this manner, each man's desert was properly taken notice of, recompensed by the consuls, and honored publicly; those who obtained any reward for services of this kind, besides the reputation and glory which they acquired among their fellow soldiers, were, when they returned from the wars, received by their friends and relations with all kinds of rejoicings and congratulations. It is no wonder, then, that a people who were so exact in rewarding merit and punishing offenders should extend their empire to such a degree as they did; they are certainly highly worthy of imitation in these respects.

Give me permission, therefore, to be a little more explicit in describing one of their punishments.[10] When a delinquent stood convicted before his general, the latter gave him a slight stroke with a rod, after which he might run away if he could; but since every soldier in the army was free to kill him, he no sooner began to run than they all fell upon him with their swords, darts, or other weapons. He seldom escaped; if he did, he was not allowed to return home, except under heavy penalties and such a burden of infamy that it would have been much better for him to have died. This custom is, in some measure, still kept alive by the Swiss in their armies; they always have a convicted offender killed by the rest of the soldiers. I think it is a very good custom because, if you want to prevent others from supporting or protecting an offender, it is certainly best to leave his punishment to them; in that case, they will always look upon him differently from the way in which they would if he were to be punished by anybody else. This rule will also hold good in popular governments, as we may learn from the example of Manlius Capitolinus

9 For rewards, Polybius, VI. 39.

10 On running the gauntlet, Polybius, VI. 37.

who, being accused by the Senate, was strenuously defended by the people until they were left to judge him themselves; then, they immediately condemned him to die.[11] Hence, this is a good method of punishing delinquents and of causing justice to be executed in security, without fear of exciting mutiny or sedition. But since neither fear of laws nor reverence to man are sufficient to bridle an armed multitude, the ancients used to call in the aid of religion and, with many imposing ceremonies and great solemnity, make their soldiers take a very strict oath to pay due obedience to military discipline. In addition, they used all other methods to inspire them with a fear of the gods, so that if they violated their oaths, they might have not only the asperity of human laws but the vengeance of heaven to dread.[12]

Battista. Did the Romans ever allow women or gambling in their camp, as we do at present?

Fabrizio. They prohibited both. The restraint was not very grievous, because their soldiers were so constantly employed either in one sort of duty or in another, that they had no time to think of women, gambling, or any of those vile avocations which commonly make soldiers idle and seditious.

Battista. They were right. But tell me, what order did they observe when they were about to decamp?

Fabrizio. The general's trumpet was sounded three times.[13] At the first sounding, they struck their tents and packed them up; at the second, they loaded their carriages; at the third, they began their march in the order I have previously de-

[11] In 390 B.C. M. Manlius Capitolinus saved the Capitol from the Gauls. For inciting the masses against their creditors, he was charged with treason and condemned to death in 384. Livy, VI. 19–20. See *Discourses*, I, 8, 58; III, 8.

[12] Once again Machiavelli stresses the importance of religion as a means of social control. See above, pp. 60, 128.

[13] Polybius, VI. 40.

scribed—with their legions in the middle of the army, and their baggage in the rear of each corps. To do this, it is necessary for one of the auxiliary regiments to move first with its own baggage, and a fourth part of the public impediments in its rear; the latter were placed in one or the other of the four divisions in the western part of the camp that I spoke of not long ago. Therefore, every legion would have its particular division assigned to its charge; so that when they are about to march, each one knew where to take its place.

Battista. Did the Romans use to make any other provisions in laying out their camps, besides those which you have already mentioned?

Fabrizio. I must tell you again that they always kept the same form in their encampments; this was their first and principal consideration. Besides this, they had two other main points in view.[14] The first was a healthy location; the next, a camp where the enemy could neither surround them, nor cut them off from water or provisions. To prevent sickness in their army, therefore, they always avoided marshy grounds and sites exposed to noxious winds; they formed their judgment not so much from the quality of the place, as from the constitution and appearance of the people who lived nearby; if they were pale or sickly, or subject to asthma, dropsy, or any other endemic disorder, they would not camp there. As to the other point—not being liable to be surrounded by an enemy—they considered where their friends and where their enemy lay, and hence judged the probability or possibility of their being, or not being, surrounded. Consequently, a general should be very well acquainted with the nature and situation of the country he is in; he should have others around him who are as knowing in these respects as he.

There are also other precautions to be used in order to prevent sickness and famine in an army: restraining all manner of excess and intemperance among the soldiers; taking care that they sleep under cover, that your camp be near trees

14 Much of the following speech follows Vegetius, III. 2–3.

affording them shade in the daytime and enough wood for fuel to prepare their food, and that they do not march when the heat of the sun is too intense. For this reason, they should decamp before daylight in the summer and take care not to march through ice and snow in the winter, unless they have frequent opportunities of making good fires, and warm clothing to guard them against the inclemency of the weather. It is also necessary to prevent them from drinking stagnant and fetid water. If any of them happen to fall ill, you should give strict orders to the physicians and surgeons of the army to take great care of them, for bad indeed is the condition of a general when he has a sickness among his men and an enemy to contend with at the same time. But nothing is more conducive to keeping an army in good health and spirits than exercise; the ancients used to exercise their troops every day. Proper exercise, then, is surely of great importance for it preserves your health in the camp and secures you victory in the field.

As for guarding against famine, it is not only necessary to take timely care that the enemy may not be able to cut you off from provisions, but to consider from whence you may be conveniently supplied and to see that the provisions you have are properly husbanded and preserved. Therefore, you should always have at least a month's provisions in reserve, and then oblige your neighboring friends and allies to furnish you daily with a certain quantity. You also ought to establish magazines and storehouses in strong places, and above all, to distribute your provisions duly and frugally among your men; give them a reasonable proportion every day and attend so strictly to this point that you may not by any means exhaust your stores and run yourself aground.

Although all other calamities in an army may be remedied in time, famine alone grows more and more grievous the longer it continues, and it is sure to destroy you eventually. No enemy will ever engage you when, in such circumstances, he is sure to conquer you without fighting. Although a victory obtained in this manner may not be as honorable as one that is gained by dint of arms, it is certain, however, and not attended with any risk. An army, then, which wantonly and extravagantly wastes its provisions without foresight or regard to rule, measure, or the circumstances of the times, cannot possibly escape famine; want of timely care will prevent its having supplies, and profusion consumes what it already has to no purpose. Consequently, the ancients took care that their soldiers should eat no more than a daily, reasonable allowance, and that only at stated times; they never were permitted to eat breakfast, dinner, or supper unless their general did the same. How well these excellent rules are observed in our armies at present, I need not tell you; everyone knows that our soldiers, instead of imitating the regularity and sobriety of the ancients, are a parcel of intemperate, licentious, and drunken fellows.

Battista. When our conversation first turned to encampments, you said you would not confine yourself to two regiments alone, but take four, the better to show how a complete army should be encamped. But I should like to know, how you would quarter your army if it consisted of a greater or smaller number of men than that, and next, what number you would think sufficient to engage any enemy?

Fabrizio. To your first question, I answer that if your army has more or less than 5,000 or 6,000 in it, you have nothing to do but add or diminish your rows of lodgments accordingly; you may do this in whatever proportion you please. The Romans, however, had two different camps when they joined two consular armies together; the rear quarters, where the impediments and unarmed people were, faced each other.

As for your second question, the ordinary armies the Romans brought into the field usually consisted of about 24,000 men, and upon the most pressing occasions, they never exceeded 50,000. With this number they opposed 200,000 Gauls who invaded them after the end of the first Carthaginian war.[15] They opposed Hannibal with the same number. Indeed,

15 The invaders were repulsed in 225–222 B.C.

both the Romans and the Greeks, depending chiefly upon their discipline and good conduct, always carried on their wars with small armies, whereas both the eastern and western nations had vast and almost innumerable hosts; the latter trusted entirely in their natural ferocity, the former availed themselves of the implicit submission which their subjects show to their princes. But neither the Greeks nor Romans were remarkable for either their natural ferocity or their implicit submission to their princes, and they were obliged to resort to good discipline; the power and efficacy of that discipline were so great that one of their small armies often defeated a prodigious multitude of the fiercest and most obstinate people.[16] In imitation, then, of the Greeks and Romans, I would not have more than 50,000 men in an army, but fewer if I might choose; for more are apt to create discord and confusion, and not only become ungovernable themselves, but corrupt others who have been well disciplined. King Pyrrhus used to say that with an army of 15,000 good soldiers, he would fight the whole world.

But let us now proceed to other matters. You have seen our army win a battle, and the accidents which may occur in time of action. You have also seen it upon a march, and been acquainted with the dangers and embarrassments it is subject to in those circumstances. Lastly, you have seen it regularly quartered in camp where it ought to stay a while not only to enjoy a little rest after its fatigues, but to concert proper measures for bringing the campaign to a happy conclusion. Many things are to be considered and digested in camp, especially if the enemy still keeps the field, or if there are any towns belonging to him not yet reduced, or if there are any towns possessed by people whose fidelity and affection you have reason to suspect; in those cases, you must make yourself master of the one and secure the attachment of the other. It is therefore necessary to show how and by what means these difficulties are to be surmounted with the same glory with which we have hitherto carried on the war.

16 See *Discourses*, III, 31, 33, 36.

To get down to particulars, then, I say that if several different men or different states should think of doing anything which may tend to your advantage and their own prejudice (such as dismantling some of their towns or banishing a great number of their inhabitants), you should abet them in it so that none of them may think you have any self-interested view of your own in so doing; thus, you may beguile them so effectively that instead of confederating together for their own safety, they will not think of giving each other the least assistance; then you may suppress them all without any material opposition. But if this method will not work, you must order each one of them to do what you would have done on the same day, so that each state—imagining that no other state has any orders of the same kind—may be obliged to obey because it has no support from its neighbors to depend upon; thus you may succeed in your designs without any resistance or combination formed against you. If you should suspect the fidelity of any people, and would protect yourself against them by taking them unawares in order to disguise your intentions more effectively, it is best to pretend having perfect confidence in them, to consult them in some design which you seem to have upon some other people, and to desire their assistance in it, as if you had not the least doubt of their sincerity or thought of molesting them; this will put them off their guard and give you an opportunity of dealing with them as you please.

If you suspect anybody in your army of giving the enemy intelligence of your designs, you cannot do better than to avail yourself of his treachery by seeming to trust him with some secret resolution which you intend to execute, while you carefully conceal your real design; hence, you may perhaps discover the traitor and lead the enemy into an error that may possibly end in its destruction.

If, in order to relieve some friend, you would lessen your army secretly, so that the enemy may not be aware of it (as Claudius Nero did), you should not lessen the number of your lodgments, but leave the vacant tents standing and the colors flying, make the same fires, and keep the same guards that you did before.[17] Similarly, if you receive fresh supplies and would not have the enemy know that you have been reinforced, you must not increase the number of your tents; for nothing is of greater importance than to keep these and other such things as secret as possible. When Metellus commanded the Roman armies in Spain, someone took the liberty of asking him what he intended to do the next day; he told him, that if he thought his tunic could know that, he would immediately burn it.[18] Marcus Crassus, asked by one of his officers when he planned to decamp, said: "Do you think you will be the only one not to hear the trumpet?" [19]

In order to penetrate the enemy's secret designs and to discover the disposition of his army, some have sent ambassadors with skillful and experienced officers in their train dressed like the rest of their attendants; these officers have taken the opportunity of viewing their army and observing their strength and weakness in so minute a manner that it has been of much service.[20] Others have pretended to quarrel with, and banish, a particular confidant who has gone over to the enemy and afterward informed them of his designs.[21] The intentions of an enemy can also be sometimes discovered by the examination of the prisoners you take.[22] When Marius commanded in the war against the Cimbri, and wanted to test the fidelity of the Gauls (who then inhabited Lombardy and were allied with the Romans), he wrote them

[17] 207 B.C. Frontinus, I. 1. 9. See above, p. 163, n. 6.

[18] Q. Caecilius Metellus Pius went to Spain as proconsul in 79 B.C.; there he carried out the campaign against Sertorius from 79–72. Frontinus, I. 1. 12.

[19] Frontinus, I. 1. 13. M. Licinius Crassus was defeated and killed by the Parthians in 53 B.C.

[20] Machiavelli evidently has in mind a ruse employed by Scipio Africanus in 203 B.C. Frontinus, I. 2. 1; Livy, XXX. 4 ff.

[21] The Carthaginian, Hamilcar Rhodinus, thus supposedly learned the designs of Alexander the Great in 331 B.C. Frontinus, I. 2. 3.

[22] According to Frontinus, I. 2. 5, Marcus Cato the Elder used this method in Spain in 195 B.C.

some letters which were left open and others that were sealed; in the former, he asked them not to open those that were sealed until a certain day, but before that time he sent for them again; finding that they had been opened, he perceived there was no confidence to be put in them.[23]

Some princes have not immediately sent an army to oppose the enemy when their territories have been invaded, but made an incursion into the enemy's country, thereby obliging him to return and defend himself.[24] This method has often succeeded, for in such cases, your soldiers—elated with victory and loaded with plunder—fight with spirit and confidence, while those of the enemy are dejected at the thoughts of being beaten instead of conquering; so, a diversion of this kind has frequently been attended with good consequences. But you must not attempt this unless your country is better fortified than the enemy's; if you do, you will certainly be ruined. If a general is blocked in his camp by an enemy, he should endeavor to set up a treaty of accommodation with him and to obtain a truce for a few days; during this period, the enemy is apt to be so careless and remiss that the general may possibly find an opportunity of slipping out of his hands. By these means, Sulla twice eluded the enemy; in this manner Hasdrubal got clear of Claudius Nero when he had surrounded him in Spain.[25] Besides these expedients, there are other methods of extricating yourself from an enemy: attacking him with only one part of your forces, so that while his attention is wholly turned to that side, the rest of your army may find means to save themselves; using some uncommon stratagem whose novelty may simultaneously fill him with terror and astonishment so that he cannot decide how to act, or whether to act at all. This is what Hannibal did when he was surrounded by Fabius Maximus; since he had a great number of oxen in his camp, he fastened lighted torches to their horns

23 104 B.C. Frontinus, I. 2. 6.

24 Scipio Africanus forced Hannibal to do this in 204 B.C. Frontinus, I. 3. 8.

25 L. Sulla in 92 and 90 B.C. Hasdrubal in 211 B.C. Frontinus, I. 5. 17–19.

at night and let them run loose about the country; at the strangeness of this spectacle, Fabius was so perplexed that he could not help letting them escape.[26]

But above all things, a general ought to endeavor to divide the enemy's strength by making him suspicious of his counselors and confidants, or by obliging him to employ his forces in different places and detachments at once—this must consequently weaken his main army very much. The first may be done by sparing the possessions of some particular men in whom he confides and not letting their houses or estates be damaged in a time of general plunder and devastation, or by returning their children and other relations when they are taken prisoners without any ransom. Thus when Hannibal had ravaged and burned all the towns and country around Rome, he spared the estate of Fabius Maximus alone;[27] Coriolanus, too, returning at the head of an army to Rome, carefully preserved the possessions of the nobility and burned those of the plebeians.[28] When Metellus commanded the Roman army against Jugurtha, he urged the ambassadors sent him by that prince to deliver their master prisoner to him; he kept up a correspondence with them for the same purpose after they had left him until Jugurtha, discovering it, grew so jealous of his counselors that he put them all to death—on one pretense or other.[29] And after Hannibal had taken refuge with Antiochus, the Roman ambassadors managed so artfully that Antiochus became suspicious of him, and would neither take his advice, nor trust him again in any matter whatever.[30]

As for dividing the enemy's strength, there can be no better way of doing it than by making incursions into his country; this will oblige him to abandon all other enterprises and return home to defend his own. This was the method which Fabius used when he had not only the Gauls but the Tuscans,

26 217 B.C. Frontinus, I. 5. 28; Livy, XXII. 16–17. See *Discourses*, III, 40.

27 217 B.C. Frontinus, I. 8. 2.

28 489 B.C. Frontinus, I. 8. 1.

29 Q. Caecilius Metellus Numidicus in 108 B.C. Frontinus, I. 8. 8.

30 Antiochus III of Syria in 191 B.C. Frontinus, I. 8. 7.

the Umbrians, and the Samnites to deal with at the same time.[31] Titus Didius had only a small army as compared with the enemy and expected to be reinforced by another legion from Rome, when he learned that the enemy planned to cut it off during its march; to prevent this, he not only had a report spread through his camp that he would engage the enemy the next day, but allowed some prisoners he had taken to escape; they informed their general of the consul's intentions; this had such an effect, that the general did not see fit to reduce his own forces by detaching any part to oppose the march of that legion; so, it joined the consul in safety, and although this stratagem did not divide the enemy's army, it proved the means of reinforcing his own.[32]

Some, in order to reduce an invader's strength, have let him enter their country and take several towns, so that when he has weakened his main army by putting garrisons into them, they might fall upon him with a greater probability of success. Others, who have had a design upon one province, have made a feint of invading another; later, turning their forces suddenly to the place where they were not at all expected, they have made themselves masters of it before the enemy could send any relief; for in such cases, the enemy—uncertain whether you might not return to attack the province first threatened— is obliged to maintain his post and not to leave one place to succor another, so that, as often happens, he is not able to secure them both.

It is of great importance to prevent the spread of mutiny or discord in an army; for this purpose, you should punish the ringleaders in an exemplary manner, but with such address that it may be done before they imagine you intend any such thing. If they are at a distance from you, it is best to call both the innocent and guilty together; for if you summon the offenders alone, they might suspect your design and become contumacious, or take some other method to elude the punish-

[31] Q. Fabius Maximus Rullianus in 295 B.C. Frontinus, I. 8. 3.
[32] In Spain, 98–93 B.C. Frontinus, I. 8. 5.

ment due them; but if they are within your reach, you may avail yourself of those who are innocent, and punish the others with their assistance. As to private discords among your soldiers, the only remedy is to expose them all to some sort of danger; for in such cases, fear generally unites them.[33]

But what most commonly keeps an army united, is the reputation of the general, that is, of his courage and good conduct; without these, neither high birth nor any sort of authority is sufficient.[34] Now the chief thing incumbent upon a general, in order to maintain his reputation, is to pay well and punish soundly; for if he does not pay his men duly, he cannot punish them properly when they deserve it. Suppose, for instance, a soldier should be guilty of a robbery; how can you punish him for that when you give him no pay? And how can he help robbing when he has no other means of subsistence? But if you pay them well and do not punish them severely when they offend, they will soon grow insolent and licentious; then you will become despised and lose your authority; later, tumult and discord will naturally ensue in your army, and will probably end in its ruin.

The commanders of armies in former times had one difficulty to struggle with from which our generals at present are in a great measure exempt; that was interpreting bad omens and auguries so that instead of seeming adverse, they might appear to be favorable and propitious. For if a thunder and lightning storm descended upon the camp, if the sun or moon were eclipsed, if there were an earthquake, or if the general happened to fall while mounting or dismounting his horse, the soldiers looked upon it as an unhappy presage and were so dismayed that they gave only faint resistance to any enemy that attacked them. As soon as such an accident occurred, therefore, they endeavored to account for it by natural causes, or to interpret it for their own purpose and advantage. When Julius Caesar landed in Africa, he happened to fall as soon

[33] See *Discourses*, III. 12, See above, pp. 76 ff., 129.
[34] See *Discourses*, III, 21.

as he set foot on shore; he immediately cried out, "Africa, I take possession of thee." [35] Others have explained the reasons for earthquakes and eclipses to their soldiers. But such events have little or no effect in our times because men are not as much given to superstition since the Christian religion has enlightened their minds and dispelled these vain fears. But should such fears ever happen to occur, we must imitate the example of the ancients upon such occasions. [36]

If famine or any other kind of distress has reduced an enemy to despair, and he advances furiously to engage, you should keep close in your entrenchments and avoid a battle if possible; this the Lacedaemonians did when they were provoked to fight by the Messenians, and Julius Caesar by Afranius and Petreius. [37] When the consul Fulvius commanded the Roman army against the Cimbri, he had his cavalry attack the enemy on several successive days, and observing that they always left their camp to pursue his troops when they retreated, he at last placed a body of men in ambush behind the enemy's camp; they rushed into it and made themselves masters of it the next time they sallied out to pursue his cavalry. [38]

Some princes, when their dominions have been invaded and their army has lain near that of the enemy, have sent out parties under the enemy's colors to plunder and lay waste their own territories; the enemy, imagining them to be friends who were coming to its assistance, has gone out to join them; but upon discovering his mistake, the enemy has fallen into confusion and given his adversary an opportunity of winning. This stratagem was practiced by Alexander of Epirus against

[35] Suetonius, *Divus Julius* 59; see Frontinus, I. 12. 2.

[36] Cf. above, p. 128, n. 45.

[37] The war with Messenia occurred sometime after 650 B.C. Caesar's action was in 49 B.C. during the Civil War. Frontinus, II. 1. 10–11; Caesar, *Civil Wars* I. 81–83.

[38] Q. Fulvius Flaccus in 181 B.C. Frontinus, II. 5. 8, is mistaken about the war being with the Cimbri. It was evidently with the Celtiberi. See Livy, XL. 30–32.

the Illyrians, and by Leptines the Syracusan against the Carthaginians—they both easily succeeded in their purpose.[39]

Many have gained an advantage by pretending to run away in great fear and by leaving their camp full of wine and provisions; the enemy has gorged himself on these and the others have returned and fallen upon the enemy while he was drunk or asleep. In this manner Cyrus was served by Tomyris, and the Spaniards by Tiberius Gracchus.[40] Others have mixed poison with the meat and drink they left behind them.

I told you a little while ago that I did not remember having read that the ancients placed any sentinels outside of the ditch surrounding their camp at night, and that I supposed it was to prevent the mischief they might occasion; it has often happened that sentinels stationed at outposts during the daytime to observe the enemy's movements have been the ruin of an army since they have sometimes been surprised and forced to make the signals for their friends to advance; these have thereby been drawn into a snare, and either killed or taken prisoner.

In order to deceive an enemy, it may not be amiss to vary or to omit some particular custom or signal that you have constantly used before, as a certain great general did of old; he, having had some of his advance parties always give him notice of the enemy's approach by fires at night and smoke during the day, thought proper to vary that custom at last; he ordered those parties to keep constant fires all night long and to make smoke throughout the day, but to extinguish them when they perceived the enemy in motion; thus the enemy, advancing again and not seeing the usual signals made to give notice of his approach, imagined he was not discovered

39 Alexander II of Epirus. Leptines, brother of the tyrant, Dionysius I of Syracuse, in 397–396 B.C. Frontinus, II. 5. 10–11.

40 Tomyris, queen of the Massagetae, a Scythian people, in 529 B.C. Tiberius Sempronius Gracchus in Spain in 179–178 B.C. Frontinus, II. 5. 5. Machiavelli may well have used another source for Tomyris. See Burd, p. 237.

and pushed on with such precipitation to the attack, that he fell into disorder and was routed by his adversary who was prepared to receive him.[41]

Memnon the Rhodian, in order to draw the enemy out of a strong and advantageous location, got one of his own men to go over to the enemy as a deserter with the report that his army was in a mutiny and that the greater part of it was going to leave him; to confirm this, he caused a great uproar and commotion to be counterfeited every now and then in his camp; hence the enemy thought he would easily win, left his entrenchments to attack Memnon, and was completely defeated.[42]

Great care is also to be taken not to reduce an enemy to utter despair. Julius Caesar was always very attentive to this point in his wars with the Germans, and used to open a way for them to escape after he began to perceive that, when they were hard pressed and could not run away, they would fight most desperately; he thought it better to pursue them when they fled, than to run the risk of not beating them while they defended themselves with such obstinacy.[43]

Lucullus, observing that a body of Macedonian cavalry which he had in his army were going over to the enemy, had a charge sounded immediately, and ordered all the rest of his army to advance; the enemy, supposing he designed to attack them, presently fell upon the Macedonians with such fury that they were obliged to defend themselves and fight bravely, instead of deserting him as they intended.[44]

It is also of great importance to secure a town, when you suspect its loyalty, either before or after a victory. Pompey, doubting the loyalty of the Chauci, was anxious for them to

41 Frontinus, II. 5. 16, credits the stratagem to the Arabians, not to any particular military commander.

42 Frontinus, II. 5. 18.

43 58–53 B.C. Frontinus, II. 6. 3. Another example of the power of necessity.

44 L. Licinius Lucullus, 74–66 B.C. Frontinus, II. 7. 8. See *Discourses*, III, 13.

let him send the sick men whom he had in his army into their town to be taken care of until they were well again; but instead of sick men, he sent a parcel of the stoutest and most resolute men he had in his army in disguise; they made themselves masters of the town and kept it for him.[45] Publius Valerius, offended by the Epidaurians and mistrusting their sincerity, had a pardon proclaimed for all those who would come to a certain temple outside the gates of their town to accept it; when all the inhabitants went there for that purpose, he shut the doors of the temple and let no one return to the town except those whom he trusted.[46] Alexander the Great, anxious to depart for Asia and to make sure of Thrace, took all the nobility and leading men of that province along with him and, allowing them pensions, left the common people to be governed by men of their own condition; thus, the nobility were content with their appointments and the common people had no leaders to oppress or incite them to rebellion —the whole province remained quiet.[47]

But of all the methods that can be taken to gain the hearts of a people, none contribute so much as remarkable examples of continence and justice; such was the example of Scipio in Spain when he returned a most beautiful young lady, safe and untouched, to her father and husband; this was a circumstance which was more conducive to the reduction of Spain than any force of arms could have ever been.[48] Caesar acquired such reputation for his justice in paying for the wood which he cut down to make palisades for his camps in Gaul, that it greatly facilitated the conquest of that province.[49] But I think I now have nothing more to add to these particular documents, or to the subject in general, unless it is to say

[45] 76–72 B.C. Frontinus, II. 11. 2.

[46] Frontinus, II. 11. 1.

[47] 334 B.C. Frontinus, II. 11. 3.

[48] 210 B.C. The husband was Allucius, a native chieftain. Frontinus, II. 11. 5. See *Discourses*, III, 20, 34.

[49] The reference in Frontinus, II. 11. 7, is to the Emperor Domitian in A.D. 83.

something concerning the nature of attacking and defending towns; this I shall do as briefly and clearly as I can, if I have not already trespassed too much upon your patience.

Battista. You are so very kind and obliging, sir, that we shall desire you to indulge our curiosity in these points, without any fear of being thought troublesome to you, since you are so good to make a free offer of what we should otherwise have been ashamed to ask. We shall esteem it a very great favor, therefore, as well as a pleasure, if you will be so kind as to go on with the subject. But before you proceed to what you were speaking about, let us entreat you to tell us whether it is better to continue a war throughout the winter (according to the custom of our times), or to fight only in the summer, quartering your troops before the winter comes on, as the ancients used to do.

Fabrizio. Indeed, sir, if you had not asked this timely and pertinent question, I believe I should have forgotten to say anything about a matter which still deserves much consideration and attention. Therefore, I must beg leave to tell you again that the ancients were wiser and conducted their affairs with more prudence than we do at present, but this is especially true of their wars; for although we are indeed guilty of great errors in many respects, we certainly are guilty of more and greater in war. Nothing can be more dangerous or indiscreet than for a general to carry on a war in wintertime; for in that case, the aggressor is sure to run a greater risk of being ruined than those on the defensive. For since the main end and design of all the care and pains expended in maintaining good order and discipline is to fit and prepare an army to engage an enemy properly, a general ought always to have that point in view—a total victory usually ends a war. Therefore, he who has an orderly and well-disciplined army under his command will certainly have an advantage over another general who has not, and he will be more likely to come away with a victory. Now, it must be considered that nothing is a greater impediment to good order and discipline than rough locations and wet or cold weather, for in a bad site you cannot arrange your forces according to your usual order and bad weather will oblige you to divide them. In such a case, you cannot act with your whole force against an enemy, since they are quartered in villages, towns, and fortresses, at a distance from each other without any order or regularity, and in such a manner as necessity prescribes. So, all the pains you have taken to discipline your men and make them observe good order will signify nothing in such a season. But it is no great cause for wonder that the generals of our times carry on their wars in the winter; since they are strangers to all sorts of discipline and military knowledge, they are neither sensible to the losses and inconveniences which must necessarily result from dividing their forces, nor do they trouble their heads in endeavoring to establish that discipline and good order among their men—which they themselves never learned. They ought to reflect, however, upon the numberless hardships and losses occasioned by a winter campaign; they ought to remember that the defeat of the French near the Garigliano in 1503 resulted not so much from the bravery of the Spaniards, as from the rigor of the season.[50] For, as I told you before, those resolving to carry on a war in an enemy's country during the winter must of necessity have the worst of it, because if they keep all their men together in a camp, they must suffer much from rain and cold, and if they divide them into different quarters, they must greatly weaken their army. Whereas, those waiting for them at home may immediately unite their forces; not only may they choose their time and place of attack, but

[50] The Spanish king, Ferdinand of Aragon, agreed to support Louis XII's claim to Naples and share it with him, under the terms of the Treaty of Granada in 1500. By July 1502, having successfully asserted their claims, the two kings were arguing over the spoils. After losing ground, Spain won at Cerignola in April 1503, then at Naples, again at Garigliano, and finally forced the French to capitulate at Gaeta on New Year's Day, 1504. Thus Spain conquered, kept, and controlled Naples and southern Italy, while France controlled Milan and the north. At Garigliano, December 28, 1503, Gonzalo de Córdoba descended upon the French with a surprise attack over difficult terrain during adverse weather conditions.

they may keep their men safe and fresh under cover until they have an opportunity of falling upon some of the enemy's quarters; divided and dispersed, as it were, he cannot be supposed to make any great resistance. In this manner we may account for the defeat of the French which I just now mentioned. In this manner, too, those having any knowledge of the conduct of military affairs will always be served if they are invaded in winter. Therefore, if any general would plunge himself into such circumstances that neither the number, discipline, good order, nor bravery of his troops can be of any service to him, let him carry on a field war in the winter. The Romans, however, in order to make the most of those qualifications which they took so much pains to acquire, always avoided winter campaigns with as much care as they did rough, confined, and inconvenient sites, or any other impediment that might prevent them from availing themselves of their valor and good discipline. This is all that I have to say at present in answer to your last question. Let us now proceed, if you please, to the method of attacking and defending towns, and to the manner of building and fortifying them.

BOOK SEVEN

FABRIZIO. Towns and fortresses, you must know, may be strong either by nature or by art. Those surrounded by rivers or morasses,[1] like Mantua or Ferrara, or situated upon a rock or steep hill, like Monaco and Santo Leo,[2] are strong by nature; those situated upon hills that are not difficult of ascent, are deemed weak since the invention of mines and artillery. Hence, those building fortresses in these times often choose a flat site and make it strong by art.

For this purpose, their first care is to fortify their walls with angles, bastions, casemates, half-moons, and ravelins, so that no enemy can approach them without being taken in both front and flank.[3] If the walls are built very high, they will be too much exposed to artillery; if they are built very low, they may be easily scaled; if you dig a ditch on the outside of the walls to make an escalade more difficult and the enemy should fill it up (which may easily be done by a numerous army), he will immediately become masters of them. Therefore, in my opinion—with submission to better judges—the best way to prevent either eventuality would be to build high walls and to dig a ditch on the inside rather than on the outside. This is the strongest method of fortifying a town; not only does it cover the besieged from artillery fire, but it makes the besiegers' scaling the walls or filling up the ditch a very difficult matter. Your walls, then, should be of a due height; two yards thick at least, to stand the fire of the enemy's batteries; also, there should be towers all along them, at a distance of 400 feet from each other. The ditch on the inside ought to be no less than 60 feet wide and 24 feet deep; all the earth dug out

1 Vegetius, IV. 1.
2 The fortress of Santo Leo in the Duchy of Urbino.
3 Vegetius, IV. 2.

of it should be thrown up on that side next to the town, supported by a wall built in the ditch, and carried the height of a man above the surface. This will make the ditch so much the deeper. In the bottom of the ditch I would have casemates about 400 feet from one another in order to rake those that might get down into it.

The heavy artillery used for the town's defense should be planted on the inside of the wall supporting the ditch; since the other wall is to be a high one, you cannot use very large pieces there without much difficulty and inconvenience. If the enemy attempts an escalade, the height of the first wall protects you. If he batters you with artillery, he must first beat down that wall; but once it is beaten down—since a wall always falls toward the side from which it is battered and since its ruins have no ditch in which to be buried—the outside must naturally add to the depth of the ditch behind the enemy; so, he cannot easily advance any further because he is stopped there not only by those ruins but by both the ditch on the inside of them and the artillery planted on the other side of that ditch. The only expedient the enemy has left upon such occasions is to fill up the ditch; this is a very difficult matter for him because of the great width and depth of the ditch, the danger of approaching it from the bastions and other fortifications with which it is flanked, and the labor of climbing over the ruins with the burden of fascines upon the backs of his men; so, I think a town fortified in this manner may be considered impregnable.

Battista. Don't you think the town would be stronger if there were another ditch outside the wall?

Fabrizio. Most certainly. But I meant that if there were to be only one ditch, it would be best to have it on the inside.

Battista. Would you choose to have water in the ditches, or would you rather have them dry?

Fabrizio. People differ in their opinions on that matter, because ditches with water in them secure you against mines, and those having none are harder to fill up. But, on the whole, I should prefer dry ditches, because they are a better security than the other type: for ditches with water in them have sometimes been frozen over so that in winter time, the towns they were designed to secure have been taken without much difficulty—as happened at Mirandola when Pope Julius laid siege to it.[4] But to guard against mines, I would make my ditches so deep that if any one should attempt to work under them, they would be prevented by water.

I would also build a castle, or any kind of fortress, with the same sort of walls and ditches; this would make them very difficult, if not impossible, to be taken. Next, I would advise those in charge of defending a town that is about to be besieged by no means to permit any bastions or other works to be erected on the outside of the walls or at a little distance from the town. I would also advise those building fortresses not to make any place of retreat in them where the besieged may retire when the walls are either beaten down or possessed by the enemy. The reason for my first caution is that the governor of a besieged town ought not to do anything at the very beginning of the siege which will certainly lessen his reputation, for the diminution of that will make all his orders little regarded and discourage the garrison. But such will always be the case if you build little forts outside the town you are to defend because they are sure to fall into the enemy's hand; it is impossible in these times to maintain such inconsiderable places against a train of artillery, so that their loss will be the loss of your reputation and, therefore, most probably of the town itself. When the Genoese rebelled against Louis XII, king of France, they built some trifling redoubts upon the hills lying around Genoa; these were immediately taken by the French and occasioned the loss of that city.[5]

As to the second piece of advice relating to fortresses, I

---

[4] In the winter of 1511 Pope Julius II captured the fortress of Mirandola.

[5] Genoa rebelled in 1506, and the French recaptured the city in 1507. See *Discourses*, II, 24, and *Prince*, 20 for Machiavelli's principal discussions of fortresses. For Roman methods of capturing cities, see *Discourses*, II, 32.

say nothing can expose a fortress to greater danger than having places of retreat into which the garrison may retire when they are hard pressed; if it were not for the hopes of finding safety in one post, after they have abandoned another, they would exert themselves with more obstinacy and resolution in defending the first; when that is deserted, all the rest will soon fall into the enemy's hands. Of this we have a recent and memorable instance in the loss of the citadel at Forli, when the Countess Caterina was besieged there by Cesare Borgia, son of Pope Alexander VI, at the head of a French army.[6] That fortress was so full of such places of retreat that a garrison might retire out of one into another, and out of that into many more successively: first, there was the citadel, and next, a castle, separated from the citadel by a ditch with a drawbridge over it upon which you might pass out of one into the other; in this castle were three divisions separated from one another by ditches full of water with drawbridges over them. The duke, therefore, made a breach in the wall of one of these divisions with his artillery; Giovanni da Casale, who was the governor, instead of defending the breach, retreated into another division; thereupon the duke's forces immediately entered that division without opposition and, having gotten possession of the drawbridges, soon made themselves masters of all the rest. The loss of that fortress, then, which was thought impregnable, resulted from two errors; first, making so many conveniences for retreating from one place to another; second, not having any of those places able to command its bridges. So, the ill-contrivance of the fortress and the want of wisdom among the garrison defeated the magnanimous resolution of the countess who had the courage to wait for an army there, which neither the King of Naples

[6] In 1488 Count Giralamo Riario of Forli was murdered in his palace. His wife, Caterina, tricked the conspirators by retiring to the citadel and holding out until relief came from her uncle, Duke Ludovico Sforza of Milan. However, in December 1499, when Forli was overwhelmed by Cesare Borgia, the Countess was simply trapped in the citadel—no one came to her rescue—and surrendered, January 12. See *Prince*, 13, 20; *Discourses*, III, 6; *History of Florence*, VIII, 34.

nor the Duke of Milan dared. However, although her efforts did not succeed, she gained much glory by so generous a stand, as appears from the many copies of verses written in her praise upon that occasion.

If I were to build a fortress, then, I would make its walls very strong and fortify it with such ditches as I have just now described. But I would have no retreating places nor anything else on the inside but houses; those, too, would be so low that the governor, in the middle, seeing every part of the walls at one glance, might know where to send relief immediately when necessary, and the garrison might be convinced that when the walls and ditch were lost, they had no other refuge left. If by any means I should happen to be prevailed upon to make places of retreat, I should build them so that each one of them would be able to command its own drawbridge which I should build upon piles in the middle of the ditches that separated them from one another.

Battista. You say that small forts are not defensible in these times; but, if I am not mistaken, I have heard others assert that the smaller a fort was, the better it might be defended.

Fabrizio. Their assertion is ill-grounded then, because no place where the besieged have no room to secure themselves by throwing up other ditches and ramparts when the enemy has got possession of the first can be called strong today. For such is the force of artillery that whoever depends upon only one wall and one ditch will have reason to lament his error. Since forts and bastions (provided they do not exceed the usual dimensions, for then they may be deemed castles and fortresses) have no room for raising new works in them, they must immediately be taken when they are assaulted. Therefore, it is best not to build any such forts at a distance from a town, but to fortify its entrance and cover the gates with ravelins so that nobody can come in or go out of them in a straight line. In addition, there should be a ditch between the ravelin and the gate with a drawbridge on it. It is also a good thing to have a portcullis at every gate for readmitting your men after they have made a sally and for hindering the enemy from entering with them if they should be pursued. This is why portcullises,[7] which the ancients called *cataractae,* were invented; on such occasions, you could not receive any benefit from either the drawbridge or the gate itself, since both of them were crowded with men.

Battista. I have seen portcullises in Germany made of wooden bars in the form of an iron grate, but those now used in Italy are all made of whole planks. What is the reason for this difference? Which is the most serviceable?

Fabrizio. Again I must tell you that the ancient military customs and institutions are almost abolished in every part of the world, but in Italy they seem to be totally extinct; if we have any good thing to boast of, it is entirely borrowed from those beyond the Alps. You must have heard, and perhaps some of the company may remember, how feebly and slightly we used to fortify our towns and castles before Charles VIII, king of France, came into Italy in 1494. The merlons, or the spaces in the walls between the embrasures, were not more than a foot thick; the embrasures themselves were made very narrowly on the outside and wide within, with many other defects which it would be too tedious to enumerate; for when the merlons are made so slight, they are soon beaten down, and embrasures of similar construction are immediately laid open. But now we have learned from the French how to make our merlons strong and substantial; and although our embrasures are still wide within and grow narrower and narrower toward the middle of the wall—after which they begin to open again and grow wider and wider toward the outside—the artillery cannot be so easily dismounted nor the men driven from the parapets. The French have many other improvements and inventions which our soldiers have never seen, and therefore cannot imitate; among these I might mention the portcullises, of which you just now spoke, made in the form of an iron grate—they are much better than ours.

7 Vegetius, IV. 4.

If you use one made of whole planks to defend a gate, when it is let down you shut yourself up tight and cannot annoy the enemy through it; so, he may either hew it down with axes or set fire to it without any danger; but if it is made like a grate, you may easily defend it against him either with spikes or by firing shot through the interstices of the bars.

Battista. I have observed another invention from beyond the Alps which has been recently imitated in Italy: making the spokes of the wheels of our artillery carriages incline obliquely from the exterior rim to the hub. Now, I should very much like to know the reason for this because I always thought straight spokes were stronger than any others.

Fabrizio. You must not look upon this deviation from the usual custom as the effect of whim or caprice, or for the sake of ornament; where strength is absolutely necessary, little account ought to be taken of beauty. The true reason, then, for what you have observed is that such wheels are safer and stronger than our own; when the carriage is loaded, it either is even or inclines to one side; when it is even, each wheel sustains an equal share of the weight and is not too overburdened by it; but when it inclines to either side, the total weight lies wholly on one of the wheels. Therefore, if the spokes are straight, they are soon broken because if the wheel inclines, the spokes must also incline and cannot support the weight that presses upon them. So, by setting the spokes of their wheels obliquely to the hub, the French judge rightly; when the carriage inclines to one side and the weight bears directly, instead of obliquely, upon the spokes, they will then become straight in a line with it; consequently, they will be better able to support the whole than they were to bear one-half of the load when the carriage was even. But to return to our towns and fortresses.

The French have still another method for securing the gates of their towns and for letting their men in and out of them more easily and conveniently when they are besieged—one I have not yet seen practiced in Italy. They erect two perpendicular piles or pillars at the end of the drawbridge on the outside of the ditch; upon each of these they balance a beam so that one-half of it hangs over the bridge and the other half hangs outside it. Those parts hanging outside are joined together with crossbars like a grate; at the end of each beam hanging over the bridge, they fix a chain and fasten it to the bridge so that when they intend to close off that end of the bridge, they loosen the chains and let the grate fall; when they want to open it, they draw the chains and hoist the grate up again; thus, they can raise it to such a height that only infantry or cavalry if necessary, may pass under, or they may shut the passage up so tightly that nobody at all can get through, since the grate is raised and lowered like the opening of an embrasure. This I take to be a better contrivance than the portcullis because the grate does not fall perpendicularly like a portcullis; therefore it is not so likely to be obstructed by an enemy.

Those, then, that would fortify a town properly should observe these directions; in addition to these, they should not let any lands be tilled nor any buildings be erected within at least a mile of it. The whole country around it should be quite clear and open, free from all thickets, or banks, or plantations, or houses which may hinder the prospect of the besieged and afford shelter to an enemy in his approaches. Remember, too, that a town whose ditches have banks higher than the ordinary surface of the earth and whose ditches are outside, may be considered very weak; instead of doing you any good, they serve only to cover the enemy and to mask his batteries. There they may easily open upon you from that point. But now let us proceed to show what is to be done within a fortified town for its greater security against an enemy.

I shall not trespass so much upon your time and patience as to tell you that besides the directions already given, it is absolutely necessary to be well supplied with ammunition and provisions for the garrison because everybody must know this, and it is clear that without such stores, all other precautions and preparations are to no purpose. In general, I shall merely say that there are two rules which should never be forgotten upon such occasions: the first is, provide yourself with everything you think you may want; the second, prevent the enemy from availing himself of anything that may be of service to him in the country around you. Consequently, if there is forage, cattle, or anything else you cannot carry off into the town, you ought by all means to destroy it.

You also ought to take care that nothing is done in a tumultuous or disorderly manner, and that every man knows his station and what part he is to act, on any given occasion. Therefore, it is necessary to give strict orders that all the old men, women, children, and sick people should remain in their houses in order to leave every passage clear and open for those who are young and fit for action; to be ready for any sudden emergency, some of these should always be under arms at the walls, others at the gates, and still others in the town's main districts. There ought to be special parties, too, which should not be confined to any specific location, but appointed to aid any district where there should be occasion for it so that when such a disposition is made, it is hardly possible that any tumult should occur which may throw you into confusion. There is another thing to be remembered in both besieging and defending a town: nothing encourages an enemy so much as his knowing that the town is not accustomed to sieges, for it often happens that a town is lost through fear alone, without waiting for an assault. The besiegers, therefore, should endeavor by all means to appear as powerful and formidable as they can and take every opportunity of making the most ostentatious display of their strength; the besieged, on the other hand, ought to post the stoutest of their men in places where they are attacked with the greatest fury, men who are neither to be imposed upon by appearances, nor to be driven from their posts by anything but outright force of arms. For if the enemy fails in the first attempt, the besieged will take courage; the enemy, perceiving they are not to be dismayed by show alone, will be obliged to resort to other methods.

The instruments the ancients used in the defense of a town were many; [8] the main ones were those that hurled darts and huge stones to a great distance and with astonishing force; they also used several instruments in besieging towns, like the battering ram, the tortoise, and many others. Today, instead of these, great guns are used both by besiegers and by those besieged. But let us return to our topic.

A governor of a town, then, must take care neither to be surprised by famine nor to be overpowered by attacks. As to famine, I told you before that he ought to lay in a plentiful stock of provisions and ammunition before the siege begins; but should the siege prove a very long one, and should this stock eventually fail, he must then devise some extraordinary method of procuring supplies from his friends and allies, especially if a river runs through the town, as did the inhabitants of Casilinum from the Romans. When that town was so closely besieged by Hannibal that they could be sent no other kind of food, people threw great quantities of nuts into a river running through the middle of their town; these nuts were carried down by the stream, escaped the enemy's notice, and supplied the besieged with food for a considerable time. [9] The inhabitants of some besieged towns, in order to make the enemy despair of reducing them by famine, have either thrown a great quantity of bread over their walls, [10] or gorged an ox with corn and then turned it out to fall into the enemy's hand so that when he killed it and found its stomach so full of corn, he might imagine they had abundance in the town. [11]

On the other hand, some great generals have used many artifices and expedients to distress a town. Fabius Maximus let the Campanians sow their fields before he besieged their city so that they would diminish their stores. [12] When Dionysius lay

8 Vegetius, IV. 22.

9 216 B.C. Today Casilinum is Capua. Frontinus, III. 14. 2.

10 Frontinus, III. 15. 1. A trick the Romans used when they were besieged by the Gauls in 390 B.C.

11 Frontinus, III. 15. 5, refers to the Thracians in this regard.

12 215 or 211 B.C. Frontinus, III. 4. 1; cf. Livy, XXIII. 46; XXV. 13. Frontinus has evidently confused two occasions.

before Rhegium, he offered the people terms of accommodation; during the treaty he prevailed upon them to furnish him with a large quantity of provisions, but when he had thus reduced their stock and increased his own, he immediately blocked up the town so tightly on all sides that he soon forced them to give it up.[13] Alexander the Great, anxious to conquer Leucadia, first made himself master of the neighboring towns and turned all the inhabitants into Leucadia; at last the town was so full of people, that he immediately reduced it by famine.[14]

As to assaults, I told you before that it is of the utmost importance to repel the first attack; the Romans took many towns by suddenly assaulting them on every side, which they called *aggredi urbem corona*,[15] as Scipio did when he made himself master of New Carthage in Spain.[16] If such an assault, therefore, can be sustained, the enemy will find it a difficult matter to succeed afterward.[17] Should the enemy get into a town after he has forced the wall, the inhabitants may find some remedy, if they are not abandoned; even in that case, it has often happened that the assailants have all been driven out again or killed, especially when the inhabitants have gotten into garret windows or upon the tops of houses and turrets and fought them from there. To prevent this, the assailants usually either set open the gates to make way for the others to escape safely, or gave orders—loud enough to be heard by everyone —not to hurt anybody except those armed, and to spare all those who would lay down their arms. This has frequently been of great service upon such occasions.

It is also an easy matter to make yourself master of a town if you come suddenly and unexpectedly upon it; that is, if you are at such a distance from it with your army, do not

[13] Dionysius I of Syracuse in 391 B.C. Frontinus, III. 4. 3.

[14] 266–263 B.C. Frontinus, III. 4. 5, refers not to Alexander the Great, but to Alexander I, son of Pyrrhus and king of Epirus.

[15] "Attacking the city by crown."

[16] 210 B.C., now Cartagena. Livy, XXVI. 44 ff.; Polybius, X. 12 ff. See *Discourses*, II, 32.

[17] For the following, Vegetius, IV. 25.

think that the inhabitants will suspect you of any such intention, or that you can attack them without their having sufficient notice of your approach. Hence, if you can make a long and hasty march or two and fall upon it unawares, you are almost sure to succeed. I would willingly pass over in silence some transactions that have occurred in our own time, since it would be disagreeable to talk of myself and my own exploits; and I do not really know what to say of others. Nevertheless, I cannot help proposing, in this respect, the example of Cesare Borgia, usually called Duke Valentine, as one worthy of imitation; when he lay with his army at Nocera and feigned an attack upon Camerino, he suddenly invaded the Duchy of Urbino and conquered a state in one day without any difficulty; another man could not have reduced it without wasting much time and money upon it.[18]

Similarly, it behooves those besieged to beware of the enemy's tricks and stratagems; therefore, they ought not to trust any appearance—however usual and familiar to them—but suspect there is some mischief lurking behind it.[19] Domitius Calvinus lay siege to a town and used to march around it every day with a good part of his army. Hence the besieged, imagining he did it only as a drill, began to grow remiss in their guards; when Domitius perceived this, he made an assault upon the town and conquered it.[20] Some generals who have had intelligence of troops marching to relieve a place they had besieged, have dressed a body of their own soldiers in the enemy's uniform and supplied them with the same colors; when they were admitted into the town, they immediately conquered it.[21] Cimon, the Athenian, one night set fire to a temple that stood outside the gates of a town he intended to surprise; thereupon, all the people ran out of it

[18] June 21, 1502. See *Discourses*, II, 24.

[19] See above, p. 143, n. 9.

[20] Gnaeus Domitius Calvinus, consul in 54 and 40 B.C. Frontinus, III. 2. 1.

[21] Stratagem of the Arcadians against the Messenians, as related in Frontinus, III. 2. 4.

to extinguish the flames and left the town to the mercy of the enemy.[22] Others, having met with a party of foragers who were sent out of a fortress, have killed them all and disguised some of their own men in their clothes; later, these men have given up the place to them.[23]

Besides these artifices, the ancients used others to draw the garrison out of a town they wanted to capture. When Scipio commanded the Roman armies in Africa, he was very anxious to make himself master of some strongholds that were well garrisoned by the Carthaginians. To do this, he feigned assaults on them, but soon desisted and marched away again to a great distance, as if he were afraid of the enemy. Hannibal, therefore, deceived by appearances, immediately drew all the garrisons out of these strongholds in order to pursue him with greater force and to have greater hopes of entirely crushing him; but when Scipio was informed of this, he sent Masinissa, his lieutenant, to seize them.[24] Pyrrhus, laying siege to the capital of Illyria—now Slavonia—where there was a very strong garrison, pretended to despair of reducing it; turning his arms against other towns which were not so well defended, he forced the enemy to draw the greater part of the garrison out of the capital to relieve these towns; then, he suddenly returned thither with his army, and took the capital without any difficulty.[25]

Many generals have poisoned wells and springs and diverted the course of rivers to make themselves masters of a town, but they have not always succeeded in so doing.[26] Others have en-

[22] *Ca.* 470 B.C. The temple of Diana in Caria, Asia Minor. Frontinus, III. 2. 5.

[23] Employed by Antiochus in besieging the town of Suenda in Cappadocia. Frontinus, III. 2. 9.

[24] 202 B.C. Masinissa, king of the Numidians, was an ally of Rome. Frontinus, III. 6. 1.

[25] 296–280 B.C. Illyria is now the area northwest of Belgrade. Frontinus, III. 6. 3.

[26] Frontinus offers six examples in III. 7. The next stratagems may have been taken from a variety of passages in Frontinus, for example, II. 3. 1; III. 3. 1, 5.

deavored to dismay the inhabitants by causing a report to be spread that they have lately gained some considerable advantage, and daily expect a powerful reinforcement. Some have made themselves masters of towns by holding a private correspondence with, and corrupting one party of, the inhabitants; they have used several different methods to do this. Others have sent one of their chief confidants among them; he, under the pretense of desertion, has gained great credit in the town and afterward betrayed it by giving intelligence to his friend about how the guards were posted, by preventing a gate—opened for some occasion such as a carriage breaking down in it—from being shut again, or by some other means for facilitating the enemy's entrance into the town. Hannibal prevailed upon an officer to betray a garrison belonging to the Romans: the officer got leave to go hunting at night under a pretense that he dared not do so in the daytime lest he should be taken by the enemy; returning before morning, he contrived matters so well that he got several of Hannibal's men admitted with him in disguise; these immediately killed the guards and delivered up one of the gates to Hannibal.[27]

Some towns have been taken by letting their garrison make a sally on the enemy and then pursuing them to too great a distance when they pretended to fly before them; thus, they have been drawn into an ambush and cut off. Many generals, and Hannibal among them, have let a besieged enemy get possession of their camp in order to throw themselves between them and the town, and so prevent their retreat. Others have imposed upon them by pretending to raise the siege, as Phormion the Athenian, did; after he had lain some time before the city of Chalcedon and ravaged all the country around it, the inhabitants sent ambassadors whom he received with much courtesy; he made them so many fair promises that, having lulled them into security, he decamped and marched away to a distance from the city; but while they were weak enough to imagine they had entirely gotten rid of him and

[27] Tarentum in 212 B.C. Frontinus, III. 3. 6. See Livy, XXV. 8–9; Polybius, VIII. 26.

had laid aside all care of their defense upon the strength of his promises, he suddenly returned and, falling upon them when they did not expect such a visit, immediately took the city.[28]

The inhabitants of a besieged town ought likewise to secure themselves by all means against any of their own townsmen whose fidelity they have reason to suspect, but they may sometimes work upon them more effectively by kindnesses than by severity and harsh treatment. Marcellus knew that Lucius Bancius of Nola was inclined to favor Hannibal, yet he treated him with so much generosity that instead of an enemy he became his firm friend.[29] They should also be at least as much upon their guard when the enemy is at some distance as when he is near at hand, and be particularly careful in guarding those places they think are least exposed to danger; many towns have been lost by being assaulted in a part which has been thought the most secure. The reason for this is either because that part has been really strong of itself, and therefore neglected, or because the enemy has artfully made a show of storming one part with great noise and alarm, while he was assaulting another in good order and silence. The besieged, therefore, above all things, should take the utmost care to have their walls always well guarded, but especially at night. Not only should they post men there, but they should also post fierce and keen-nosed dogs to smell out an enemy at a distance and to give an alarm by their barking; for dogs, and geese too, have sometimes saved a fortress, as they rescued the Capitol at Rome when it was besieged by the Gauls.[30] When the Spartans laid siege to Athens, Alcibiades ordered that whenever he should hoist a light in the night, every guard should do the same upon pain of severe punishment in case of neglect.[31] The Athenian Iphicrates, finding a sentinel asleep

28 432 B.C. Frontinus, III. 11. 1.

29 M. Claudius Marcellus in 216 B.C. Frontinus, III. 16. 1; Livy, XXIII. 15–16.

30 Vegetius, IV. 26.

31 During the Peloponnesian War. Frontinus, III. 12. 1.

at his post, immediately killed him and said he had only left him as he found him.[32]

Some who have been besieged have found different methods of conveying intelligence to their friends, such as writing them letters in ciphers, when they dared not trust the messenger with a verbal errand, and concealing the letters in different ways. The nature of the ciphers has been devised and agreed upon by the parties beforehand, and the methods of concealing them various. Some have written what they had to say in the scabbard of a sword, others have put their letters into unbaked bread, which they have baked and given to the bearer as food for the road, others have concealed them in their private parts, and still others under the collar of the messenger's dog. Some have written letters about ordinary affairs and interlined them with their main purpose written with a certain substance which will not appear until they have been dipped in water and held to a fire. This method has been very artfully practiced in our own time by someone who, having occasion to communicate a secret to some of his friends living in a besieged town and not daring to trust any messenger with it, sent letters of excommunication written in the usual style, but interlined in the manner I have been mentioning; when these were hung from the doors of the churches there, they were soon taken down and the contents of them perfectly understood by those who knew from whom they came by some particular marks; this is a very good way, for he who carries such letters cannot know their secret contents, nor can there be any danger of his being discovered by an enemy.

In short, there are a thousand other methods of giving and receiving secret intelligence which any man may invent himself or learn from others. But it is a much easier matter to convey intelligence to those besieged than for them to send any to their friends, because nothing can be carried out of a town, except by those pretending to be deserters; this is a very uncertain and hazardous method, especially if the en-

[32] The Athenian general Iphicrates was holding Corinth in 393–391 B.C. Frontinus, III. 12. 2.

emy is vigilant and circumspect. Whereas, those who want to carry intelligence to the besieged having nothing more to do than to get into the enemy's camp, which they may do under almost any pretense, and take their opportunity of slipping from there into the town.

But now let us proceed to the present method of repairing and defending a breach in the walls of a town. If you should happen to be blocked up in a place where there is no ditch on the inside of the walls, in order to prevent the enemy from entering at a breach that may be made by their artillery, you must make a ditch at least 60 feet wide behind the part they are battering, and throw up all the earth that is dug out of it toward the town to form a good rampart and to add to the depth of the ditch; you must carry this out with such diligence that when the wall is beaten down, the ditch is at least 10 or 12 feet deep. It is also necessary—while you have time—to flank the ditch with a casemate at each end. If the wall is substantial enough to hold out until these works are finished, you will be stronger on that side than in any other part of the town, for then you will have a complete ditch there of that sort which I recommended a little while ago. But if the wall is so weak that you cannot have time to do all this, you must then depend upon your men and exert your utmost vigor to defend the breach. This method was used by the Pisans when the Florentines laid siege to their city; indeed they were very well enabled to do it, for their walls were so strong that they had enough time, and the soil upon which their city is built is very proper for making ditches and ramparts; but if either of those conveniences had failed them, they would inevitably have been undone. However, it is best, as I said before, to have such ditches made within a town and all around its walls in good times, for then you need not be afraid of any enemy.

The ancients sometimes made themselves masters of a town by using subterranean passages; they did this either by secretly working an underground passage into the middle of the place and entering their men that way—as the Romans did at Veii, or by undermining the walls so as to make them tumble down.[33] The latter method is now most in use; this is the reason why towns situated on high places are considered weaker than others—they are more subject to being undermined; when they are, if the passages are filled with gunpowder and a lighted match put to a train leading to them, they not only blow up the walls, but split the rocks upon which they are built and tear an entire fortress to bits. The way to prevent this is to build on a plain and to make the ditch that surrounds your fortress so deep that an enemy cannot work under it without coming to water—the best defense against passages. But if you are in a town standing upon a rock or hill, the only remedy is to dig several deep wells along the foot of the wall on the inside; these may serve to give vent to the powder when a mine is sprung. Indeed, there is another expedient, and a very good one too: to countermine the enemy, provided you can discover their mines; but that is a very difficult matter, if they take proper care to conceal them.

The governor of a besieged town also ought to take great care that he be not surprised while the garrison is either refreshing or reposing after an assault, or when the guards are relieved—generally at break of day in the morning and then by twilight in the evening—but especially while they are eating; at those times, many towns have been surprised and many sallies, which have proved fatal to the besiegers, have been made; hence, it is highly necessary always to keep both a strict guard in every quarter and the greater part of the garrison under arms. Another thing I must not forget to tell you is that the chief difficulty in defending a town or a camp is occasioned by your being obliged to divide your men; since the enemy may assault you at any time or any place he thinks proper with all his forces at once, you must keep a constant guard at every place so that when he attacks you with his whole strength, you can defend yourself with only a part of your own. The besieged are likewise often in danger of being totally ruined at one stroke, whereas the besiegers have nothing to fear but a repulse; consequently, some who have been

33 Vegetius, IV. 24.

blocked up either in a town or in a camp have made a sudden sally with all their forces, although they were inferior to the enemy, and utterly dispersed them. This is what Marcellus did at Nola,[34] and Julius Caesar in Gaul; [35] the latter, attacked in his camp by a very powerful army, and finding that he was neither able to defend himself there nor to fall upon the enemy with his whole strength because he was forced to divide it to protect every part of his camp, threw open the entrenchments on one side and, facing about in that direction with all his men, exerted himself with such *virtù* that he totally defeated the enemy.

Similarly, the constancy and resolution of the besieged often dismay and weary the besiegers. In the wars between Pompey and Caesar, when their two armies were lying near one another, and Caesar's was in great want of provisions, a piece of the bread which Caesar's men were forced to eat was brought to Pompey; finding that it was made of herbs, Pompey gave strict orders that none of his own soldiers should see it, lest they should be daunted when they perceived with what sort of an enemy they had to deal.[36] In their wars with Hannibal, the Romans honored nothing so much as their unshaken firmness and constancy, for they never sued for peace nor showed the least signs of fear, even in the lowest ebb of their fortune. On the contrary, when Hannibal was almost at their gates, they sold the ground upon which he was encamped at a much greater price than they would have asked for it at any other time; they were so inflexible in the prosecution of the enterprises they had in hand, that they would not raise the siege of Capua to defend Rome itself, at a time when it was daily threatened with a siege.[37]

I am aware, after all, that I have told you many things you

---

[34] M. Claudius Marcellus defended Nola against Hannibal after the defeat at Cannae in 216 B.C. Livy, XXIII. 14–16.

[35] 57 B.C. Not Caesar, but his legate in Gaul, Servius Sulpicius Galbus. Caesar, *Gallic War* III. 2–6.

[36] Suetonius, *Divus Julius* 68.

[37] 211 B.C. Frontinus, III. 18. 2–3; Livy, XXVI. 7–8, 11.

must have known before and, perhaps, may have considered as well as myself; but this I did, as I told you I should, so that you might perfectly comprehend the nature of true military discipline and the art of war, and for the instruction of others who may not have had the same opportunity of learning them that you have. And now, gentlemen, I think I have but little more to add to what I have said upon this subject, except to lay down some general rules of military discipline which nevertheless you may probably think very obvious and common.[38] You must know, then, that:

[1] Whatever is of service to the enemy must be prejudicial to you; whatever is prejudicial to him must be of service to you.

[2] He who is most careful to observe the motions and designs of the enemy and takes the most care in drilling and disciplining his army, will be least exposed to danger and will have the most reason to expect success in his undertakings.

[3] Never come to an engagement until you have inspired your men with courage and see them in good order and eager to fight, nor hazard a battle until they seem confident of victory.

[4] It is better to subdue an enemy by famine than by sword, for in battle, *fortuna* has often a much greater share than *virtù*.

[5] No enterprise is more likely to succeed than one concealed from the enemy until it is ripe for execution.

[6] Nothing is of greater importance in time of war than knowing how to make the best use of a fair opportunity when it is offered.

[7] Few men are brave by nature, but good discipline and experience make many so.

[8] Good order and discipline in an army are more to be depended upon than ferocity.

[9] If any of the enemy's troops desert him and come over to you, it is a great acquisition—provided they prove faithful; for their loss will be more felt than that of those killed in

[38] The following twenty-seven precepts are taken from Vegetius, III. 26.

battle, although deserters will always be suspected by their new friends and odious to their old ones.

[10] In drawing up an army in order of battle, it is better to keep a sufficient reserve to support your front line than to extend it so as to make only one rank, as it were, of your army.

[11] If a general knows his own strength and that of the enemy perfectly, he can hardly miscarry.

[12] The *virtù* of your soldiers is of more consequence than their number; sometimes the location of the place is of greater advantage and security than the *virtù* of your soldiers.

[13] Sudden and unexpected accidents often throw an army into confusion, but things that are familiar and have come on gradually are little regarded; therefore, when you have a new enemy to deal with, it is best to accustom your men to their sight as often as you can by slight skirmishes before you come to a general engagement with them.

[14] He whose troops are in disorder while pursuing a routed enemy will most probably lose the advantage he had previously gained and be routed in his turn.

[15] Whoever has not taken proper care to furnish himself with a sufficient stock of provisions and ammunition bids fair to be vanquished without striking a stroke.

[16] He who is stronger in infantry than cavalry, or in cavalry than infantry, must choose his ground accordingly.

[17] If you would know whether you have any spies in your camp during the day, you have nothing more to do than to order every man to his tent.

[18] When you are aware that the enemy is acquainted with your designs, you must change them.

[19] After you have consulted with many about what you ought to do, confer with very few concerning what you are actually resolved to do.

[20] While your men are in quarters, you must keep them in good order by fear and punishment; but when they are in the field, by hopes and rewards.

[21] Good commanders never come to an engagement un-

less they are compelled to by absolute necessity, or occasion calls for it.

[22] Take great care that the enemy may not be apprised of the order in which you design to draw up your army for battle; make such a disposition that your first line may fall back with ease and convenience into the second, and both of them into the third.

[23] In time of action, be sure not to call off any of your battalions to a service different from what they were destined to do at first, lest you should occasion disorder and confusion in your army.

[24] Unexpected accidents cannot be easily prevented, but those foreseen may easily be obviated or remedied.

[25] Men, arms, money, and provisions are the sinews of war, but of these four, the first two are the most necessary; for men and arms will always find money and provisions, but money and provisions cannot always raise men and arms.

[26] A rich man without arms must be a prey to a poor soldier well armed.

[27] Accustom your soldiers to abhor fastidious living and luxurious dress.

Let these general rules suffice at present as altogether necessary to be remembered. I am indeed aware that I might have introduced several other topics in the course of this conversation which would have fallen in properly enough with our subject; for instance, I might have shown how, and in how many different dispositions, the ancients drew up their armies, how they clothed their soldiers, and how they employed them at different times. I could have added several other particulars, which I thought might be omitted, not only because you may have various other means of informing yourselves about these things, but also because I did not propose, at first, to enter into the minute details of ancient military discipline, but only to point out the methods by which much better order and greater *virtù* might be established in our armies than there is anywhere to be found at present. Consequently, I thought I had no occasion to make any further mention of ancient rules and institutions, except what was absolutely necessary for the introduction of such an establishment.

I know full well that I might have taken an opportunity of enlarging more copiously upon the method of drilling and disciplining cavalry, and of discoursing upon the nature of sea service; for those who write upon the art of war tell us there are armies for sea and land, infantry, and cavalry.[39] However, I shall say nothing about naval affairs because I do not pretend to have any knowledge about them; I leave that to the Genoese and Venetians who have done such wonderful things through their experience in those matters. Nor shall I say any more about cavalry, because as I told you before, that part of our soldiery is the least corrupted; if your infantry, in which the strength of an army chiefly consists, is well disciplined, your cavalry must of necessity be so too. I would advise anyone, however, who is anxious to raise and keep up a good body of cavalry, first, to fill his country with stallions of the best breed that can be procured, and to encourage the farmers to raise foals and colts—as your countrymen do calves and young mules; second, in order to promote their sale, to make everyone keeping a mule also keep a horse, and to oblige him who would keep only one beast to use a horse; moreover, he should oblige all those wearing garments made of fine cloth to keep at least one horse. This method was used by a certain prince in our own memory, and in a very little time he saw his country abound with excellent horses. As to anything else relating to cavalry, I must refer you to what I have said today on that subject and the currently established practice.

But before we part, perhaps you may want to know what qualifications a general ought to possess. I shall satisfy you in a few words, for I cannot choose a more proper man than one who is master of the qualifications I have already particularized and recommended; and yet, even those are not sufficient unless he has abilities to strike out something new of his own occasionally. For no man ever excelled in his profes-

[39] Vegetius completed his work with a consideration of naval warfare.

sion who could not do that, and if a ready and quick invention is necessary and honorable in any profession, it must
certainly be so in the art of war above all others. Thus we see
how any invention or new expedient, trifling though it may
be, is celebrated by historians. Alexander was admired for
having a cap held up at the point of a lance as a signal for
decamping, instead of the usual sounding of a trumpet, in order to decamp in silence and unobserved.[40] The same prince
is similarly commended for ordering his men to kneel down
on the left knee to receive the enemy so that they might be
able to sustain the attack with greater firmness; thus, he not
only won a victory, but such honor that statues were erected
to him in that attitude.

But, since it is now high time to end this conversation, I
shall conclude it by returning to the point from which we
began, lest I should expose myself to the ridicule usually and
justly bestowed upon those who make long digressions and
wander from their subject until they are lost. If you remember,
Cosimo, you seemed to wonder that I, who professed to hold
the ancients in such admiration and so liberally bestowed my
censure upon others for not imitating them in matters of the
greatest consequence, have not myself copied their example
in the art of war, which is my profession, and in which I have
spent so much of my time and studies. In answer to this, I told
you that men who have any great design in view ought first
to make due preparations and qualify themselves properly to
carry it into execution when they have a fair opportunity of
so doing. Now, I must let you judge from the long conversation we have had today whether or not I am master of
sufficient abilities to reduce our present military discipline to
the standard of the ancients; from this conversation you can
tell how often I must have revolved this matter in my mind,
and you can form a pretty good idea about how much I have
it at heart and whether I would not actually have attempted
to execute my design, if ever I had been favored with a proper

40 Quintus Curtius, V. 2.

opportunity. However, for your further satisfaction and my own justification, and to discharge my promise in some measure, I shall show you how difficult a matter it is in some respects, and how easy a one in others, to copy the ancients in this point at present.

I say, then, that nothing in the world can be more easily effected than the reduction of military discipline to the standard of the ancients, if a prince or state is able to raise an army of 15,000 or 20,000 strong, young men in his own dominions. On the other hand, if this power is lacking, nothing can be more difficult. Now to explain myself more fully, you must know that some generals have done great things and gained much glory with armies already formed and well disciplined, as we might instance in several of the Roman citizens, and in others who have commanded armies they found already disciplined; therefore, they had nothing more to do but to keep them so and to lead them like able commanders. Others, who have been no less renowned for their exploits, have not only been obliged to discipline their armies, but even to raise them out of the earth, as it were, before they could face an enemy; these certainly deserve a much greater degree of approbation than those who have commanded veteran and well-disciplined armies with *virtù*. Among such, we may count Pelopidas; Epaminondas; Tullus Hostilius; Philip of Macedon, the father of Alexander the Great; Cyrus king of Persia; and Gracchus the Roman.[41] All of these generals had their armies to raise and discipline before they could lead them into the field; yet they were enabled to effect these things by their own wisdom and by having subjects of such a disposition that they could discipline and train them as they pleased. But it would have been utterly impossible for any one of them, however great his merit and qualifications, ever

[41] Pelopidas, *ca.* 410–364 B.C., Theban general, friend of Epaminondas, and leader in the drive to expel the Spartans from Thebes. Tiberius Sempronius Gracchus, the conqueror of Hanno during the Second Punic War.

to have performed anything memorable in a foreign country whose inhabitants were corrupt and averse to all good order and necessary obedience.

In Italy, therefore, it is not enough to know how to command an army already raised and disciplined. A general must first raise and discipline it himself before he puts himself at its head. Nobody can do that unless he is a prince possessing large territories and a great number of subjects, which I am not. Nor did I ever yet, nor can I, command any but foreign armies composed of soldiers who owed me no natural obedience; whether it is possible to establish such discipline as I have been recommending among troops of that kind, I submit to your consideration. Do you think I could ever make these men carry heavier arms than they were used to, and not only arms but provisions for two or three days, and a spade or mattock in the bargain? Could I ever make them dig or keep them whole days together at their maneuvers in order to prepare them for the field? Could I keep them from the gambling, drinking, whoring, swearing, and insubordination common among soldiers in these times? How long would it be before I could establish such order, discipline, and obedience among them that if there should happen to be a tree full of ripe fruit in the middle of the camp, not one of them would dare to touch it [42]—as we read happened among several ancient armies? What rewards could I promise them of sufficient weight to make them love me, or what threats could I use to make them fear me when they know that once the war is over, I shall have nothing more to do with them? How could I ever make those who have no shame in them ashamed of anything? How can they respect me when they hardly know my face? By what God or what Saint must they swear: him whom they worship, or those whom they blaspheme? What God they worship I know not; nor do I know what Saint they do not blaspheme. How could I hope they would ever

----

[42] Marcus Scaurus, consul in 115 B.C., relates in his memoirs that the fruit-laden tree was untouched after the withdrawal of the army. Frontinus, IV. 3. 13.

keep any promise when I saw they did not pay the least regard
to their word? How could I imagine they would revere man
when they show so much dishonor to God? What good form,
then, could I impress upon such matter? [43] If you object that
the Swiss and Spaniards are good soldiers, I freely confess that
I think them much better than the Italians; but if you have
attended to what I have been saying and considered the discipline of both those nations, you will find they fall very far
short of the ancients in many respects. The superiority of the
Swiss is a result of their ancient institutions and the lack of
cavalry, as I told you before; that of the Spaniards, to necessity, for as they generally carry on their wars in foreign countries, they cannot hope to escape if they lose a battle; therefore, they must either conquer or die—this is what makes them
resolute soldiers. However, they are very deficient in several
other respects: their chief, if not their only, excellence consists in standing firm to receive a charge from the push of a
pike or the point of a sword; should any man attempt to instruct them in what they are still lacking, especially if he were
a foreigner, he would find all his endeavors were of no purpose.

As for the Italians, their princes have been weak and pusil-
lanimous for so long a time that they were not able to introduce any good military institution; not being reduced to it
by necessity, like the Spaniards, they could not do it by themselves; so that without a single example of *virtù*, they are now
the scorn and derision of the world. Indeed, the people are
not to be blamed for this, but rather their princes, who have
been justly punished for it and lost their dominions without
being able to strike a stroke in their defense. [44] To confirm
what I have said, let me ask you to recall how many wars there

---

[43] The distinction between "form" and "matter," important in Scholastic
doctrine, indicates that Machiavelli conceived of leadership as creative.
The leader impresses a form upon the raw matter, the people. Cf. *Prince*,
6; *Discourses*, III, 8. See Introduction, pp. liii–liv; and below, p. 210 and
n. 45.

[44] See *Discourses*, III, 29.

have been in Italy since it was invaded by Charles VIII of France; although wars generally make men good soldiers, yet the longer these wars lasted, the worse were our officers and men. This resulted from the nature of their military discipline and institutions, which have long been very bad—and still are; what is even worse, there is nobody able to reform them. It is in vain, therefore, to think of ever restoring the reputation of Italian arms by any method other than what I have prescribed and by the cooperation of some powerful princes in Italy; then the ancient discipline might be reintroduced among raw, honest men who are their own subjects, although it never can among a parcel of corrupted, debauched rascals and foreigners. Just as no good sculptor can hope to make a beautiful statue out of a block of marble that has been previously mangled and spoiled by some bungler, so he will be sure to succeed if he has a fresh block to work upon.[45]

Before our Italian princes had been scourged by men from beyond the Alps, they thought it sufficient for princes to write handsome letters, or to return civil answers to them, to excel in drollery and repartee, to undermine and deceive one another, to decorate themselves with jewels and lace, to eat and sleep in greater magnificence and luxury than their neighbors, to spend their time in wanton dalliance and lascivious pleasures, to keep up a haughty kind of state and grind the faces of their subjects, to indulge themselves in indolence and inactivity, to dispose of their military honors and preferments to pimps and parasites, to neglect and despise merit of every kind, to browbeat those who endeavored to point out anything that was salutary or praiseworthy, and to have their words and sayings looked upon as oracles. They did not forsee (weak and infatuated as they were) that by such conduct they were making a rod for their own backs and exposing themselves to the mercy of the first invader. All this resulted in the dreadful alarms, the disgraceful defeats, and the astonishing losses they sustained in 1494; hence it happened that

[45] In *Discourses*, I, 11, a similar metaphor is used in regard to the founder of a civil order. See Introduction, pp. liii–liv; also the terms "form" and "matter" above, p. 209 and n. 43.

three of the most powerful states in Italy were so often ravaged and laid waste in those times.[46]

But it is still more deplorable to see that those remaining princes are so far from taking warning from the downfall of others, that they pursue the same course and live in the same sort of misrule and fatal security; they do not consider that princes in former times who were anxious to acquire new dominion or, at least, to preserve their own, strictly observed all those rules I have laid down and recommended in the course of this conversation, and that their chief endeavors were to inure their bodies to all manner of hardship and fatigue and to fortify their minds against danger and the fear of death. Thus, Julius Caesar, Alexander of Macedon, and all such men and excellent princes always fought at the head of their own armies, always marched with them on foot, and always carried their own arms; if any of them ever lost his power, he simultaneously lost his life with it and died with the same *virtù* which he had displayed while he lived. So that however much we condemn the inordinate thirst for dominion in some of them, we cannot reproach any of them with softness and effeminacy, or accuse them of having lived in so delicate or indolent a manner as to enervate and make them unfit to reign over mankind. If, then, our princes would read and duly consider the lives and fortunes of these great men, one would think it impossible they should not alter their conduct, or that their dominions should long continue in the feeble and languishing condition they are in at present.

But since you complained of your militia [47] in the beginning of this conversation, I must tell you that if you had formed it upon the model, and drilled it in the manner, I have recommended, and it had not answered your expectation, you would indeed then have just reason for your complaint; but as you have neither formed nor disciplined it in that manner, you yourself are more properly to be blamed if it has proven an abortion instead of a perfect birth. The Venetians, and also the Duke of Ferrara,[48] made a good beginning, but they

---

[46] Milan, Venice, and Florence.

[47] The Florentine militia ordinance of 1506.

[48] The Venetians in 1509, and Ercole d'Este, duke of Ferrara in 1479.

did not persevere; so, if they too miscarried, it is to be imputed to their own mismanagement and not the defects of their men. I shall venture to affirm that the first state in Italy that will take up this method and pursue it will soon become master of the whole province; things will turn out in his state as they did with Philip of Macedon who, having learned the right method of forming and disciplining an army from Epaminondas the Theban, grew so powerful—while the other Greek states were buried in indolence and luxury, and wholly taken up with plays and banquets—that he conquered them all in a few years and left his son such a foundation to build upon that the son was able to conquer the whole world.[49] Therefore, whoever despises this advice, whether he be a prince or the governor of a commonwealth, has but little regard for himself or for his country.

For my own part, I cannot help complaining of fate, which either should not have let me know these things, or given me power to put them in execution; this is something I cannot hope for now that I am so far advanced in years. Hence, I have freely communicated my thoughts on this matter to you as young men well qualified not only to instill such advice into the ears of your princes, if you approve of it, but to assist them in carrying it into execution whenever a proper opportunity arises. Let me urge you not to despair of success since this province seems destined to revive the arts and sciences which have seemed long since dead, as we see it has already raised poetry, painting and sculpture—as it were—from the grave. As to myself, I cannot expect to see so happy a change at my time of life. Indeed if *Fortuna* had indulged me some years ago with a territory fit for such an undertaking, I think I should soon have convinced the world of the excellence of the ancient military discipline, for I would either have increased my own dominions with glory or, at least, not have lost them with infamy and disgrace.

[49] Philip II, father of Alexander the Great. Plutarch, *Pelopidas* XXVI.

APPENDIX I

Diagrams

NOTE ON THE DIAGRAMS

Machiavelli's description of the various marching formations, battle orders, and the arrangement of an encampment, may be clarified by reference to the following figures and diagrams. Most of them are based upon the diagrams drawn to accompany Burd, "Le fonti letterarie," for which the GENERAL KEY below is designed. The others are based on Farneworth and on the French translation of *The Art of War* by J. V. Périès (Paris: Michaud, 1823). Each of these latter figures is accompanied by its own key. Although the symbols in the keys vary, the terms to which they refer have been standardized.

Machiavelli's army numbers 24,000 men. One-half consists of the citizens' militia. The other half is composed of the forces from the allies, organized ideally along the lines of the militia. The model is the Roman consular army of two legions plus allies, as Machiavelli conceived of it—if not completely accurately. The militia is formed into two regiments of 6,000 men, each to be commanded by a colonel. A regiment, Machiavelli's equivalent to the legion, comprises 10 battalions of 450 men (400 heavily armed and 50 velites), each commanded by a lieutenant colonel. Under the lieutenant colonel is one captain for each group of 100 heavily armed soldiers, assisted by one corporal per 10 men. One captain and 5 corporals command the 50 velites attached to the battalion.

GENERAL KEY

C – Battalion Captain
Co – Battalion Lieutenant Colonel
P – Pikeman
S – Shieldbearer armed with a sword
X_p – Corporal armed with a pike
X_s – Corporal armed with a sword and shield
B – Standard-bearer/colors
D – Fife and Drum corps
V – Velites, men with light-arms

FIGURE I

FRONT   FRONT

<table>
<tr><td colspan="3">C¹</td><td></td><td colspan="3">C⁵</td></tr>
</table>

C¹			C⁵	
Xₚ P P P P	1		P P P P P	1
Xₚ P P P P	2		P P P P P	2
Xₚ P P P P	3		P P P P P	3
Xₚ P P P P	4		P P P P P	4
Xₚ P P P P	5		P P P P P	5
Xₛ S S S S	I		S S.S S S	I
Xₛ S S S S	II		S S S S S	II
Xₛ S S S S	III		S S S S S	III
Xₛ S S S S	IV		S S S S S	IV
Xₛ S S S S	V	α′	S S S S S	V	γ′
Xₛ S S S S	VI		S S S S S	VI
Xₛ S S S S	VII		S S S S S	VII
Xₛ S S S S	VIII		S S S S S	VIII
Xₛ S S S S	IX		S S S S S	IX
Xₛ S S S S	X		S S S S S	X
Xₛ S S S S	XI		S S S S S	XI
Xₛ S S S S	XII		S S S S S	XII
Xₛ S S S S	XIII		S S S S S	XIII
Xₛ S S S S	XIV		S S S S S	XIV
Xₛ S S S S	XV		S S S S S	XV

C³			C⁴	
P P P P P	1		P P P P Xₚ	1
P P P P P	2		P P P P Xₚ	2
P P P P P	3		P P P P Xₚ	3
P P P P P	4		P P P P Xₚ	4
P P P P P	5		P P P P Xₚ	5
BCoD			S S S S Xₛ	I
			S S S S Xₛ	II
S S S S S	I		S S S S Xₛ	III
S S S S S	II		S S S S Xₛ	IV
S S S S S	III		S S S S Xₛ	V
S S S S S	IV	β′	S S S S Xₛ	VI	δ′
S S S S S	V		S S S S Xₛ	VII
S S S S S	VI		S S S S Xₛ	VIII
S S S S S	VII		S S S S Xₛ	IX
S S S S S	VIII		S S S S Xₛ	X
S S S S S	IX		S S S S Xₛ	XI
S S S S S	X		S S S S Xₛ	XII
S S S S S	XI		S S S S Xₛ	XIII
S S S S S	XII		S S S S Xₛ	XIV
S S S S S	XIII		S S S S Xₛ	XV
S S S S S	XIV			
S S S S S	XV			

(*Diagram 1*)

FIGURE I *(Con't.)*

FRONT

↑ ↑

C¹   C⁴

*   *

V	1	X_p P P P P P P P P P P P P P P P P X_p	1	V
V	2	X_p P P P P P P P P P P P P P P P P X_p	2	V
V	3	X_p P P P P P P P P P P P P P P P P X_p	3	V
V	4	X_p P P P P P P P P P P P P P P P P X_p	4	V
V	5	X_p P P P P P P P P P P P P P P P P X_p	5	V

BCoD

LEFT FLANK

V	I	X_s S S S S S S S S S S S S S S S S X_s	I	V	
V	II	X_s S S S S S S S S S S S S S S S S X_s	II	V	RIGHT FLANK
V	III	X_s S S S S S S S S S S S S S S S S X_s	III	V	
V	IV	X_s S S S S S S S S S S S S S S S S X_s	IV	V	
V	V	X_s S S S S S S S S S S S S S S S S X_s	V	V	
V	VI	X_s S S S S S S S S S S S S S S S S X_s	VI	V	
V	VII	X_s S S S S S S S S S S S S S S S S X_s	VII	V	
V	VIII	X_s S S S S S S S S S S S S S S S S X_s	VIII	V	
V	IX	X_s S S S S S S S S S S S S S S S S X_s	IX	V	
V	X	X_s S S S S S S S S S S S S S S S S X_s	X	V	
V	XI	X_s S S S S S S S S S S S S S S S S X_s	XI	V	
V	XII	X_s S S S S S S S S S S S S S S S S X_s	XII	V	
V	XIII	X_s S S S S S S S S S S S S S S S S X_s	XIII	V	
V	XIV	X_s S S S S S S S S S S S S S S S S X_s	XIV	V	
V	XV	X_s S S S S S S S S S S S S S S S S X_s	XV	V	

C²   C³

V V V V V V V V V

REAR GUARD

(Diagram 2)

Diagram 1. The Marching Order of 400 Heavily Armed Men. This marching formation is Machiavelli's fundamental tactical unit. The Arabic numerals indicate the ranks where pikemen stand; the Roman numerals, where the shieldbearers stand. There are 4 captains (C¹, C², C³, C¹), each leading a consecutively marked group of men; the latter are indicated by α′, β′, γ′, and δ′. As in Diagrams 3 and 5 below, these groups should not be read as marching side by side, but as *following* one another in a line: δ′ follows γ′, which follows β′, which follows α′.

Diagram 2. The Battle Order of 400 Heavily Armed Men. The same men, augmented by 50 velites, moved into a battle formation. The captain of α′(C¹) halts; the captain of β′(C²) and his men advance on the right of α′ and square off with both α′ and γ′, and δ′ advances to the right of these three and aligns his men with them. The asterisks represent the position formerly occupied by captains C² and C³. For Machiavelli, the advantages of this formation are: the placement of the pikemen in the front to hold off a cavalry attack, and the placement of the shieldbearers, the strongest unit, in the most strategic location.

FIGURE II

C¹

X_p	X_p	X_p	X_p	X_p	1	
P	P	P	P	P	2	
P	P	P	P	P	3	
P	P	P	P	P	4	
P	P	P	P	P	5	
P	P	P	P	P	6	
P	P	P	P	P	7	
P	P	P	P	P	8	
P	P	P	P	P	9	α'
P	P	P	P	P	10	
P	P	P	P	P	11	
P	P	P	P	P	12	
P	P	P	P	P	13	
P	P	P	P	P	14	
P	P	P	P	P	15	
P	P	P	P	P	16	
P	P	P	P	P	17	
P	P	P	P	P	1s	
P	P	P	P	P	19	
X_p	X_p	X_p	X_p	X_p	20	

C²

X_s	X_s	X_s	X_s	X_s	I	
S	S	S	S	S	II	
S	S	S	S	S	III	
S	S	S	S	S	IV	
S	S	S	S	S	V	
S	S	S	S	S	VI	
S	S	S	S	S	VII	
S	S	S	S	S	VIII	
S	S	S	S	S	IX	β'
S	S	S	S	S	X	

BCoD

S	S	S	S	S	XI
S	S	S	S	S	XII
S	ȧ	S	S	S	XIII
S	S	S	S	S	XIV
S	S	S	S	S	XV
S	S	S	S	S	XVI
S	S	S	S	S	XVII
S	S	S	S	S	XVIII
S	S	S	S	S	XIX
X_s	X_s	X_s	X_s	X_s	XX

C³

X_s	X_s	X_s	X_s	X_s	I	
S	S	S	S	S	II	
S	S	S	S	S	III	
S	S	S	S	S	IV	
S	S	S	S	S	V	
S	S	S	S	S	VI	
S	S	S	S	S	VII	
S	S	S	S	S	VIII	γ'
S	S	S	S	S	IX	
S	S	S	S	S	X	
S	S	S	S	S	XI	
S	S	S	S	S	XII	
S	S	S	S	S	XIII	
S	S	S	S	S	XIV	
S	S	S	S	S	XV	
S	S	S	S	S	XVI	
S	S	S	S	S	XVII	
S	S	S	S	S	XVIII	
S	S	S	S	S	XIX	
X_s	X_s	X_s	X_s	X_s	XX	

C⁴

X_s	X_s	X_s	X_s	X_s	1	
S	S	S	S	S	II	
S	S	S	S	S	III	
S	S	S	S	S	IV	
S	S	S	S	S	V	
S	S	S	S	S	VI	
S	S	S	S	S	VII	
S	S	S	S	S	VIII	
S	S	S	S	S	IX	δ'
S	S	S	S	S	X	
S	S	S	S	S	XI	
S	S	S	S	S	XII	
S	S	S	S	S	XIII	
S	S	S	S	S	XIV	
S	S	S	S	S	XV	
S	S	S	S	S	XVI	
S	S	S	S	S	XVII	
S	S	S	S	S	XVIII	
S	S	S	S	S	XIX	
X_s	X_s	X_s	X_s	X_s	XX	

(*Diagram 3*)

FIGURE II (Con't.)

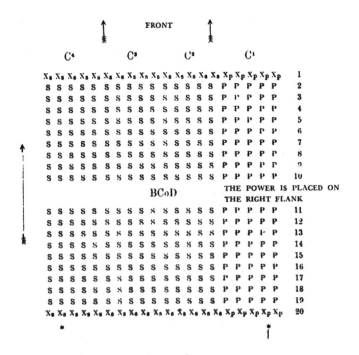

(Diagram 4)

Diagram 3. Marching Formation of Soldiers Expecting a Sudden, Flank Attack. Note the rearrangement of the pikemen as well as that of the corporals armed with pikes, and those with swords and shields.

Diagram 4. The Same as #3, Now in Battle Formation. Group β' moves either to the right or to the left of α' depending upon which flank the attack is expected: here, preparing for an attack from the right, β' moves to the left of α'. Then group γ' will move to the left of β'; δ', to the left of γ' The * and ‡ indicate the new position of C² and C³ after the soldiers have formed to the left.

FIGURE III

C¹   BCoD

```
P  P  S  S  S   I                S  S  S  S  S   I
P  P  S  S  S   II               S  S  S  S  S   II
P  P  S  S  S   III              S  S  S  S  S   III
P  P  S  S  S   IV               S  S  S  S  S   IV
P  P  S  S  S   V             ↑  S  S  S  S  S   V
P  Xp S  S  S   VI               S  S  S  S  S   VI
P  Xp S  S  S   VII              S  S  S  S  S   VII   γ'
P  Xp S  S  S   VIII             S  S  S  S  S   VIII
P  Xp S  S  S   IX               S  S  S  S  S   IX
P  Xp S  S  S   X                S  S  S  S  S   X
P  P  Xs S  S   XI               S  S  S  S  S   XI
P  P  Xs S  S   XII   α'          S  S  S  S  S   XII
P  P  Xs S  S   XIII             S  S  S  S  S   XIII
P  P  Xs S  S   XIV              S  S  S  S  S   XIV
P  P  Xs S  S   XV               S  S  S  S  S   XV
P  P  Xs S  S   XVI
P  P  Xs S  S   XVII                    C³
P  P  Xs S  S   XVIII            S  S  S  P  P   1
P  P  Xs S  S   XIX              S  S  S  P  P   2
P  P  Xs S  S   XX               S  S  S  P  P   3
P  P  Xs S  S   XXI              S  S  S  P  P   4
P  P  Xs S  S   XXII             S  S  S  P  P   5
P  P  Xs S  S   XXIII            S  S  S  Xp P   6
P  P  Xs S  S   XXIV             S  S  S  Xp P   7
P  P  Xs S  S   XXV              S  S  S  Xp P   8
                                S  S  S  Xp P   9
       C²                       S  S  S  Xp P   10
                             ↑  S  S  Xs P  P   11
S  S  S  S  S   I                S  S  Xs P  P   12   δ'
S  S  S  S  S   II               S  S  Xs P  P   13
S  S  S  S  S   III              S  S  Xs P  P   14
S  S  S  S  S   IV               S  S  Xs P  P   15
S  S  S  S  S   V                S  S  Xs P  P   16
S  S  S  S  S   VI               S  S  Xs P  P   17
S  S  S  S  S   VII  β'           S  S  Xs P  P   18
S  S  S  S  S   VIII             S  S  Xs P  P   19
S  S  S  S  S   IX               S  S  Xs P  P   20
S  S  S  S  S   X                S  S  Xs P  P   21
S  S  S  S  S   XI               S  S  Xs P  P   22
S  S  S  S  S   XII              S  S  Xs P  P   23
S  S  S  S  S   XIII             S  S  Xs P  P   24
S  S  S  S  S   XIV              S  S  Xs P  P   25
S  S  S  S  S   XV
                  (Diagram 5)         C⁴
```

Diagram 5. The Marching Formation of a Battalion Prepared to Convert into Either a Winged Battalion or a Hollow Square. Note that α' and δ' consist of 25 ranks.

Diagram 6. To form a winged battalion, the captain of α' halts and β' moves along the right side until its first rank is parallel to the eleventh rank of α'. Then γ' aligns with β'. Finally, δ', with its 25 ranks also moves to the right—thus forming the wing. C² moves to the *.

Diagram 7. To form a hollow square based on the preceding formation, ranks 18 through 25 move around to the front of the first rank. The placement of the standard-bearer/colors, lieutenant colonel, and drums is not specified in Burd, and is derived from Farneworth and Périès. Nor is it

```
          C¹                                                        C³
   1   P  P  S  S  S                                    S  S  S  P  P
   2   P  P  S  S  S                                    S  S  S  P  P
   3   P  P  J  S  S                                    S  S  S  P  P
   4   P  P  S  S  S                                    S  S  S  P  P
   5   P  P  S  S  S                                    S  S  S  P  P
   6   P  Xp S  S  S                                    S  S  S  Xp P
   7   P  Xp S  S  S                                    S  S  S  Xp P
   8   P  Xp S  S  S                                    S  S  S  Xp P
   9   P  Xp S  S  S       C²              BCoD         S  S  S  Xp P
  10   P  Xp S  S  S                                    S  S  S  Xp P
  11   P  P  X₈ S  S  S  S  S  S  S  S  S  S  S  S  S  S  X₈ P  P
  12   P  P  X₈ S  S  S  S  S  S  S  S  S  S  S  S  S  S  X₈ P  P
  13   P  P  X₈ S  S  S  S  S  S  S  S  S  S  S  S  S  S  X₈ P  P
  14   P  P  X₈ S  S  S  S  S  S  S  S  S  S  S  S  S  S  X₈ P  P
  15   P  P  X₈ S  S  S  S  S  S  S  S  S  S  S  S  S  S  X₈ P  P
  16   P  P  X₈ S  S  S  S  S  S  S  S  S  S  S  S  S  S  X₈ P  P
  17   P  P  X₈ S  S  S  S  S  S  S  S  S  S  S  S  S  S  X₈ P  P
  18   P  P  X₈ S  S  S  S  S  S  S  S  S  S  S  S  S  S  X₈ P  P
  19   P  P  X₈ S  S  S  S  S  S  S  S  S  S  S  S  S  S  X₈ P  P
  20   P  P  X₈ S  S  S  S  S  S  S  S  S  S  S  S  S  S  X₈ P  P
  21   P  P  X₈ S  S  S  S  S  S  S  S  S  S  S  S  S  S  X₈ P  P
  22   P  P  X₈ S  S  S  S  S  S  S  S  S  S  S  S  S  S  X₈ P  P
  23   P  P  X₈ S  S  S  S  S  S  S  S  S  S  S  S  S  S  X₈ P  P
  24   P  P  X₈ S  S  S  S  S  S  S  S  S  S  S  S  S  S  X₈ P  P
  25   P  P  X₈ S  S  S  S  S  S  S  S  S  S  S  S  S  S  X₈ P  P

   *                           (Diagram 6)                          C⁴
```

```
          C                                                         C
  18   P  P  X₈ S  S  S  S  S  S  S  S  S  S  S  S  S  S  X₈ P  P
  19   P  P  X₈ S  S  S  S  S  S  S  S  S  S  S  S  S  S  X₈ P  P
  20   P  P  X₈ S  S  S  S  S  S  S  S  S  S  S  S  S  S  X₈ P  P
  21   P  P  X₈ S  S  S  S  S  S  S  S  S  S  S  S  S  S  X₈ P  P
  22   P  P  X₈ S  S  S  S  S  S  S  S  S  S  S  S  S  S  X₈ P  P
  23   P  P  X₈ S  S  S  S  S  S  S  S  S  S  S  S  S  S  X₈ P  P
  24   P  P  X₈ S  S  S  S  S  S  S  S  S  S  S  S  S  S  X₈ P  P
  25   P  P  X₈ S  S  S  S  S  S  S  S  S  S  S  S  S  S  X₈ P  P
   1   P  P  S  S  S                                    S  S  S  P  P
   2   P  P  S  S  S                                    S  S  S  P  P
   3   P  P  S  S  S                                    S  S  S  P  P
   4   P  P  S  S  S                                    S  S  S  P  P
   5   P  P  S  S  S                                    S  S  S  P  P
   6   P  Xp S  S  S                                    S  S  S  Xp P
   7   P  Xp S  S  S                 BCoD               S  S  S  Xp P
   8   P  Xp S  S  S                                    S  S  S  Xp P
   9   P  Xp S  S  S                                    S  S  S  Xp P
  10   P  Xp S  S  S                                    S  S  S  Xp P
  11   P  P  X₈ S  S  S  S  S  S  S  S  S  S  S  S  S  S  X₈ P  P
  12   P  P  X₈ S  S  S  S  S  S  S  S  S  S  S  S  S  S  X₈ P  P
  13   P  P  X₈ S  S  S  S  S  S  S  S  S  S  S  S  S  S  X₈ P  P
  14   P  P  X₈ S  S  S  S  S  S  S  S  S  S  S  S  S  S  X₈ P  P
  15   P  P  X₈ S  S  S  S  S  S  S  S  S  S  S  S  S  S  X₈ P  P
  16   P  P  X₈ S  S  S  S  S  S  S  S  S  S  S  S  S  S  X₈ P  P
  17   P  P  X₈ S  S  S  S  S  S  S  S  S  S  S  S  S  S  X₈ P  P

          C                      (Diagram 7)                        C
```

clear how the captains should be rearranged; presumably they should
stand as indicated.

FIGURE IV

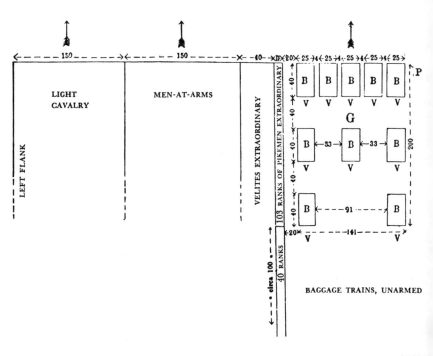

Legend: The rectangles marked B represent the battalions in formations similar to the one shown in Diagram 2, Figure I. Machiavelli did not specify the depth of the light cavalry, of the men-at-arms, or of the velites extraordinary.

G = Regimental Colonel

P = General Leading the Entire Army

Two Regiments in Battle Formation

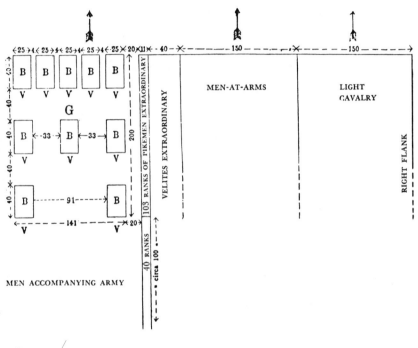

FRONT

MEN-AT-ARMS

LIGHT CAVALRY

RIGHT FLANK

VELITES EXTRAORDINARY

103 RANKS OF PIKEMEN EXTRAORDINARY

40 RANKS

← circa 100 →

MEN ACCOMPANYING ARMY

GUARD

Scale: 1 millimeter = approx. 2 feet

FIGURE V

Marching Formation of an Army Comprising Two Regiments Totaling 20 Battalions
Together With Supporting Units in a Hollow Square

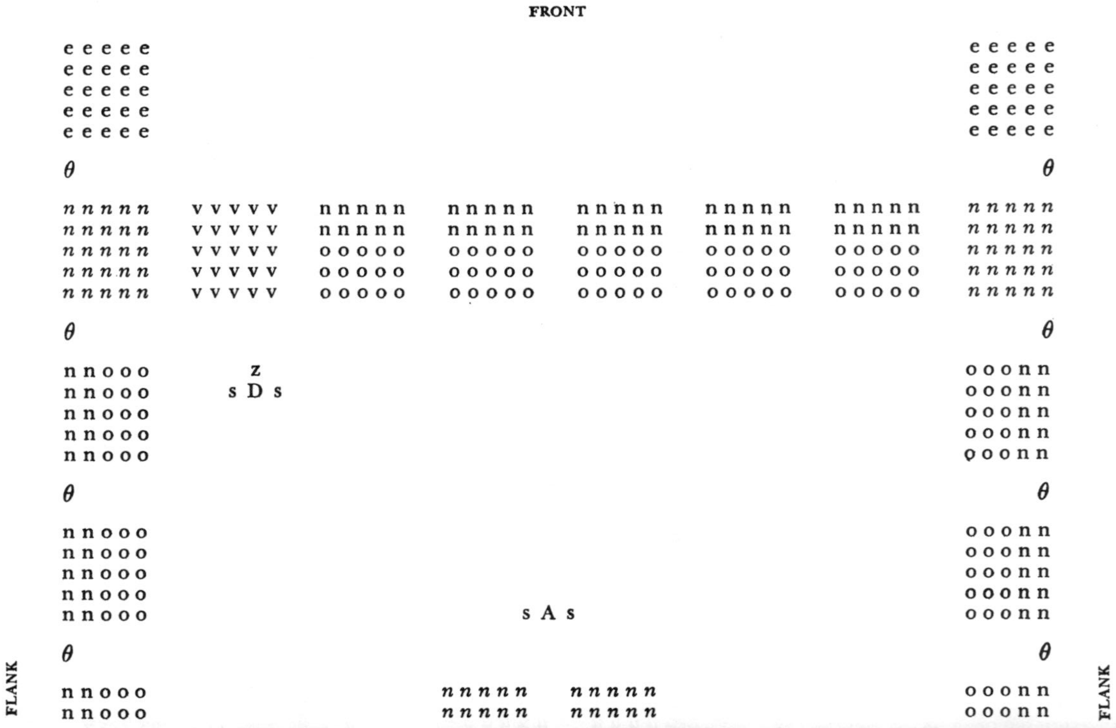

```
LEFT                                                                  RIGHT
n n o o o                  n n n n n   n n n n n              o o o n n
n n o o o                  n n n n n   n n n n n              o o o n n
n n o o o                  n n n n n   n n n n n              o o o n n

θ                                                                     θ

n n o o o                     BATTLE TRAINS                   o o o n n
n n o o o                                                     o o o n n
n n o o o                                                     o o o n n
n n o o o                                                     o o o n n
n n o o o                                                     o o o n n

θ                                                                     θ

n n o o o                                                     o o o n n
n n o o o                                                     o o o n n
n n o o o                                                     o o o n n
n n o o o                                                     o o o n n
n n o o o                                                     o o o n n
                                                    z
θ                                                 s D s               θ

n n n n n  o o o o o  o o o o o  o o o o o  o o o o o  o o o o o  v v v v v  n n n n n
n n n n n  o o o o o  o o o o o  o o o o o  o o o o o  o o o o o  v v v v v  n n n n n
n n n n n  o o o o o  o o o o o  o o o o o  o o o o o  o o o o o  v v v v v  n n n n n
n n n n n  n n n n n  n n n n n  n n n n n  n n n n n  n n n n n  v v v v v  n n n n n
n n n n n  n n n n n  n n n n n  n n n n n  n n n n n  n n n n n  v v v v v  n n n n n

θ                                                                     θ

r r r r r                                                     r r r r r
r r r r r                                                     r r r r r
r r r r r                                                     r r r r r
r r r r r                                                     r r r r r
r r r r r                                                     r r r r r
```

Legend:

e = Light Cavalry	o = Shieldbearer armed with a sword	D = Regimental Colonel
n = Ordinary Pikemen	r = Men-at-Arms	A = Commanding General
n = Pikemen Extraordinary	s = Fife and Drum Corps	θ = Artillery
v = Velites, men with light-arms	z = Standard-bearer/Colors	

FIGURE VI

Two Regiments in Marching Formation

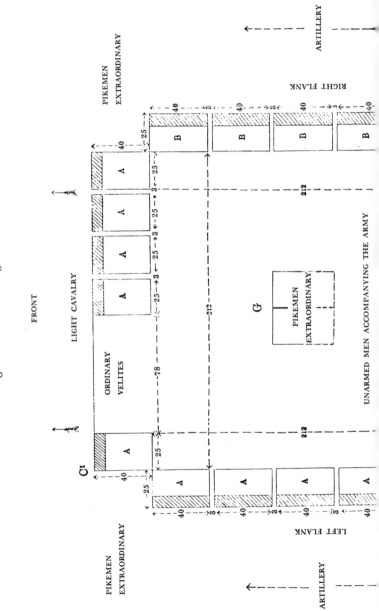

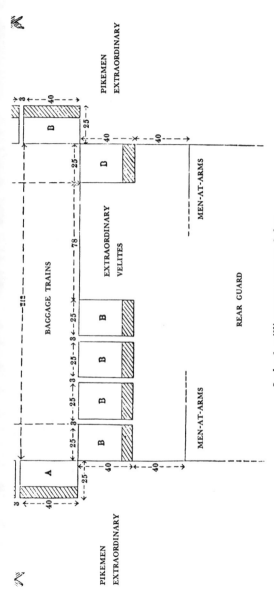

Scale: 1 millimeter = approx. 2 feet

Legend: This formation is designed to give maximum effectiveness against any sudden attack. The rectangles marked A represent the subdivisions of the first regiment; those marked B represent the subdivisions of the second regiment. Machiavelli does not give the dimensions of the space in the center occupied by the pikemen extraordinary. The shaded areas indicate where each group's pikemen are.

C¹ = General Leading the First Regiment

C² = General Leading the Second Regiment

G = General Leading the Entire Army

FIGURE VII

A Fortified Camp and Lodgings

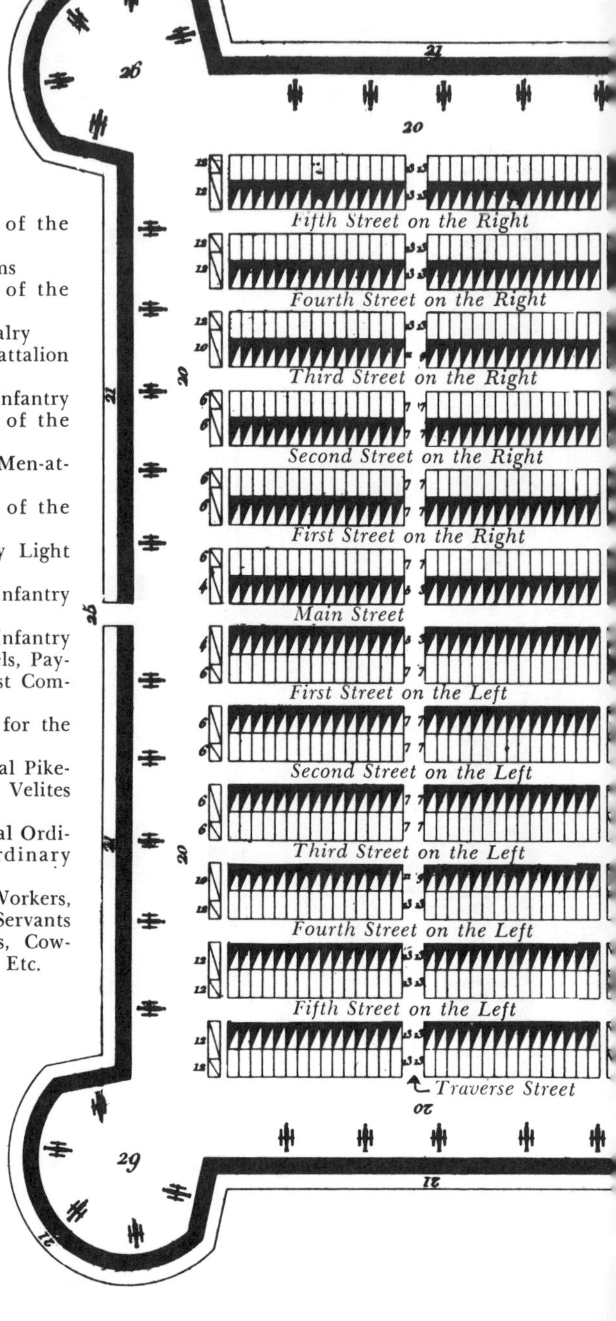

KEY

1. Tent for the General
2. Tents for the Officers of the Men-at-Arms
3. Tents of the Men-at-Arms
4. Tents for the Officers of the Light Cavalry
5. Tents for the Light Cavalry
6. Tents for the Infantry Battalion Commanders
7. Tents for the National Infantry
8. Tents for the Officers of the Auxiliary Men-at-Arms
9. Tents for the Auxiliary Men-at-Arms
10. Tents for the Officers of the Auxiliary Light Cavalry
11. Tents for the Auxiliary Light Cavalry
12. Tents for the Auxiliary Infantry Battalion Commanders
13. Tents for the Auxiliary Infantry
14. Lodgings for the Colonels, Paymasters, Regimental First Company, and Volunteers
15. Supplemental Lodgings for the Auxiliary Cavalry
16. Lodgings for the National Pikemen Extraordinary and Velites Extraordinary
17. Lodgings for the National Ordinary Pikemen and Ordinary Velites
18. Lodgings for Clerks, Workers, Craftsmen and Officers' Servants
19. Lodgings for Shepherds, Cowherds, Butchers, Bakers, Etc.
20. Drill Area
21. The Camp's Ditches
22. Southern Gate
23. Western Gate
24. Northern Gate
25. Eastern Gate
26. Southeast Bastion
27. Southwest Bastion
28. Northwest Bastion
29. Northeast Bastion

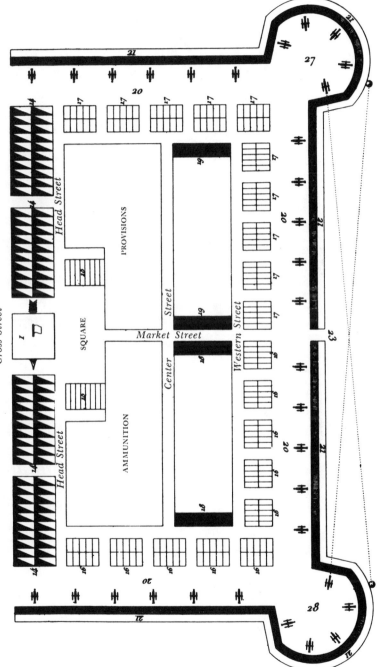

APPENDIX II

TO THE MOSTE

HIGHE, AND EXCELLENT PRINCES,

ELIZABETH

BY THE GRACE OF GOD, QUENE
OF ENGLANDE, FRAUNCE, AND IRELANDE,
DEFENDER OF THE FAITHE, AND OF THE CHURCHE
OF ENGLANDE, AND IRELANDE, ON YEARTH
NEXT UNDER GOD, THE SUPREME
GOVERNOUR

ALTHOUGH COMMONLIE every man, moste worthie and re-noumed Soveraine, seketh specially to commend and ex-tolle the thing, whereunto he feleth hymself naturally bent and inclined, yet al soche parciallitie and private affection laid aside, it is to bee thought (that for the defence, mainte-naunce, and advauncemente of a Kyngdome, or Common weale, or for the good and due observacion of peace, and ad-ministracion of Justice in the same) no one thinge to be more profitable, necessarie, or more honourable, then the knowledge of service in warre, and dedes of armes; bicause consideryng the ambicion of the worlde, it is impossible for any realme or dominion, long to continue free in quietnesse and savegarde, where the defence of the sweard is not alwaies in readinesse. For like as the Grekes, beyng occupied aboute triflyng matters, takyng pleasure in resityng of Comedies, and soche other vain thinges, altogether neclecting Marciall feates, gave occasion to Philip kyng of Macedonia, father to Alexander the Great, to oppresse and to bring theim in servitude, under his sub-jeccion, even so undoubtedly, libertie will not be kepte, but men shall be troden under foote, and brought to moste hor-rible miserie and calamitie, if thei givyng theim selves to pastymes and pleasure, forssake the juste regarde of their owne defence, and savegarde of their countrie, whiche in temporall regimente, chiefly consisteth in warlike skilfulnesse. And therefore the aunciente Capitaines and mightie Conquerours, so longe as thei florished, did devise with moste greate diligence, all maner of waies, to bryng their men to the perfect knowledge of what so ever thing appertained to the warre: as manifestly appereth by thc warlike games, whiche in old time the Princes of Grecia ordained, upon the mount Olimpus, and also by thorders and exercises, that the aunciente Romaines used in sundrie places, and specially in Campo Martio, and in their wonderful sumptuous Theaters, whiche chiefly thei builded to that purpose. Whereby thei not onely made their Souldiours so experte, that thei obtained with a fewe, in faightyng againste a greate houge multitude of enemies, soche marveilous victories, as in many credible Histories are mencioned, but also by the same meanes, their unarmed and rascalle people that followed their Campes, gotte soche understandyng in the feates of warre, that thei in the daie of battaile, beeyng lefte destitute of succour, were able without any other help, to set themselves in good order, for their defence againste the enemie, that would seke to hurte theim, and in soche daungerous times, have doen their countrie so good service, that verie often by their helpe, the adversaries have been put to flight, and fieldes moste happely wone. So that thantiquitie estemed nothing more happie in a common weale, then to have in the same many men skillful in warlike affaires: by meanes whereof, their Empire continually inlarged, and moste wonderfully and triumphantly prospered. For so longe as men for their valiauntnesse, were then rewarded and had in estimacion, glad was he that could finde occasion to venter, yea, and spende his life, to benefite his countrie: as by the manly actes that Marcus Curcius, Oracius Cocles, and Gaius Mucius did for the savegarde of Rome, and also by other innumerable like examples, dooeth plainly appeare. But when through long and continuall peace, thei began to bee altogether given to pleasure and delicatenesse, little regardyng Marciall feates, nor soche as were expert in the practise thereof: Their dominions and estates, did not so moche before increase and prospere, as then by soche meanes and oversight, thei sodainly fell into decaie and utter ruine. For soche truly is the nature and condicion, bothe of peace and warre, that where in governemente, there is not had equalle consideracion of them bothe, the one in fine, doeth woorke and induce, the others oblivion and utter abholicion. Wherfore, sith the necessitie of the science of warres is so greate, and also the necessarie use thereof so manifeste, that even Ladie Peace her self, doeth in maner from thens crave her chief defence and preservacion, and the worthinesse moreover, and honour of the same so greate, that as by prose we see, the perfecte glorie therof, cannot easily finde roote, but in the hartes of moste noble couragious and manlike personages, I thought most excellente Princes, I could not either to the specialle gratefiyng of your highnesse, the universall delight of all studious gentlemen, or the common utilitie of the publike wealth, imploie my labours more profitablie in accomplishyng of my duetie and good will, then in settyng foorthe some thing, that might induce to the augmentyng and increase of the knowledge thereof: inespecially thexample of your highnes most politike governemente over us, givyING plaine testimonie of the wonderfull prudente desire that is in you, to have your people instructed in this kinde of service, as well for the better defence of your highnesse, theim selves, and their countrie, as also to discourage thereby, and to be able to resist the malingnitie of the enemie, who otherwise would seeke peradventure, to invade this noble realme or kyngdome.

When therfore about x. yeres paste, in the Emperours warres against the Mores and certain Turkes beyng in Barberie, at the siege and winnyng of Calibbia, Monesterio and Africa, I had as well for my further instruction in those affaires, as also the better to acquainte me with the Italian tongue, reduced into Englishe, the booke called The arte of Warre, of the famous and excellente Nicholas Machiavell, whiche in times paste he beyng a counsailour, and Secretarie of the noble Citee of Florence, not without his greate laude and praise did write: and havyng lately againe, somwhat perused the same, the whiche in soche continuall broiles and unquietnesse, was by me translated, I determined with my self, by publishyng thereof, to bestowe as greate a gift (sins greater I was not able) emongeste my countrie men, not experte in the Italian tongue, as in like woorkes I had seen before me, the Frenchemen, Duchemen, Spaniardes, and other forreine nacions, moste lovyngly to have bestowed emongeste theirs: The rather undoubtedly, that as by private readyng of the same booke, I then felt my self in that knowledge marveilously holpen and increased, so by communicatyng the same to many, our Englishemen findyng out the orderyng and disposyng of exploictes of warre therein contained, the aide and direction of these plaine and briefe preceptes, might no lesse in knowledge of warres become incomperable, then in prowes also and exercise of the same, altogether invincible: which my translacion moste gracious Soveraine, together with soche other thynges, as by me hath been gathered, and thought good to adde thereunto, I have presumed to dedicate unto youre highnes: not onely bicause the whole charge and furniture of warlike counsailes and preparacions, being determined by the arbitremente of Governours and Princes, the treatise also of like effecte should in like maner as of right, depende upon the protection of a moste worthie and noble Patronesse, but also that the discourse it self, and the woorke of a forrein aucthour, under the passeport and safeconduite of your highnes moste noble name, might by speciall aucthoritie of the same, winne emongest your Majesties subjectes, moche better credite and estimacion. And if mooste mightie Queen, in this kind of Philosophie (if I maie so terme it) grave and sage counsailes, learned and wittie preceptes, or politike and prudente admonicions, ought not to be accompted the least and basest tewels of weale publike. Then dare I boldely affirme, that of many straungers, whiche from forrein countries, have here tofore in this your Majesties realme arrived, there is none in comparison to bee prefered, before this worthie Florentine and Italian, who havyng frely without any gaine of exchaunge (as after some acquaintaunce and familiaritie will better appeare) brought with hym moste riche, rare and plentifull Treasure, shall deserve I trust of all good Englishe hartes, most lovingly and frendly to be intertained, embraced and cherished. Whose newe Englishe apparell, how so ever it shall seme by me, after a grosse fasion, more fitlie appoincted to the Campe, then in nice termes attired to the Carpet, and in course clothyng rather putte foorthe to battaile, then in any brave shewe prepared to the bankette, neverthelesse my good will I truste, shall of your grace be taken in good parte, havyng fashioned the phraise of my rude stile, even accordyng to the purpose of my travaile, whiche was rather to profite the desirous manne of warre, then to delight the eares of the fine Rethorician, or daintie curious scholemanne: Moste humblie besechyng your highnes, so to accept my labour herein, as the first fruictes of a poore souldiours studie, who to the uttermoste of his smalle power, in the service of your moste gracious majestie, and of his countrie, will at al tymes, accordyng to his bounden duetie and allegeaunce, promptlie yeld hym self to any labour, travaile, or daunger, what so ever shal happen. Praiyng in the mean season the almightie God, to give your highnes in longe prosperous raigne, perfect health, desired tranquilitie, and against all your enemies, luckie and joifull victorie.

Your humble subject and dailie oratour,

PETER WHITEHORNE

INDEX

The Index for the Introduction and the text includes primarily proper names (persons, places, and events), including Machiavelli's sources. For students of political thought, some important concepts have been indexed. Readers who are interested in military matters will find the table of contents a useful supplement to the Index.

Other titles of interest

**FIFTEEN DECISIVE
BATTLES OF THE WORLD
From Marathon to Waterloo**
Sir Edward S. Creasy
420 pp., 2 illus.
80559-6 $15.95

GREAT CAPTAINS UNVEILED
B. H. Liddell Hart
New introduction by
Russell F. Weigley
289 pp., 1 illus., 5 maps
80686-X $13.95

HANNIBAL
Enemy of Rome
Leonard Cottrell
287 pp., 27 illus., 10 maps
80498-0 $13.95

JULIUS CAESAR
Man, Soldier, and Tyrant
J. F. C. Fuller
336 pp., 17 illus.
80422-0 $14.95

LAWRENCE OF ARABIA
B. H. Liddell Hart
458 pp., 17 photos, 10 maps
80354-2 $14.95

CAESAR
Theodore Ayrault Dodge
816 pp., 253 illus.
80787-4 $22.50

ALEXANDER
Theodore Ayrault Dodge
723 pp., 234 illus., maps, and charts
80690-8 $19.95

HANNIBAL
Theodore Ayrault Dodge
702 pp., 227 charts, maps,
plans, and illus.
80654-1 $19.95

**THE DISCOVERY AND
CONQUEST OF MEXICO**
Bernal Díaz del Castillo
Translated by A. P. Maudslay
New introd. by Hugh Thomas
512 pp., 33 illus., 2 maps
80697-5 $16.95

**THE CONDUCT OF
WAR 1789–1961**
J. F. C. Fuller
352 pp.
80467-0 $14.95

**THE EVOLUTION OF
WEAPONS AND WARFARE**
Colonel Trevor N. Dupuy
358 pp.
80384-4 $13.95

**THE GENERALSHIP OF
ALEXANDER THE GREAT**
J. F. C. Fuller
336 pp., 35 illus.
80371-2 $14.95

INVINCIBLE GENERALS
Philip J. Haythornthwaite
240 pp., 160 illus.,
29 maps and plans
80577-4 $16.95

**MASTERS OF THE ART
OF COMMAND**
Martin Blumenson and
James L. Stokebury
410 pp., 11 maps
80403-4 $14.95

**A MILITARY HISTORY OF THE
WESTERN WORLD**
J. F. C. Fuller
**Vol. I: From the Earliest Times to
the Battle of Lepanto**
602 pp.   80304-6 $15.95
**Vol. II: From the Defeat of the
Spanish Armada to the
Battle of Waterloo**
562 pp.   80305-4 $15.95
**Vol. III: From the American
Civil War to the
End of World War II**
666 pp.   80306-2 $15.95

**SCIPIO AFRICANUS
Greater than Napoleon**
B. H. Liddell Hart
New foreword by Michael Grant
304 pp., 3 illus., 7 maps
80583-9 $14.95

Available at your bookstore

OR ORDER DIRECTLY FROM 1-800-386-5656

VISIT OUR WEBSITE AT WWW.PERSEUSBOOKSGROUP.COM